Bed and Breakfast Ireland

D0963841

Bed and Breakfast Ireland

Elsie Dillard & Susan Causin

Appletree Press
Belfast

Chronicle Books
San Francisco

First published in Ireland in 1996 by
The Appletree Press Ltd
19-21 Alfred Street
Belfast BT2 8DL

A catalogue record for this book
is available from the British Library.
ISBN 0-86281-497 9

First published in the United States in 1996 by
Chronicle Books
275 Fifth Street
San Francisco
California 94103

Second Edition
Library of Congress Cataloguing-in-Publication
Data available.
ISBN 0-8118-1158-1

Distributed in Canada by Raincoast Books
8680 Cambie Street
Vancouver, B.C. V6P 6M9

Copyright © Elsie Dillard and Susan Causin, 1996
Illustrations © Karen Karmack, 1996

All rights reserved. No part of this publication may
be reproduced or transmitted in any form or by any
means, electronic or mechanical, photocopying,
recording or any information and retrieval system,
without prior permission in writing from publisher.

9 8 7 6 5 4 3 2 1

Printed in Ireland

Contents

Our Favourite Bed and Breakfasts

Introduction

It is easy to fall in love with Ireland. Even though we are not strangers to Ireland, once again we found ourselves overwhelmed with the warmth of welcome and the beauty of the countryside and thoroughly enjoyed our travels to every corner of the country. Our researches covered the four seasons, and we highly recommend a visit to Ireland in the off-season, when it is easy to get around and there are still plenty of things to interest the visitor. There are limited motorway facilities in Ireland, but the roads are well maintained, even in the most rural areas, and are seldom crowded.

Every property listed in this book was personally visited by us. There are no charges whatsoever for inclusion in this guide. Our criteria for entry are based primarily upon the warmth of welcome and cleanliness of the property, with many other factors of course taken into consideration. We have covered most parts of the country, including areas not considered as tourist regions, in order to accommodate business travellers, visiting friends and family gatherings.

Children are welcome unless otherwise stated. Smoking is allowed unless we have mentioned that it is not permitted, and pets are only welcome outside unless altogether excluded as indicated. Parking is always available unless mentioned otherwise. We have included information on the number of ground floor rooms, which is helpful for the elderly or infirm. Almost all bedrooms have washbasins and if other facilities in bedrooms, such as hairdryers, TVs, phones or tea/coffee-making services are available, this too has been mentioned. Unlicensed premises often allow guests to bring their own wine.

When booking, confirm prices; although at the time of publication these figures were correct, prices may vary. It is advisable when booking to also verify specifics such as child reductions, single supplements, special break prices, opening times, meals and dietary requirements, and whether a deposit is required. Obtaining driving directions is also recommended.

Wherever possible we have given the names of the owners. However, it is possible that change of ownership may have occurred, which could lead to significant differences in the standard of accommodation, welcome, cleanliness, price.

At the time of publication, and to the best of our knowledge, the facts in this book were correct. However, changes do occur for which we cannot be responsible. Visitors may want to read *Discover Ireland*, Aer Lingus's most popular holiday brochure, which includes a variety of programmes for touring Ireland.

We would like to thank Bord Failte Eireann and the Northern Ireland Tourist Board for their help in making this book possible, and Holiday Auto for providing us with a safe and reliable car.

We would welcome any comments you have on your personal experiences about properties in this book and we would be delighted to receive your recommendations for consideration for future inclusion. Please send your comments and recommendations to Elsie Dillard and Susan Causin, 48 Nursery Road, Great Cornard, Sudbury, Suffolk CO10 3NJ, or in North America to P. O. Box 5107, Redondo, Washington, 98054.

Note:

A 'single supplement' refers to the practice of charging a single visitor who stays in a double room the single room rate plus a small additional charge.

The prices listed for accommodation in the Republic of Ireland are given in Irish pounds (or *punts*). The prices listed for accommodation in Northern Ireland are given in pounds sterling (British pounds). Prices and exchange rates fluctuate, so be sure to check the rates when you book your room, as well as the method of payment. Some establishments might not accept credit cards. All prices refer to prices per person.

Dublin and the East

County Dublin

From above Killakee, on the northern slopes of the Dublin Mountains, there is a wonderful view of both city and county. You can see to the northeast the majestic sweep of Dublin Bay, the beautiful peninsula of Howth Head, and to the south of the bay, South Killiney Head. The city stretches across the plain, divided by the River Liffey, and the large green patch in the north west is Phoenix Park, one of Europe's finest city parks, covering some 290 acres.

The county north of Howth has long sandy beaches and fishing villages, which, in spite of their proximity to the city, still retain their character and charm, and a wealth of archaeological sites. The castle at Howth dates from 1464, but has been altered over the centuries. The gardens, which are open to the public, are famous for their rhododendrons and eighteenth-century formal garden. Malahide Castle belonged to the Talbot family from 1185 to 1976, when the property was sold to Dublin County Council. It now houses a large part of the National Portrait Collection.

To the south of the Liffey, Blackrock and Dalkey retain their village identity, and the popular Victorian holiday resort of Dun Laoghaire is one of the main sea-gateways to Ireland.

The city of Dublin is beautifully situated and the people have a friendliness and wit that captivates most visitors. Relatively speaking, it is a small and compact city. The city centre, stretching between Parnell Square and St Stephen's Green north to south, and Dublin Bay and Phoenix Park east to west, can be covered easily by foot. Most points of interest in the city lie between these boundaries. Like in any European capital city, there is so much to see that it would take weeks to do it full justice, to take in not just the principal sights of churches, museums and galleries, but to have the time to browse and absorb the atmosphere, the people, shops, theatres and pubs. Amongst the sights that come top of the list to visit are the National Museum, the National Gallery and the Municipal Gallery, as well as St Patrick's Cathedral, dating from 1190; Christchurch Cathedral, restored in the nineteenth century; St Michan's, where intact bodies still lie in vaults; the fine eighteenth-century church of St Anne's; and St Werburgh's Church – amongst the most noteworthy churches to visit.

Dublin Castle, with its beautifully decorated State Apartments, was used by the British for state functions, and since 1938 has been the scene of the inauguration of the Presidents of Ireland. The General Post Office in O'Connell Street is where the Free Republic was proclaimed, and the Custom House is one of the most impressive buildings in Dublin. Parliament House, now the Bank of Ireland, was built in 1785 by James Gandon, Dublin's most famous architect. The Book of Kells is kept in the Library at Trinity College, which is a restful spot away from the bustle of the city.

DUBLIN CITY

Aberdeen Lodge

53-55 Park Avenue, Ailesbury Road, Dublin 4, Co Dublin
Tel: (01) 283 8255, Fax: (01) 283 7877

A substantial, brick-built Edwardian house in an elegant residential area, easily accessible both to the centre of Dublin and Dun Laoghaire. The building was originally two houses and was very run down when the Halpins acquired it. The whole house has been completely renovated and has been open for business for the last three years. The house features hardwood floors, original ceiling work and fire-places. It has been plainly decorated in pastel colours and the furniture was custom-made for the rooms. The bed-rooms at the back of the house overlook the cricket grounds, with a glimpse of the mountains. The sitting room and dining room are comfortable, pleasant rooms, and dinner can be served by arrangement. There is extra parking and a large garden at the back.

OWNER The Halpin family   OPEN All year   ROOMS 16 double/twin (all en-suite)   TERMS IR£40.00; reductions for children; single supplement; dinner à la carte.

Ariel House

52 Lansdowne Road, Ballsbridge, Dublin 4, Co Dublin
Tel: (01) 668 5512, Fax: (01) 668 5845

A Victorian residence in an excellent location close to city centre. Ariel House has recently been completely refurbished and has new furniture, baths and showers, curtains, carpets and beds, although much of its former character has been preserved. There is a new addition that houses 17 period Victorian bedrooms. All bedrooms are equipped with TVs, direct dial telephones, trouser presses, irons and hairdryers. Very high standards pervade through-

out the house, which cleverly combines the graciousness of a bygone era with all modern comforts. The owners, Michael and Marese, take great pride in their house and have created an informal, relaxed and friendly atmosphere. There are antique furnishings in the public rooms and beautifully decorated porcelains. Breakfast is served in the Garden Restaurant. Ariel House has a bar and wine licence. If you are looking for a special place to stay, this would make an excellent choice. Reservations recommended. Located 1 mile (1½ km) southeast of the city centre, 4 minutes by rapid rail. All major credit cards accepted. No pets. Smokers' rooms available.

OWNER Michael O'Brien   OPEN All year, except Christmas
ROOMS 28 double/family/twin (all en-suite)   TERMS Rooms from
IR£36.00 p.p.; reductions for children; single supplement; breakfast extra.

Belcamp Hutchinson

Carr's Lane, Balgriffin, Malahide, Co Dublin
Tel: (01) 846 0843, Fax: (01) 848 5703

This superb, ivy-clad Georgian house is hidden away down a narrow lane off the main Malahide Road. The house is named after Francis Hely-Hutchinson, third Earl of Donoughmore. Count Waldburg, who lived here for some years, has only recently opened it to guests. He renovated the house with the utmost care, ensuring it had all modern comforts yet preserving its features and elegance. Each bedroom has been decorated with a different colour scheme – blue, burgundy, wedgewood, terracotta or green. It is superbly furnished and extremely comfortable, and all the spacious bedrooms have bathrooms, TVs, telephones and hospitality trays. It stands in 18 acres of fields and gardens, including a walled garden, which is being repaired. Dinner (book in advance) is served in the elegant, dark-green dining room. Convenient to the Airport and central Dublin, Belcamp Hutchinson is a comfortable and relaxing place to stay.

OWNER Doreen Gleeson and Karl Waldburg   OPEN All year
ROOMS 5 double/twin (all en-suite)   TERMS IR£36.00; dinner IR£22.00.

Breffni House

45 Upper Drumcondra Road, Dublin 9, Co Dublin
Tel: (01) 836 0714

A warm and friendly welcome awaits you at this creeper-covered Victorian house set back off the road. This is an excellent location for either the airport or downtown Dublin, and there is a frequent bus service. An extremely high standard prevails; the rooms are immaculate, individually decorated with pretty pastel wallpaper. Freshly prepared and substantial breakfasts are served in the cosy dining room, which has bright, attractive table cloths. The B&B has been in operation for 10 years, when the Sheridans took over the house and completely refurbished it. Mr Sheridan has done all of the work himself and the result is a most charming property offering all the facilities of a hotel with personal service at reasonable prices. On the main road en route to the airport in Drumcondra, 2 miles (3 km) to the city. No pets.

OWNER Nora and Padraig Sheridan   OPEN 1 March–31 October
ROOMS 2 double, 2 twin, 2 family (all en-suite) TERMS B&B IR£17.00 p.p.; reductions for children; single supplement

Cedar Lodge

98 Merrion Road, Ballsbridge, Dublin 4, Co Dublin
Tel: (01) 668 4410, Fax: (01) 668 4533

A turn-of-the-century stucco house set back off Merrion Road. The Doody family have lived in the house for some years, and when they decided to open it for guests, they built on a wing at the back of the house. The new wing has been very well designed and executed, providing spacious en-suite bedrooms, attractively decorated, with TVs, telephones and tea- and coffee-making facilities. The breakfast room, with separate tables, is also in this part of the house. Mary Doody is a very friendly lady, and you can be assured of a warm welcome at Cedar Lodge. There is a large garden at the back of the property. Frequent buses take you to the city centre.

OWNER Mary and Gerard Doody   OPEN All year   ROOMS 5 double, 5 twin, 2 triple (all en-suite)   TERMS IR£35.00 p.p.s.; single supplement

Elva

5 Pembroke Park, Ballsbridge, Dublin 4, Co Dublin
Tel: (01) 660 2931, Fax: (01) 660 5417

An impressive Victorian residence in a central location, just 5 minutes from town centre. There is a good bus service into town. The door has some beautiful stained glass work and leaded windows, and other original features include decorative ceiling cornices and fireplaces in the bedrooms and lounge. There are antique funishings throughout the house and the atmosphere is warm and friendly. The bedrooms all have TVs, hairdryers, telephones and tea- or coffee-making facilities. Pleasant hosts and personal attention guaranteed. No pets. No smoking.

OWNER Sheila Matthews   OPEN 1 February–30 November
ROOMS 1 double, 1 single, 1 twin (all en-suite)   TERMS B&B IR£22.50–£25.00 p.p.; single supplement

Glenogra House

64 Merrion Road, Ballsbridge, Dublin 4, Co Dublin
Tel:(01) 668 3661, Fax: (01) 668 3661

Glenogra House is a beautifully appointed Georgian residence in an excellent location, close to the city centre, DART and all amenities. The house has recently been completely refurbished to a high standard of comfort in pleasing fabrics and colours. The bedrooms are a good size, and all have TVs, telephones, hairdryers and tea- and coffee-making facilities. The dining room, where breakfast only is served, is rather ornate, with pillars, a fireplace and a decorative ceiling. Mr and Mrs McNamee offer all the facilities of a hotel, combined with the warmth and personal service of a private residence. Off-street car parking is available. No smoking in the dining room and no pets. Visa, American Express and Access cards accepted.

OWNER Seamus and Cherry McNamee   OPEN All year, except Christmas, New Year and spring break   ROOMS 8 double, 2 twin (all en-suite)   TERMS B&B IR£35.00 p.p.; reductions for children; single supplement

Glenveagh

31 Northumberland Road, Ballsbridge, Dublin 4, Co Dublin
Tel: (01) 668 4612, Fax: (01) 668 4559

Glenveagh is a Victorian house retaining many original features, including beautiful cornices and a ceiling rose. There are antique furnishings, including a grandfather clock in the hallway. The bedrooms are well appointed, all en-suite with TVs, hairdryers, direct-dial telephones and writing desks. The house is spacious, beautifully maintained and extremely comfortable, combining the facilities of a hotel with the warmth and friendliness of a private house. Joe and Bernadette are a gracious couple who enjoy welcoming people to Dublin and are happy to offer advice on what to see. There is an excellent bus service to town, and the house is minutes from the DART station. Off-street parking available. No smoking in the dining room and no pets. Visa and Access cards accepted.

OWNER Joe and Bernadette Cunningham   OPEN All year, except Christmas   ROOMS 5 double, 3 twin, 3 family (all en-suite) TERMS B&B IR£35.00 p.p., single supplement; reductions for children

Greenmount

124 Howth Road, Dublin 3, Co Dublin
Tel: (01) 339522

A spacious Victorian house standing in its own grounds with splendid mature trees and a lawn. Guests are welcome to use the garden on pleasant days. The house is spacious and there is a warm, informal atmosphere. There are no en-suite rooms, but all the bedrooms have washbasins and there are 2 bathrooms exclusively for guests' use. Greenmount has one enormous family room; children are welcome and a cot is provided. There is a large lounge/dining room where freshly prepared breakfasts are served; special diets and vegetarians catered for. The lounge has a marble Georgian fireplace, rescued from a house in the process of being demolished. Located 10 minutes from the city centre; guests are advised to leave their cars at the B&B and take the local bus to town. Pets by arrangement. TV on request.

OWNER Mrs Gladys Duggan OPEN All year ROOMS 1 double/ twin, 2 family TERMS B&B IR£19.00 p.p.; single supplement; reductions for children

Haddington Lodge

49 Haddington Road, Ballsbridge, Dublin 4, Co Dublin
Tel: (01) 660 0974

A Georgian house in a good location, close to Jury's Hotel and 15 minutes' walk from the town centre. All the rooms have been completely refurbished and are individually decorated with soft, restful colours. Each bedroom has an electric blanket, TV and hairdryer, and some rooms overlook a pretty courtyard with shrubs and trees. Haddington Lodge started life as two separate houses, but they were cleverly converted to one house 4 years ago, when Mrs Egan opened up the premises for guests. The TV lounge is quite small, and leads onto the dining room, where breakfasts are served. Vegetarians catered for if prearranged. There is some private parking; street parking is also available. No pets. There is a self-catering unit available. Special off-season breaks upon request.

OWNER Mrs Mary Egan OPEN 1 February–1 December
ROOMS 1 double, 3 twin, 1 family (all en-suite) TERMS B&B
IR£19.50 p.p.; single supplement

Joyville

24 St Alphonsus Road, Drumcondra, Dublin 9, Co Dublin
Tel: (01) 830 3221

Owners Roma and John Gibbons are a most gracious couple who extend a warm welcome in their pleasant, red-brick Victorian house. Joyville is situated opposite St Alphonsus Convent and Church, 1 mile (1½ km) to the town centre. There is a good local bus service; guests would be well advised to take local transport to avoid the parking and traffic problems. Street parking is available. The bedrooms are average in size, spotlessly clean, with orthopaedic beds.

There are no en-suite rooms, but there are two shower rooms and two WCS exclusively for guests' use. There is a family lounge, with a lovely marble fireplace, which guests are welcome to share. No pets. Four miles from the airport and 1 mile (1¹/₂ km) to the city centre. Smoking not encouraged.

OWNER Roma and John Gibbons OPEN All year, except Christmas ROOMS 1 double, 3 twin TERMS B&B IR£14.00 p.p.; single supplement

Merrion Hall

54-56 Merrion Road, Ballsbridge, Dublin 4, Co Dublin
Tel: (01) 668 3661, Fax: (01) 668 4280

A substantial Victorian brick-built house set back off the main road, opposite the Royal Dublin Showgrounds (RDS). The building was originally two semi-detached houses and was amalgamated into one two years ago, at which time the whole house was renovated. The rooms are spacious and comfortable, and the hosts are welcoming, caring people. The dining room, where a buffet-type breakfast is served, has a bay window overlooking the garden. The large, comfortable drawing room has high ceilings with the original plasterwork. The bedrooms all have bathrooms, TVS, telephones, hairdryers and tea- and coffee-making facilities. There is a garden and car park at the back of the house. Winner of the Galtee Irish Breakfast of the Year Award, 1989, and RAC 'Best Small Hotel/Guest-house in Ireland', 1995. Frequent buses into the city centre. Access and Visa accepted.

OPEN All year ROOMS 15 twin/triple/double (all en-suite) TERMS IR£25.00–£37.50; reductions for children; single supplement

Merrion Lodge

148 Merrion Road, Ballsbridge, Dublin 4, Co Dublin
Tel: (01) 269 1565, Fax: (01) 283 9998

Built in 1931, this brick and stucco house in its own grounds is on busy Merrion Road. It has an extensive walled garden to the rear and is in an elegant residential neighbourhood and very handy for the Royal Dublin Showgrounds (RDS). There is a regular bus service, and the DART rail station is a 5-minute walk away. The bedrooms are comfortable and well equipped with telephones, tea- and coffee-making facilities

and are all en-suite. There is a comfortable lounge/breakfast
room with a bay window. All major credit cards accepted.

OWNER Phil and Kevin Dowling OPEN All year ROOMS 5 double/
twin (all en-suite) TERMS IR£25.00–£35.00 p.p.; single supple-
ment

Number 31

31 Leeson Close, Dublin 2, Co Dublin
Tel: (01) 676 5011, Fax: (01) 676 2929

A rare find in the centre of Georgian Dublin, Number 31 is
tucked away just off Leeson Street, an oasis of peace and quiet
in this busy area. Built by the famous Dublin architect Sam
Stephenson as his home, this spacious house has many inter-
esting features. The low entrance opens up into a spacious
drawing room with a sunken sitting area featuring a bar, fire-
place, high ceilings and tall windows. There are terraces and
patios – 2 of the bedrooms have their own – and different
levels. Breakfast can be served either in the upstairs dining
room or in the enclosed conservatory. The comfortable
bedrooms all have phones, bathrooms, hairdryers and tea-
and coffee-making facilities. This bed and breakfast has only
been open for business since the summer of 1991, when
Brian and Mary Bennett moved here from Monkstown.
Secure garage parking is available. Not suitable for children
under 10. Visa, Mastercard, Access, American Express
accepted. Leeson Close is situated opposite number 42
Lower Leeson Street.

OWNER Brian and Mary Bennett OPEN All year, except
Christmas ROOMS 5 double/twin (all en-suite) TERMS B&B from
IR£34.00 p.p.

Parknasilla

15 Iona Drive, Drumcondra, Dublin 9, Co. Dublin
Tel: (01) 830 5724

A friendly welcome awaits one at this Edwardian detached
house located in a quiet residential street. Mrs Ryan is a
friendly, chatty person, who likes to make sure her guests
have everything they need. The location is excellent for both
the centre and the airport, with many buses travelling in
each direction. The accommodation is simple but comfort-
able, with a TV lounge and breakfast room. No pets.

OWNER Mrs Teresa Ryan OPEN All year, except Christmas
ROOMS 1 double, 1 twin, 1 family, 1 single (2 en-suite)
TERMS B&B IR£14.50–£17.00 p.p.; reductions for children; single
supplement

DUBLIN COUNTY

Avondale House

Scribblestown, Castleknock, Co Dublin
Tel: (01) 8386545, Fax: (01) 4539099

Built as a farmhouse in the early eighteenth century, this
unpretentious-looking house was split into two in 1953.
Avondale House is in a rural setting on the banks of the
River Tolka, overlooking Phoenix Park, and is only a 15-
minute drive from the centre of Dublin. There is also a
regular train service into Dublin from Ashtown Station,
which is within walking distance. The interior has been most
attractively and imaginatively decorated and furnished. The
Gothic bedroom on the ground floor has parts of a carved
wooden organ surrounding the fireplace, wardrobe and large
bed. The twin-bedded room is on the first floor. Both rooms
have private bathrooms. The Carrolls are friendly, welcom-
ing people and Avondale House is an interesting place to
stay in close proximity to Dublin.

OWNER Frank and Josie Carroll OPEN All year, except Christmas
and New Year ROOMS 1 double, 1 twin (both with private bath)
TERMS IR£35.00; single supplement; dinner from IR£20.00

Chestnut Lodge

2 Vesey Place, Monkstown, Dun Laoghaire, Co Dublin
Tel: (01) 280 7860, Fax: (01) 280 1466

A delightful terraced Regency building facing a park, with a
pleasant walled back garden, only minutes from Dun
Laoghaire. Nancy Malone, who used to work in television,
started doing bed and breakfast a few years ago. The house
has beautifully proportioned rooms, with high, ornate
ceilings. It is a most comfortable, elegantly furnished and
well-equipped house, and the bedrooms all have TVS,
hairdryers and telephones. Breakfast, which includes home-
made preserves and bread, is beautifully presented in the
dining/sitting room, and there is also a separate drawing
room. Located between Salthill and Dun Laoghaire, access
into central Dublin is quick on the DART train service.

Highly recommended as a Dublin base, or as a touring point from Dun Laoghaire. Visa and Access accepted.

OWNER Nancy Malone   OPEN All year   ROOMS 2 double, 2 twin (all en-suite)   TERMS B&B IR£25.00–£27.50 p.p.; reductions for children; single supplement

Ivylea

220 Swords Road, Santry, Dublin 9, Co Dublin

Tel: (01) 842 1000 or 842 3457

A modern, clean and homely property on the main airport road, situated 1½ miles (2½ km) from the airport and 2 miles (3 km) from the city centre. There are plenty of buses from the house to town and to the airport. The bedrooms are freshly decorated, all have tea- and coffee-making facilities and TVs. The front of the house and driveway have recently been redesigned for easier access, and there is an enclosed, private car park. New to the area is a shopping complex and leisure centre. Tressa Brazil keeps very busy, so advance reservations are recommended. No pets.

OWNER Tressa Brazil   OPEN All year   ROOMS 1 double, 1 single, 2 twin (3 en-suite)   TERMS B&B IR£15.00 p.p.; reductions for children; single supplement

Kingswood Country House and Restaurant

Naas Road, Clondalkin, Dublin 22, Co Dublin

Tel: (01) 4592428

This unpretentious, 250–year-old country house stands, in its own gardens, in a quiet road just off the main Dublin to Naas road. The house is comfortable and has a relaxed atmosphere. The Kingswood restaurant is very popular with businesspeople. Vegetables and herbs are grown for use in the restaurant, and both lunch and dinner are available. The house at one time belonged to the famous singer, Josef Locke. Major credit cards accepted.

OWNER The O'Byrne family   OPEN All year   ROOMS 7 double/twin (all en-suite)   TERMS IR£27.50–£35.00; single supplement; lunch IR£12.95; dinner IR£21.00

Rosmeen House

13 Rosmeen Gardens, Dun Laoghaire, Co Dublin
Tel: (01) 280 7613

A beautifully appointed, turn-of-the-century Spanish-style
villa set in its own grounds, in a quiet cul-de-sac, minutes
from the ferry, bus and train terminals. The house has
recently been refurbished and a conservatory added. The
bedrooms are prettily decorated and a good size, with
comfortable beds. There is one en-suite ground-floor room.
There is a well-furnished, comfortable lounge, a separate
dining room, and a lovely antique grandfather clock in the
hallway. Joan Murphy is a very friendly host, ably assisted by
her sister Maureen. Excellent breakfasts are served, and
continental or vegetarian breakfasts are available. Plenty of
parking. No smoking in the dining room or lounge and no
pets.

OWNER Joan Murphy   OPEN January–mid December
ROOMS 1 double, 1 twin, 1single, 2 family (2 en-suite)   TERMS B&B
IR£16.00–£20.00 p.p.; reductions for children; single supplement

Counties Louth and Meath

The Boyne Valley cuts right through the centre of this area –
one of the most historic and evocative places in Irish history,
and for thousands of years the centre of political power.
Innumerable remains from every century lie scattered across
this fertile green valley.

Dominating the town of Trim are the ruins of King
John's Castle, the largest Anglo-Norman castle in Ireland,
dating from 1172. The Duke of Wellington's family came
from here, as did the family of Bernardo O'Higgins, a
prominent figure in Chilean history.

Apart from a few earthworks, there is not much left to see
at the Hill of Tara, the seat of Ireland's kings since prehis-
toric times. Imagination is needed to conjure up the sight of
great buildings and a mass of warriors and nobles who
inhabited this place in days gone by.

At the attractive village of Slane, the old castle overlooks
the river, and a little farther along the valley is Brugh na
Boinne, the Palace of the Boyne, an enormous cemetery
with graves dating back to the Neolithic era, the main sites
of which are at Newgrange, Knowth and Dowth.

The pretty village of Kells, which is in the Blackwater

Valley, was the site of the settlement of the Columban monks, who moved here from Iona in 807. St Columba's house still stands, and in the church is a copy of the famous Book of Kells.

Monasterboice and Mellifont are the sites of two ancient ecclesiastical centres, and at Drogheda one can see the preserved head of St Oliver Plunkett, former Archbishop of Armagh, in the Church of St Peter.

The Cooley Peninsula is an attractive and unspoilt area with lovely views, and the old town of Carlingford has lots of historical sites, including King John's Castle.

ARDEE

Red House

Ardee, Co Louth

Tel: (041) 53523

This attractive, red-brick Georgian house just off the main Dundalk-to-Ardee road is approached through parklike grounds. It is a relaxed, informal place with very friendly owners and a welcoming atmosphere. There is a large entrance hall, formal dining room, comfortable sitting room and enormous bedrooms. Outside, one end of the stable courtyard has been turned into an indoor swimming pool and sauna, and beyond is a hard tennis court, which is floodlit at night. Guests are welcome to bring their horses and dogs, and local attractions include Newgrange. An 18-hole golf course is 1 mile (1½ km) away. Dinner served for a minimum of 6 people, by special arrangement. Visa accepted.

OWNER Jim and Linda Connolly   OPEN March–November
ROOMS 1 double, 2 twin (1 en-suite)   TERMS B&B IR£30.00–£40.00 p.p.; reductions for children; single supplement; evening meal IR£20.00

BALTRAY

Aisling House

Baltray, Drogheda, Co Louth

Tel: (041) 22376

Aisling House is in a peaceful spot adjacent to the beach and 100 yards from the Louth Golf Club and Restaurant. The house is bright and clean, and the bedrooms all have TVS and are simply furnished. There is a lovely, bright lounge to relax in. Breakfasts are served in the dining room, which overlooks the garden. The golf club restaurant is open to non-golfers, and there are several other eating establishments close by. An ideal base for touring the Boyne Valley. No smoking in the dining room. Located on the Boyne road 3 miles (4½ km) from Drogheda.

OWNER Mrs Josephine McGinley   OPEN 1 March–1 October
ROOMS 1 double, 2 twin, 1 family (3 en-suite)   TERMS B&B
IR£13.50–£15.50 p.p.; single supplement

CARLINGFORD

Shalom

Glan Road, Carlingford, Co Louth
Tel: (042) 73151

Built as a family home in 1978 and added on to a couple of times, Shalom is an interesting house, with all sorts of angles and strange-shaped rooms. It is located close to the shore and near the outer end of the harbour. The 2 dining rooms, where breakfast only is served, are on the upper floor, to take advantage of the sea view. The house has a friendly, welcoming atmosphere, with modern fittings and strong colours. All rooms have tea- and coffee-making facilities and TVS. No pets in the house.

OWNER Jackie and Kevin Woods   OPEN All year, except Christmas
ROOMS 4 double, 1 twin, 2 family (all en-suite)   TERMS B&B
IR£15.00 p.p.; reductions for children under 10

Viewpoint

Omeath Road, Carlingford, Co Louth
Tel: (042) 73149, Fax: (042) 73733

A modern house, built by the owners as their own house, standing above the road on the edge of Carlingford and enjoying spectacular views over the town, harbour and across to the Mourne Mountains. All the bedrooms are motel style, with their own entrances, bathrooms, TVS and tea- and coffee-makers. They are comfortably furnished, some with views, and mostly painted in dark colours (one completely black, which is one of the most popular rooms). A new dining room has just been built to take better advantage of the surrounding views. No pets. Visa accepted.

DROGHEDA

Faulty Piers

Smithstown, Drogheda, Co Louth

Tel: (041) 29020

Handy for travellers, this unassuming little bungalow lies just off the main Dublin-to-Belfast road and is only 30 minutes from Dublin airport. The bedrooms are small, neat and freshly decorated, and the en-suite rooms have very small shower rooms. There is rural countryside to the back of the house. The dining room is for breakfast only and both a smoking and non-smoking lounge are provided. No smoking outside the lounge; no pets. Acess, Visa and Mastercard accepted.

OWNER Noeleen and Tom Dunne   OPEN April–October ROOMS 3 double, 1 single, 1 family, 1 twin (4 en-suite) TERMS B&B IR£15.00 p.p.; reductions for children; single supplement

Harbour Villa

Mornington Road, Drogheda, Co Louth

Tel: (041) 37441

Sheila Dwyer will offer a true Irish welcome at Harbour Villa, her vine-covered, old-style country home on the River Boyne, just a mile (1½ km) from Drogheda. The gardens are lovely and there is a garden house containing a sun-lounge where guests can relax, away from the wind, and admire the flowers. There is a grass tennis court for guests' use. The bedrooms are small, clean and simply furnished. The comfortable lounge has the original marble fireplace. There are no TVs here; instead, people are encouraged to chat, enjoy the scenery or take a walk in the countryside. No pets. No smoking in dining room.

OWNER Mrs Sheila Dwyer   OPEN All year   ROOMS 4 double, 1 triple/twin   TERMS B&B IR£15.00 p.p.; single supplement

The Glebe House

Dowth, near Drogheda, Co Meath

Tel: (041) 36101, Mobile: (088) 520183

In the heart of the Boyne valley, between historic
Newgrange and Dowth, this attractive, whitewashed, small
country house is covered in wisteria, clematis and honey-
suckle. Surrounded by a pretty garden, there are lovely
views over the tennis court to distant hills. Mrs Addison is a
delightful, welcoming host, who, apart from her B&B
business, specialises in small functions and private dinner
parties. The reception rooms are welcoming and warm, with
fireplaces in both the large formal drawing room and small,
cosy study/sitting room. The bedrooms are pretty and
comfortable. Dinners are available if arranged in advance
and cream teas are served to the public. Visa and Access
accepted.

OWNER Mrs Elizabeth Addison   OPEN 1 April–20 December
ROOMS 5 double/twin (4 en-suite)   TERMS IR£19.00; single
supplement in August only

DULEEK

Annesbrook

Duleek, Co Meath

Tel: (041) 23293, Fax: (041) 23024

An impressive gate and a long wooded drive bring you to
Annesbrook, an interesting house, the core of which is
seventeenth-century, with additions at different periods.
The pedimented portico of the house and the ballroom
were added on to impress George IV when he came here in
1821. Another distinguished visitor was William Thackeray.
However, the formal hospitality of those days has been
replaced by a relaxed and welcoming family atmosphere. All
of the bedrooms are spacious and comfortable, with folders
detailing events of local interest and suggested walks and
drives to places of interest. Each bedroom has tea- and
coffee-making facilities and hairdryers. The reception rooms
have big log fires. Evening meals must be ordered prior to
11.30 am and feature home-grown organic vegetables
picked fresh daily from the walled garden. There is a wine
licence. No smoking in the dining room and no pets. French
spoken. The house can be found 4^1/$_2$ miles (6^1/$_2$ km) north

of Ashbourne. Visa, Access and Eurocard accepted.

OWNER Kate Sweetman   OPEN 1 May–30 September
ROOMS 5 double/twin/family (all en-suite)   TERMS B&B IR£25.00–£30.00 p.p.; reductions for children; single supplement; evening meals by arrangement.

DUNSHAUGHLIN

Gaulstown House

Dunshaughlin, Co Meath

Tel: (01) 8259147

A small, attractive, whitewashed farmhouse standing in a small garden. Gaulstown House is located in a rural, peaceful scene and is surrounded by fields of grazing sheep and horses. There is quite an extensive range of farm buildings to the rear of the house which are going to be converted into additional accommodation. Mrs Delany is a most friendly lady who has won all kinds of prizes for her baking. Evening meals might well include home-reared lamb. The house is immaculately kept, the rooms are fresh and bright, and there is a comfortable drawing room. No smoking, and pets outside only.

OWNER Kathryn Delany   OPEN 1 April–31 October   ROOMS 3 double/twin/family (2 en-suite, 1 with private bath)   TERMS B&B IR£15.00–£17.00 p.p.; reductions for children; single supplement; evening meal IR£13.00

KELLS

Lennoxbrook

Carnaross, Kells, Co Meath

Tel: (046) 45902

A substantial farmhouse standing just off the main road in its own grounds. The back part of the house is over 200 years old, and the surrounding farmland is let out. Mrs Mullan looks after 3 small children and runs the bed and breakfast. The house is homely, the bedrooms are plain but comfortable and dinner is available if booked in advance. No smoking except in the drawing room. The house is on the main road between Virginia and Kells.

OWNER Pauline Mullan   OPEN All year, except Christmas
ROOMS 2 double, 1 twin, 1 triple, 1 single   TERMS B&B IR£15.00 p.p.; reductions for children; evening meal IR£12.00

Gainstown House

Navan, Co Meath

Tel: (046) 21448

An attractive country house dating from the early nineteenth century and standing in pleasant lawned gardens, surrounded by 200 acres of pastureland. A patio at the rear of the house overlooks the garden. Pleasantly decorated, the drawing room (with open fireplace) leads off the large entrance hall; evening meals are served in the dining room. The house is located 2 miles (3 km) from Navan, 1 mile (1¹/₂ km) off the Navan to Trim road and is signposted. Fishing, golf, swimming and riding are all available locally. No pets. Smoking in public rooms only.

OWNER Mrs Mary Reilly OPEN 1 June–1 September ROOMS 2 family 1 double, 1 twin (1 en-suite) TERMS B&B IR£13.00–£17.00 p.p.; reductions for children; single supplement; evening meal IR£15.00

Lios na Greine

Bailis, Athlumney, Navan, Co Meath

Tel: (046) 28092

Lios na Greine, meaning "enclosure of the sun", is a neo-Georgian-style house in a sunny location. It is set back off the road, 1 mile (1¹/₂ km) from the town centre on the Duleek to Ashbourne airport road. The house is immaculate and the decor is of a high standard, with matching wallpapers, fabrics and cosy duvets. There is a comfortable TV lounge, where tea is served in the evening. Breakfast is served family-style in the bright and cheerful dining room, as are evening meals (advance notice required). There is one room on the ground floor and a pleasant garden with furniture for guests' use. An ideal base for exploring Newgrange and the Boyne Valley.

OWNER Mrs Mary Callahan OPEN All year ROOMS 1 double, 2 family (all en-suite) TERMS B&B IR£15.00 p.p.; reductions for children; single supplement; evening meal IR£13.00

Crannmór

Dunderry Road, Trim, Co Meath
Tel: (046) 31635

Crannmór is situated about a mile from historic Trim, which boasts the largest Norman castle in Ireland. When the Finnegans bought Crannmór 5 years ago, there was no water or electricity installed. Three of the fresh and bright guest rooms are located in what was once the stable block. They are on the ground-floor level, and one is particularly suitable for disabled guests. The fourth room is on the first floor in the main part of the house. The breakfast/sitting room is a most charming room, with comfortable chairs, a fireplace and antique furniture. The house is surrounded by pleasant gardens, decorated with old-fashioned farming equipment, and six acres of fields. Crannmór is a friendly, comfortable place to stay and take advantage of all the activities and sights around Trim, which include the annual Trim Fair, "The Power and the Glory" – a multi-media exhibition explaining the background of Trim's medieval ruins – and Butterstream Gardens.

OWNER Colin and Anne Finnegan   OPEN 1 April–30 September (other times by prior arrangement) ROOMS 4 double/twin/family (all en-suite)   TERMS IR£16.00; reductions for children; single supplement

County Wicklow

Lying just to the south of Dublin, this is an area of hills and mountains, lakes and streams – a pleasant, peaceful place to escape to after the bustle of the city.

From Dublin one comes first to Bray, a large seaside resort, and then to Enniskerry. Here one can visit the gardens of Powerscourt Estate. The house, which had been one of the most beautiful in Ireland, was destroyed by fire in the 1950s, leaving only the shell still standing.

Glendalough is a beautiful, scenic place in the mountains, set between two small lakes, with the ruins of St Kevin's Kitchen, the church and cathedral founded by St Kevin in 520. Just beyond is the small twelfth-century priory of St Saviour. The county town, Wicklow, is on the coast, and further south is Arklow, a popular resort and fishing centre.

At Blessington is Russborough House, a beautiful Palladian-style house, containing a marvellous art collection,

and the Poulaphouca Reservoir, which has been formed by
damming the River Liffey.

ANNAMOE

Carmel's Bed and Breakfast

Annamoe, Co Wicklow
Tel: (0404) 45297

A warm and welcoming house, set back off the main road in
an acre of immaculately kept gardens. The house was built
as a family home in 1970 by the Hawkins and added on to
in 1981. The bedrooms are small but clean and comfort-
able. There are no guests here; everyone is a family friend.
Cups of tea or coffee are given upon arrival and/or during
the evening. All of the bedrooms are on the ground floor.
This is a lovely spot in which to spend a few days. Close by
is the Glendalough Fun Park, and hiking and walking can be
enjoyed nearby. Mr and Mrs Hawkins are local people
willing to assist with sightseeing and local events. No smok-
ing in the dining room. 2 miles (3 km) from Glendalough.

OWNER Carmel Hawkins OPEN 1 March–31 October ROOMS 2
double, 2 twin (en-suite) TERMS B&B IR£16.00 p.p.; reductions
for children; single supplement

ARKLOW

Fairy Lawn

Wexford Road, Arklow, Co Wicklow
Tel: (0402) 32790

An attractive brick-and-plaster house set back off the road.
The owners, Mr and Mrs Kelly, do their own decorating,
and the bright, airy bedrooms are all colour-coordinated
with matching fabrics. Mr Kelly is a keen gardener, as
evidenced by the beautiful landscaped gardens and colourful
window boxes. Breakfast only is served, but there are lots of
venues for meals in the area. There's a comfortable guest
lounge with a TV. Situated ½ mile from Arklow on the road
to Gorey.

OWNER Rita Kelly OPEN All year ROOMS 2 double, 1 twin, 1
family (3 en-suite) TERMS B&B IR£13.50–£15.00 p.p.;
reductions for children

Keppels Farmhouse

Ballanagh, Avoca, Arklow, Co Wicklow
Tel: (0402) 35168

Built around 1880, Keppel's Farmhouse is set in quiet countryside with beautiful views over the Vale of Avoca. A new wing, with a large dining room where evening meals are served, a lounge and two bedrooms upstairs, has recently been built on to the house. The bedrooms are spacious, clean and bright, full of fresh country air; all have hairdryers and en-suite facilities. Guests are welcome to walk around the farm, watch the cows being milked and observe the famous Avoca Handweavers nearby.

OWNER Charles and Joy Keppel   OPEN mid-April–mid-October
ROOMS 2 doubles, 2 twins, 1 family (all en-suite)   TERMS IR£16.00; reductions for children; single supplement; dinner IR£13.00

Lakevilla

Seaview Avenue, Ferrybank, Arklow, Co Wicklow
Tel: (0402) 32734

A modern house built in 1962 with later additions, a few minutes' walk to the beach and all amenities. The small garden is well maintained and the window boxes are a blaze of colour in summer. Una Dennehy is a cordial lady, dedicated to ensuring that everything possible is done for her guests. The bedrooms are small but comfortable, with plenty of wardrobe space. There is a comfortable guest lounge with TV. Tea- and coffee-making facilities are available on the landing. There is a pitch-and-putt course and leisure centre across the street and 2 golf courses within 2 miles (3 km). No pets. Self-catering available. The house is signposted at Ferrybank. Credit cards accepted.

OWNER Una Dennehy   OPEN 15 April–30 September
ROOMS 2 double, 1 twin, 1 family   TERMS B&B IR£13.50 p.p.; reductions for children; single supplement

Moneylands Farm

Arklow, Co Wicklow
Tel: (0402) 32259

This small farm is located down a quiet country lane on the outskirts of Arklow and has views of the sea. Mr and Mrs

Byrne are a kindly couple who only recently started doing bed and breakfast. There is a lovely ground-floor family room which has a small sitting area and French doors that open on to the garden. The comfortable lounge leads through to the large conservatory where breakfast is served. Evening meals are served if arranged in advance.

OWNER Michael and Lillie Byrne   OPEN 1 February–30 November
ROOMS 3 doubles/twins (all en-suite)   TERMS IR£13.50–£15.00; reductions for children; single supplement; dinner IR£10.00–£12.00

Plattenstown House

Arklow, Co Wicklow
Tel: (0402) 32582

This old farmhouse was built in 1853 for Lady Jane O'Grady. It is set in 50 acres of farmland, supporting cows and goats, and has a lovely, peaceful front garden. The attractive, whitewashed farm buildings are at the back of the house. The comfortable drawing room is for non-smokers, while smokers can use the small sitting room with fireplace and TV. There are beaches three to four miles away and pleasant forest walks. Visa and Access accepted.

OWNER Mr and Mrs G. R. McDowell   OPEN 1 April–31 October
ROOMS 4 doubles (all en-suite)   TERMS from IR£18.00; reductions for children; single supplement; dinner IR£13.00.

BLESSINGTON

The Manor

Manor Kilbride, Blessington, Co Wicklow
Tel: (01) 4582105, Fax: (01) 4582607

This delightful, rambling house was built in 1830 around a much older building, which had been here since Cromwell's time. It is set in 40 acres of gardens and trees and has a small river and private lake stocked with brown trout, and, for the more energetic, an heated indoor swimming pool. The drawing room is completely panelled, and the dining room, which is part of the older house, has also been re-stored. The paintings in these rooms date from 1840. A cow shed has been turned into a most attractive self-catering cottage. The Manor is just 18 miles from Dublin.

OWNER Charles and Margaret Cully   OPEN 1 April–1 October
ROOMS 4 doubles (all en-suite)   TERMS IR£45.00–£55.00

Derrybawn House

Rathdrum, Glendalough, Co Wicklow
Tel: (0404) 45134

About a mile (1¹/₂ km) from Glendalough, Derrybawn
House is set in 90 acres of sheep-grazing parkland with a
lovely river running through the property. Built about
1780, the house was burnt down during the 1798 Rising
and rebuilt in the style of a north Italian villa in the early
nineteenth century. The wisteria-covered house is sur-
rounded by a sheltered garden with great banks of rhodo-
dendrons, with hills rising behind. There are some very
attractive, compact rooms in the back of the house, fur-
nished in pine. The rooms in the main part of the house are
larger and furnished with antique furniture. All rooms are
en-suite. Upstairs there is a large room with a full-sized
snooker table, armchairs and wood-burning stove, while on
the ground floor one will find the formal dining room, where
breakfast and dinner (by arrangement only) are served, and
an attractive small sitting room with an open fire. No
children under 12.

OWNER Donald and Lucy Vambeck   OPEN All year, except
Christmas   ROOMS 6 double/twin (all en-suite)   TERMS B&B
IR£25.00 p.p.; single supplement; evening meal from IR£17.00

Laragh Trekking Centre

Glendalough, Co Wicklow
Tel: (0404) 45282, Fax: (0404) 45204

This long, low building is in a lovely position in the
Glendalough National Park and offers woodland views. The
McCallions have been here six years, and have extended the
house at either end. David runs the trekking centre and
Noreen, who trained in the hotel industry, is in charge of the
house. You can be assured of a warm welcome and excellent
meals. The bright lounge has a fireplace and a balcony with
chairs for sitting outside. The small dining room is very
pretty, with individual tables. There is also an outside patio.
Laragh is the only trekking centre licensed to trek in the
National Park, and there are also wonderful walks from the
house. Access and Visa accepted.

OWNER David and Noreen McCallion   OPEN All year
ROOMS 6 family/double/twin (all en-suite)   TERMS B&B IR£18.50–
£25.00; single supplement; dinner IR£13.50

RATHDRUM

Avonbrae House

Rathdrum, Co Wicklow

Tel: (0404) 46198

Nestling in the foothills of the Wicklow Mountains, just
outside the village of Rathdrum, is Avonbrae House. The
Geoghegan family are pleased to be your hosts in this
walker's paradise. The hiker will find tracks and boreens
(little roads) across mountains, over hills, beside the lake
and along the seashore. Detailed maps are provided, with
discussions on each day's itinerary the night before, and the
Geoghegans specialise in conducting guided hill-walking
tours. A very inviting house with warm, comfortable bed-
rooms (all with telephones), open fires, grass tennis court
and a heated swimming pool, open from Easter to the
beginning of November. The Geoghegan family have
organised some excellent 5- and 7-day holidays, with break-
fast, dinner and packed lunches included. Special rates for 6
or more. Transport to and from Rathdrum railway station,
or bus, can be arranged. There is free fishing (mostly brown
trout) close by. No pets. The house is located 400 metres
outside Rathdrum on the Glendalough road. Visa, Access
and American Express cards accepted.

OWNER Mrs Dorothea Geoghegan   OPEN Easter–mid November
ROOMS 1 double, 3 twin, 2 family, 1 single (all en-suite)
TERMS B&B IR£19.00 p.p.; reductions for children; single supple-
ment; evening meal IR£14.00

Whaley Abbey

Rathdrum, Co Wicklow

Tel: (0404) 46529, Fax: (0404) 46793

Built as a shooting lodge in 1760, this historic house is set in
200 acres of park-like grounds and farmland, in the foothills
of the Wicklow mountains. The house has bright, light and
spacious rooms. It has been beautifully furnished and
decorated and is filled with interesting pictures. The ceilings
have been renovated and painted in the drawing room and

dining room and both rooms have Waterford crystal chandeliers. One large, ground-floor, double bedroom has an enormous bathroom with a corner jacuzzi bath, shower, bidet and fireplace, while another has a small conservatory which leads out to the garden and on to the tennis court. There is a small conference room at the back of the house, a comfortable sitting room with TV and a lovely courtyard. The ruins of Whaley Abbey are at the end of the driveway.

OWNER Emer Shanahan   OPEN 1 March–30 November   ROOMS 7 double/twin (all en-suite)   TERMS IR£27.00; no children under 16; single supplement; dinner IR£18.00; Sunday lunch IR£12.50

RATHNEW

Hunter's Hotel

Newrath Bridge, Rathnew, Co Wicklow
Tel: (0404) 40106

This attractive, long, low building, covered with climbing plants, was originally an old coaching inn. Built in 1720, it stands on what used to be the main road, though now it is one kilometre off the new Dublin road, three miles outside Wicklow. Owned and run by the Gelletlies, it has been in the same family since 1840. It is comfortable and old-fashioned, combining a lot of old-world charm with modern comforts. Several rooms overlook the beautiful, colourful garden and others on the ground floor are suitable for disabled guests. Tables and chairs are dotted around the garden, which lies along the banks of the River Vartry, a delightful place for afternoon tea or a pre-lunch or -dinner drink. The Mount Usher Gardens are nearby.

OWNER Gelletlie Family   OPEN All year   ROOMS 17 double/twin (all en-suite)   TERMS IR£40.00–£42.50; dinner IR£21.00

REDCROSS

Saraville

Redcross, Co Wicklow
Tel: (0404) 41745 or 41620

Right in the middle of the little village of Redcross, Saraville is a small, modernised house with some farm buildings at the back. The Flemings, a young couple with two small children, farm in a small way and keep horses. The house is immaculately clean, the cooking fresh and wholesome, with freshly squeezed orange juice for breakfast and homemade food using local produce. Children are very welcome, the hostess is charming and the atmosphere is friendly and relaxing.

OWNER Sarah Fleming   OPEN March–September   ROOMS 3 double, 1 twin (2 en-suite)   TERMS IR£13.00–£15.00; reductions for children; single supplement; dinner IR£11.50

ROUNDWOOD

Forest Way Lodge

Baltynanima, Roundwood, Co Wicklow
Tel: (0404) 2818429

A long, low house built 20 years ago as 2 bungalows. Forest Way Lodge is set in beautiful countryside in an isolated position with spectacular views. All rooms face the front, taking advantage of the wonderful landscape. In 1983, Grainne Foy bought Forest Way with her sister and trans-formed the 2 semi-detached bungalows into a single house. There is a large sitting/dining room with a fireplace, and a kitchen that guests are welcome to use at any time to make tea or coffee. The owners have their own kitchen at the other end of the house. The lodge is a relaxed, informal place, the emphasis being on activities and the outdoors. With access to 4,000 acres of forest, this is a wonderful place for walking and painting. The Foys give riding lessons, have a cross-country course and take people out trekking; guests are welcome to bring their own horses. Riding courses are offered for children aged between 10 and 16. Evening meals are by arrangement and no pets are allowed. The property can be found 1¹/₂ miles (2¹/₂ km) from Roundwood, the highest village in Ireland, on the Lough Dan road.

OWNER Mrs Grainne Foy   OPEN All year   ROOMS 2 single, 2 family TERMS B&B from IR£15.00 p.p.; evening meal IR£11.50

WICKLOW

Bella Vista

St Patrick's Road Upper, Wicklow, Co Wicklow
Tel: (0404) 67325

A modern, neat bungalow in a most spectacular position, with panoramic views of Wicklow Harbour. The lounge and dining room both overlook the harbour and, although there is a TV in the lounge, guests seem to prefer just to sit and relax and enjoy the scenery. The spotless bedrooms are comfortable, with firm beds. It's a ten-minute walk to the town centre, a little longer on the return as it is uphill all the way. Mrs Wright is a friendly lady; a cup of tea with home-baking is offered upon arrival. Mr Wright has a good sense of humour, is very knowledgeable about the area and enjoys planning itineraries for guests. No pets.

OWNER Mrs Eithne Wright   OPEN 1 June–1 September
ROOMS 2 double, 1 family (1 en-suite)   TERMS B&B IR£14.00–£16.00 p.p., reductions for children

Lissadell House

Ashtown, Wicklow, Co Wicklow
Tel: (0404) 67458

A modern house built in the Georgian style, Lissadell is surrounded by its own grounds in a peaceful spot on the outskirts of Wicklow. The Klaues used to live just down the road, and built this house for themselves in 1982. They are a most friendly couple and the house has a welcoming, homely atmosphere. The rooms are plainly decorated and furnished, and there is an elegant sitting room and dining room where home-cooked meals are served. Both rooms have French windows that open onto the lawn and garden. No smoking in the bedrooms and pets outside only. The house is signposted off the Wexford to Wicklow road.

OWNER Mrs Patricia Klaue   OPEN 1 March–1 November
ROOMS 4 family (2 en-suite)   TERMS B&B from IR£14.00–£16.00 p.p.; reductions for children; single supplement; evening meal IR£14.00

Silver Sands

Dunbur Road, Wicklow, Co Wicklow
Tel: (0404) 68243

A modern, friendly bungalow that has a reputation of being one of the warmest houses in Ireland, in terms of both temperature and welcome! The bungalow has magnificent views of the Sugar Loaf Mountains and the sea. The spacious bedrooms are tastefully decorated; some have TVs and all have hairdryers. Tea-making facilities are available. There are 3 en-suite rooms on the ground floor. Guests share the family lounge. Mr and Mrs Doyle are a down-to-earth, friendly couple, always willing to help plan outings to local events and places of interest. Breakfasts and dinners are served in the bright dining room overlooking the sea. Home-cooking includes traditional Irish recipes and home-made breads and desserts. Babysitting is available. No smoking in the dining room. Drive through Wicklow town, take the Coast road; Silver Sands is on the right, 500 yards from the monument.

OWNER Mrs Lyla Doyle   OPEN All year   ROOMS 2 double, 2 twin, 1 family (3 en-suite)   TERMS B&B IR£15.00–£16.00 p.p.; reductions for children; single supplement; evening meal IR£14.00

The South and Southwest

County Cork

Ireland's largest county is like a miniature of the whole country in terms of its history and scenery. It has a spectacular coastline alternating between long, sandy beaches and wild, rugged cliffs, high, rocky mountains, corn-covered farmland and sub-tropical gardens.

Cork is a bustling, cosmopolitan, friendly city founded by St Finbar in the sixth century on some dry land in the Great Marsh of Munster – Cork meaning 'a marsh'. The appearance of much of the city is nineteenth-century, with elegant, wide streets. Because of its watery origins, Cork is still a city of bridges. The city expanded up a hill, on the north side of which is the Tower of Shandon, with its two faces and famous chime of bells. St Finbar's Cathedral, whose French Gothic spires dominate the city, is built on the site of Finbar's monastery.

The famous Blarney stone – kissing it gives you the gift of the gab – is at the castle, one of the largest and finest tower houses in Ireland.

Nineteenth-century Cobh, with its Gothic cathedral, is Cork's harbour, some 15 miles from the city. Beyond, westward along the coast, is Kinsale, an attractive old town popular with yachtsmen, and packed with people enjoying its many restaurants and old buildings. There are marvellous cliffs at the Old Head of Kinsale and the remains of a fifteenth-century castle, plus a lovely sandy beach at Garrettstown.

Youghal, which is a most attractive seaside town, has many interesting things to see, including the Clock Gate and St Mary's Collegiate Church, and is known for its association with the potato. Sir Walter Raleigh is said to have planted the first potato in his garden during the time he was mayor of the town. Nearby is Shanagarry with its pottery, where William Penn lived, and Ballycotton, a small fishing village.

The coastal scenery west of Skibbereen is particularly beautiful, and the view from Gabriel Mountain, which can easily be climbed, is spectacular. Garnish Island has a wonderful garden, which can be visited most days. Bantry House at Bantry is a most interesting house to visit and has a superb view; and Castle Hyde, a Georgian house close to Fermoy and former home of Douglas Hyde, first President of the Irish Republic, is one of the most beautiful houses in Ireland. Macroom is set in glorious countryside, and the road across the pass of Keimaneigh and through the forest of Gougane Barra is particularly beautiful.

Glebe Country House

Ballinadee, Bandon, near Kinsale, Co Cork

Tel: (021) 778294, Fax: (021) 778456

This small, elegant Georgian rectory is in the centre of
Ballinadee, next to the church. Gill and Tim Bracken
bought the house about 5 years ago and converted the
basement for themselves and their 2 small children. Guests
have the run of the rest of the house, which includes an
attractive dining room with one large table for breakfast and
smaller, individual tables for dinner. Good, home-cooked
evening meals feature homegrown vegetables. Two of the
rooms are particularly large and all contain telephones, tea-
and coffee-making facilities, hairdryers, irons and bathrobes.
The charming, small library leads into the very attractive
garden, beyond which there are 2 self-catering apartments
converted from old coach houses. No pets. Visa and Access
cards accepted.

OWNER Tim and Gill Bracken OPEN All year ROOMS 2 double,
2 twin (all en-suite) TERMS B&B IR£22.50 p.p.; reductions for
children; single supplement; evening meal IR£16.50

St Anne's

Clonakilty Road, Bandon, Co Cork

Tel: (023) 44239

This Georgian house was in need of repair when Anne
Buckley bought it in 1991. Since then, she has completely
renovated it, and has operated the bed and breakfast for
three years. The bedrooms are bright and attractively
furnished, and both the dining room and living room have
the original fireplaces. Anne, who is an ex-school teacher, is
very charming and attentive to the needs of her guests.
Breakfast only is served, and smoking is not allowed in the
bedrooms.

OWNER Anne Buckley OPEN All year ROOMS 3 family, 1 single, 1
double (all en-suite) TERMS IR£15.00; reductions for children;
single supplement

Ard na Greine

Newtown, near Bantry, Co Cork
Tel: (027) 51169

A country house owned by Mrs Phyllis Foley, who is always
happy to advise guests on what to see and do. Complimen-
tary tea and refreshments are offered upon arrival. The
house is set in mature grounds, with panoramic views of the
countryside. This peaceful and restful location is an ideal
base for touring West Cork and South Kerry. Mrs Foley is a
keen golfer, and is willing to prearrange golfing holidays for
guests. No pets. No smoking.

OWNER Mrs Phyllis Foley   OPEN 1 April–31 October
ROOMS 2 double, 1 twin, 1 family   TERMS B&B IR£15.00 p.p.;
reductions for children; single supplement

Ballylickey Manor House

Ballylickey, Bantry Bay, Co Cork
Tel: (027) 50071, Fax: (027) 50124

On the boundary of Cork and Kerry, amidst sheltered
lawns, flower gardens and parkland, and bordered by sea,
river and mountains, stands Ballylickey House, commanding
a magnificent view over Bantry Bay. Built some 300 years
ago by Lord Kenmare as a shooting lodge, Ballylickey has
been the home of the Graves family for over 4 generations.
Robert Graves, the poet, was an uncle of the present owner.
The house was burnt down 8 years ago, but it has been
rebuilt incorporating the best of the old features with a new
standard of comfort. This elegant residence is exquisitely
decorated with many pieces of antique furniture. One of the
main features of a stay at Ballylickey is the food, which is
superbly prepared and presented, and served with great
elegance in the attractive dining room. The bedrooms are
luxurious, and all have TV, phone, hairdryer and trouser
press. Five suites include a bedroom, drawing room and
bathroom. Five of the rooms are in the manor house, and
there are four delightful garden cottages around the swim-
ming pool and gardens. A restaurant by the pool is open to
non-residents. The 10 acres of grounds include another
Georgian home for self-catering and 2 rookeries, which are
believed to bring a special blessing for a house. There are 2

golf courses nearby and miles of mountainous coastline.
Visa and Mastercard accepted.

OWNER Mr and Mrs Graves   OPEN 1 April–1 November
ROOMS 5 suites, 6 twin (all en-suite)   TERMS B&B IR£45.00–
£82.50 p.p. plus 10% service charge; evening meal IR£26.00–
£30.00

Bantry House

Bantry, Co Cork
Tel: (027) 50047, Fax: (027) 50785

Bantry House, overlooking Bantry Bay, is one of the finest
stately mansions in Ireland. Purchased by the White family
in 1739, it is furnished with the most wonderful collection of
pictures, furniture and works of art. The White family were
also responsible for laying out the formal gardens. Both the
east and west wings of Bantry House provide newly refur-
bished accommodations, all with direct-dial telephones.
Facilities for residents include a sitting room, billiard room
and a balcony TV room overlooking the Italian garden with
its fountain, parterres and "stairway to the sky". There is a
wine licence, and guests are welcome to help themselves to
drinks from the bar. Bantry House is open to the public and
overnight guests are admitted at no extra charge. There are
also a tea room and craft shop on the premises. Evening
meals are sometimes available, but must be booked by noon.
No pets.Visa, Access and American Express cards accepted.

OWNER Mr and Mrs Egerton Shellswell-White   OPEN All year
ROOMS 9 double/twin/single/family (all en-suite)   TERMS B&B
IR£45.00–£55.00 p.p.; reductions for children; single supplement;
evening meal IR£20.00

Dunauley

Seskin, Bantry, Co Cork
Tel: (027) 50290

A country house in an elevated position with magnificent
views of Bantry Bay and the Caha Mountains. Absolutely
worth the mile drive from Bantry itself. The dining-room-
cum-lounge is spacious and overlooks the panoramic view,
as do two of the bedrooms. There are 4 bedrooms on the
ground floor and they are furnished simply and comfortably.
Breakfast is a feast, including freshly squeezed orange juice

and drop scones. Dunauley was the national winner in 1990 of the Galtee Breakfast award. There is also a self-catering unit (with its own entrance) available. No smoking. No pets. Upon arriving in Bantry, follow signs for the hospital until you see Dunauley signposted.

OWNER Rosemary McAuley OPEN 1 May–30 September
ROOMS 3 double, 2 twin (2 en-suite) TERMS B&B IR£15.50–£18.00; reductions for children; single supplement

Grove House

Ahakista, Durrus, near Bantry, Co Cork
Tel: (027) 67060

A 250-year-old, white-washed stone farmhouse set amidst beautiful scenery on Sheep's Head Peninsula. An idyllic setting, perfect for nature lovers, with beautiful walks, bird-watching and a private beach for swimming or boating (a boat is provided); with advance notice, bicycle hire can also be arranged. There is a huge, old log fireplace, and the dining room has been extended to include a conservatory, with a stone floor, that also enjoys the lovely view. Down-to-earth Mary O'Mahoney is a good cook, using homegrown vegetables from the garden, and, when the fishing is good, fresh seafood. Light meals, as well as evening meals, can be provided upon request. Honey fresh from the hive, soda scones and home-baked breads are all on the menu here. Signposted from Durrus village, 5 miles away.

OWNER Mrs Mary O'Mahoney OPEN 1 May–1 October
ROOMS 2 double, 1 twin, 1 single, 1 family (1 en-suite)
TERMS B&B IR£14.00–£17.00 p.p.; reductions for children; single supplement; evening meal IR£15.00

Hillcrest House

Ahakista, Durrus, Bantry, Co Cork
Tel: (027) 67045

Situated on the Sheep's Head Peninsula 7^1/2 miles (11 km) from Durrus, Hillcrest stands in a lovely position on top of a hill with wonderful views over the coast. Mrs Hegarty has run a bed and breakfast for years, most recently in the bungalow she used to live in on the farm. Hillcrest is an attractive, old stone dairy farm that was renovated a few years ago. An extension has been built onto the house, linking it with the old barn, which now houses the large games room. There are flagstone floors, peat fires and quite spacious rooms, simply furnished and decorated. Mrs Hegarty is the recipient of the 1991 AIB Agri-Tourism award and the BHS 1991 regional award, and her daughter plays traditional Irish music on the tin whistle and accordion. Hillcrest is a 5-minute walk to a sandy beach; there is good sea fishing and mountain walking behind the house. Pets can be kept outside. Hillcrest is signposted from Durrus.

OWNER Mrs Agnes Hegarty   OPEN 1 April –1 November
ROOMS 2 double, 2 family (3 en-suite)   TERMS B&B IR£15.00–£17.00 p.p.; reductions for children; evening meal IR£13.50, high tea IR£9.50; single supplement

Larchwood House Restaurant

Pearson's Bridge, Bantry, Co Cork

Tel: (027) 66181

The Vaughans built Larchwood House as their home 14 years ago. Two years ago, Sheila decided to start a restaurant, and they began to build onto the house. The property runs down to the River Ouvane and enjoys splendid views of the Caha Mountains. The small restaurant seats about 20 people and is open to non-residents. There is a sitting room outside the restaurant, and the bedrooms are pleasant and good sized, 2 having their own entrances. Bedrooms have TVs and hairdryers. There is a wine licence. Located about 3 miles (4¹/₂ km) from Bantry; signposted at Ballylickey. No pets. Major credit cards accepted.

OWNER Sheila Vaughan   OPEN All year   ROOMS 3 double, 1 twin (all en-suite)   TERMS B&B from IR£20.00 p.p.; reductions for children; evening meal à la carte, approx. IR£22.00

The Mill

Newtown, Bantry, Co Cork

Tel: (027) 50278

Ten years ago, Mr and Mrs Kramer came to Bantry for a holiday and fell in love with the area. Returning to Holland, they sold their farm, and have since made Ireland their home. The Mill is a chalet-style house, set back from the road in beautiful, landscaped gardens, and is especially good for families. The house has been totally refurbished; the delightful bedrooms have wicker and pine furnishings.

Mr Kramer, a true craftsman, has made all the wardrobes, cabinets and dining room tables. Most rooms are on the ground floor, and all except one have en-suite bathrooms. There are plenty of excellent pubs and restaurants in the area. Close by there is golf, fishing, horse-riding, and bicycles for hire. Laundry services available. No pets.

OWNER Tosca Kramer OPEN 1 April–1 November
ROOMS 4 double, 2 family (5 en-suite) TERMS B&B IR£13.00–£15.00; reductions for children; single supplement

BLARNEY

Ashlee Lodge

Tower, Blarney, Co Cork
Tel: (021) 385346

The Callaghans built this immaculately kept house 11 years ago. Whitewashed and with a porticoed front porch, the house is 2¹/2 miles (4 km) from Blarney. There is a large, open-plan sitting/dining room with cathedral ceilings and fireplace, off of which is a pleasant little patio. Furnished with reproduction furniture, the house has been interestingly decorated. Bedrooms have tea- and coffee-making facilities. No pets. No smoking.

OWNER The Callaghan family OPEN 1 April–1 November
ROOMS 2 twin, 3 family (3 en-suite) TERMS B&B IR£15.00 p.p.; single supplement

Rosemount

The Square, Blarney, Co Cork
Tel: (021) 385584

An ideal location for visiting Blarney. Parking is usually difficult, particularly during high season, but Rosemount House offers private parking, and is a 5-minute stroll to the castle. Mr Cronin completely renovated the house, intending to sell it, but after the work was finished, Mr and Mrs Cronin decided to keep the house and start a bed-and-breakfast business. They have never regretted their decision. Mrs Cronin thoroughly enjoys her business, as do her guests, as evidenced by the many who return. The house is warm, the rooms clean and comfortable, each with its own tea-making facilities. There are a TV and VCR in the comfortable guest lounge. There is one en-suite ground-floor room.

No pets. The house can be found opposite the woollen mills.

OWNER Mrs Margaret Cronin   OPEN 1 April–31 October
ROOMS 2 double, 2 twin, 1 family (3 en-suite)   TERMS B&B
IR£14.00–£16.00 p.p.; reductions for children; single supplement

Traveller's Joy

Tower, Blarney, Co Cork
Tel: (021) 385541

One of the nicest things about Traveller's Joy is Gertie O'Shea, a warm, friendly lady who offers a home-away-from-home welcome. The bungalow is 2$^{1}/_{2}$ miles (4 km) from Blarney, in a quiet location, set in an award-winning, $^{3}/_{4}$-acre garden, with mature shrubs, colourful flowers and a fish pond. The rooms are large, basic and spotlessly clean. The family room is ideal, and there is a small room adjoining. The O'Sheas are happy to offer advice on local sightseeing and where to find the best traditional entertainment. There is a cosy guest lounge with TV. Evening meals are to be booked in advance. No smoking in the dining room. Approx. 7 miles (10 km) from Cork.

OWNER Sean and Gertie O'Shea   OPEN 1 February–20 December
ROOMS 1 double, 1 twin, 1 family, 1 single   TERMS B&B
IR£14.00–£16.00 p.p.; reductions for children; evening meal
IR£11.00, high tea IR£8.00

BUTLERSTOWN

Sea Court

Atlantic View, Butlerstown, Co Cork
(023) 40151 or 40218

David Elder is an American. He visited Ireland several times, falling in love with the land of his ancestors, and he wanted to establish roots here, so 12 years ago he bought an old Georgian mansion. It dates from 1760 and stands in 10 acres of wooded grounds on the Seven Heads Peninsula. The house, which has been listed, was in a very run-down condition, and the garden was completely overgrown. David Elder has taken on the challenge of restoration, adding modern comforts as financing permits, yet carefully preserving the character of the house. The latest restoration work includes transforming the ballroom into the Edwardian

Ballroom Suite. Most of the rooms have the original shutters, and the bedrooms are spacious, furnished with antiques. Four rooms have sea views. David loves to cook, and breakfasts are sumptuous; they include scones made to his own recipe. The house is available for self-catering from the end of August through May.

OWNER David Elder   OPEN 10 June–20 August   ROOMS 3 double, 2 twin, 1 family (5 en-suite)   TERMS B&B IR£21.00; reductions for children

CASTLELYONS

Ballyvolane House

Castlelyons, Co Cork
Tel: (025) 36349, Fax: (025) 36781

Ballyvolane is a country house in a lovely setting, surrounded by its own farmland, wooded grounds and formal,

well-maintained gardens, which are open to the public. It was built in 1728 on the site of an older house and altered later to the Italianate style. When the Greens bought the house some 30 years ago, there was a lot of work to be done, and their own sitting room/kitchen is still the old drawing room. Guests have a choice of 7 comfortable rooms, all with TV and hairdryers, and there is one on the ground floor suitable for wheelchairs. The house has been elegantly furnished and decorated, and there is both a drawing room

and large sitting area. There is also a piano in the hall.
Dinner is provided by arrangement, sometimes also for non-residents, and served either at the large dining room table, or at smaller tables for those who prefer eating on their own. One of the bathrooms contains a wonderful old bathtub, encased in wood and raised on 2 steps. There is a croquet lawn, horse-riding nearby, and lovely walks. Salmon fishing is also available. There is a wine licence and French is spoken. The house is signposted from Castlelyons. No pets. Visa, Access and American Express cards accepted.

OWNER Merry and Jeremy Green   OPEN All year
ROOMS 4 double, 3 twin (5 en-suite)   TERMS B&B IR£35.00–£44.00 p.p.; single supplement; evening meal IR£22.00; reductions for children.

CLONAKILTY

Ard na Greine

Ballinascarthy, Clonakilty, Co Cork
Tel: (023) 39104, Fax: (023) 39397

Reached down narrow lanes, Ard na Greine is a compact farmhouse standing in an elevated position with fine rural views. The comfortable bedrooms are on the small side, but have TVs and hairdryers, and four have shower rooms. There is a small sitting room and dining room. Mrs Walsh has won many awards, including the Galtee Irish Breakfast award in 1989, '90 and '91 and the Agri-Tourism award in 1990. Breakfast and dinner menus. Signposted off the Bandon to Clonakilty road. Visa accepted.

OWNER Norma Walsh   OPEN All year   ROOMS 1 double, 3 twin, 2 family (4 en-suite)   TERMS B&B IR£18.00 p.p.; reductions for children; single supplement; evening meal IR£15.00

Nordav House

off Western Road, Clonakilty, Co Cork
Tel: (023) 33655

A secluded, cosy family home on $^3/_4$ acre, set in a lovely garden bordered by trees. Colourful flowers abound in the pretty window boxes and hanging baskets. The whole house has recently been redecorated with new furnishings, and 2 extra rooms have been added to the back of the house. These 2 rooms are excellent for families, one with a well-equipped kitchenette and the other with 2 bedrooms and 2 bathrooms. There is a comfortable guests' lounge and dining room. There is also a sun lounge for guests' use. Horseback-riding can be arranged locally, and there are some lovely walks close by. Mrs McMahon has been in business for just over 10 years and is concerned that her guests are comfortable. Many visitors return on a regular basis for her special brand of hospitality. The house can be found about 70 metres off the N71, and it is just a 2-minute walk from the town centre, where restaurants, a pub and a church can be found.

OWNER David and Noreen McMahon   OPEN All year, except Christmas   ROOMS 6 double/twin/family (4 en-suite)   TERMS B&B IR£13.00–£15.00 p.p.; reductions for children; single supplement

CONNA

Conna House

Conna, Co Cork
Tel: (058) 59419

This charming Victorian country house is set in nine acres of mature woodland and lawns. The Verlings are an interesting couple who have lived in many different countries. Michael is an army officer, and Maura runs the house and is an excellent cook. The house has been most attractively furnished and decorated. Rugs cover polished floors and the pretty dining room leads from the cosy sitting room. There are plans to add on a conservatory. The restored stables can be used for self-catering. Fishing can be arranged on the Blackwater.

OWNER Michael and Maura Verling   OPEN All year   ROOMS 4 double/twin (all en-suite)   TERMS B&B from IR£22.00; reductions for children; IR£40.00 full board (including lunch & dinner); dinner IR£17.00

CORK

Lotamore House

Tivoli, Cork, Co Cork
Tel: (021) 822344, Fax: (021) 822219

Lotamore House, an impressive Georgian manor, is set in extensive grounds, with magnificent views of Blackrock Castle and Harbour. The house retains the atmosphere and furnishings of an elegant home, with window shutters, a beautiful oval ceiling rose and decorations. There are several antiques of interest, including a gold-leaf and marble hatstand. The well-appointed bedrooms, all with TVs, telephones, hairdryers and trouser presses, are colour-coordinated. Five are on the ground floor and one is large enough for wheelchair access. The spacious drawing room has a marble fireplace; a most enjoyable place to relax in after a busy day. Light snacks are also available. Lotamore House is a very popular place with businesspeople and tourists, so early reservations are recommended. Situated in a peaceful spot, just off the dual carriageway in the direction of Dublin and Waterford, 4 minutes' drive to the city centre. Visa and American Express cards accepted.

OWNER Mrs Harty   OPEN All year, except Christmas
ROOMS 14 double/twin, 1 single, 6 family (all en-suite)
TERMS B&B IR£26.00 p.p.; reductions for children; single supplement

Seven North Mall

7 North Mall, Cork, Co Cork
Tel: (021) 397191, Fax: (021) 300811

This terraced, 240-year-old, listed building is in a tree-lined mall facing the river in a very central location. When the Hegartys bought the property, it was derelict, and they resolved to do all the restoration work themselves. Now it is most comfortable and tastefully decorated. The bedrooms are spacious and have telephones, cable TVs, trouser presses, hairdryers, tea- and coffee-making facilities, and overlook either the river or the rural aspect at the back of the house. Both the sitting room and breakfast room at the back of the house have original 1740 fireplaces. There is wheelchair access to the house, and one room equipped for the disabled. No pets. Visa and Access accepted.

OWNER The Hegarty family   OPEN All year, except Christmas
ROOMS 4 family, 1 twin/single (all en-suite) TERMS IR£25.00–£30.00; single supplement; no children under 12

COURTMACSHERRY

Travara Lodge

Courtmacsherry, Co Cork
Tel: (023) 46493

Travara Lodge is a Georgian residence nestling in the sheltered foothills of Courtmacsherry and overlooking its magnificent bay. The house was named after the intrepid men of Travara who manned one of the first lifeboats out of Courtmacsherry in 1825. Mandy Guy is a hardworking entrepreneur who follows her dream. Recognising its potential, she purchased the house in a very dilapidated condition, and extensive restoration was undertaken. The bedrooms are small, but comfortable, and some have sea views. Behind the house are a small patio and herb garden. Mandy studied at the Alex Gardiner Cordon Bleu School in Dublin and has quickly built up an enviable reputation for excellent, imaginative evening meals. The restaurant specialises mainly in local seafood, and vegetarian and special diets are catered for. Off-season evening meals require advance notice. An ideal location for birdwatching, golf, riding, cycling, deep sea angling and watersports. There are bicycles for hire and drying facilities. No smoking in bedrooms. No pets. Car park available. Visa and Access cards accepted.

OWNER Mandy Guy   OPEN Easter–1 October   ROOMS 3 double, 3 twin, 1 family (all en-suite)   TERMS B&B IR£18.00–£20.00 p.p.; reductions for children; single supplement

DOUGLAS

Riverview

Douglas Village, Cork, Co Cork
Tel: (021) 893762

Riverview is a Georgian-style house built in the Victorian era. It is located near the police station on the No. 7 bus route, 2 miles (3 km) from Cork. The rooms are all a good size, with modern furnishings, comfortable beds and TVs. There is a warm, civilised atmosphere, and Mr and Mrs Edwards are a charming couple, offering guests a personal service. The lounge-cum-dining room has the original fireplace and an antique chaise-longue. Only breakfast is available, but there are lots of good pubs and restaurants close by. No pets.

OWNER Mrs Catherine Edwards   OPEN All year, except Christmas
ROOMS 1 twin, 2 family (all en-suite)   TERMS B&B IR£16.50 p.p.; reductions for children; single supplement

GLENGARRIFF

Cois Coille

Glengarriff, Co Cork

Tel: (027) 63202

This modern house stands in a commanding position: a peaceful spot by the woodlands of Glengarriff overlooking Bantry Bay and Garnish Island. It is set in a lovely hillside garden, and is within walking distance of the village. The Barry-Murphys are kind and welcoming, and have been there since 1979. The rooms are attractive and comfortable, and all are en-suite. Extensive breakfast menu.

OWNER Michael and Rita Barry-Murphy   OPEN 1 May–31 October   ROOMS 5 double/twin (all en-suite)   TERMS IR£16.50; reductions for children; single supplement

KANTURK

Glenlohane

Kanturk, Co Cork

Tel: (029) 50014

Glenlohane is a superb Georgian country house set in beautiful park grounds with some wonderful old trees and views to the distant mountains. The present owners are direct descendants of the family who built it in 1741. Desmond lived and worked in the United States and Melanie is American, and between them they have combined the very best of modern comforts with the character and atmosphere of the past. Glenlohane is an informal house, with plenty of animals around, and guests often like to observe the regular farm activities. Good food and open log fires make this a relaxing place to stay. The large, comfortable drawing room features a square bay window, a baby grand piano, a superb full-length mirror, grey marble fireplace and interesting pictures and furniture. There is also a small study filled with books, a dining room and a country kitchen. A traditional stable yard is attached to the house, and the farm includes sheep and cattle. Riding can be arranged, providing sufficient notice is given, and the local Duhallow Hunt is the oldest pack in Ireland. Fishing is available only one mile away on the River Blackwater, and there are a variety of golf courses and lovely walks nearby. Mastercard and Visa accepted.

OWNER Desmond and Melanie Sharp-Bolster   OPEN All year,
except Christmas   ROOMS 4 double/twin (all en-suite)
TERMS IR£45.00–£50.00; dinner IR£20.00

KILLEAGH

Ballymakeigh House

Killeagh, Co Cork

Tel: (024) 95184, Fax: (024) 95370

This is a truly delightful place. Ballymakeigh House is a
charming, 250-year-old farmhouse located in the rich
farmlands of East Cork. Guests are welcome to walk around
the intensive dairy farm, observe cows being milked or relax
with a book in the sunny conservatory. There is a hard
tennis court (coaching available on request), and a games
room with snooker and table tennis. Michael and Margaret
Browne are gracious hosts and are proud of their 1992 Agri-
Tourism award. Margaret also received the 'Housewife of
the Year' award. Furnishings include marble tables, wrought-
iron chairs and log fireplaces. The public rooms and bed-
rooms have recently been redecorated and upgraded, with
all bedrooms now en-suite and containing their own
hairdryers. The kitchen has been extended and an extra
room added, and the gardens are taking shape. Margaret is
an excellent cook, and was the proud recipient of the Na-
tional Breakfast Award in 1994. Her meals are imaginative
and beautifully presented, featuring fresh vegetables, herbs
and fruit from the garden, and fresh cream and milk from
the farm. Vegetarian and special diets catered for. There is a
wine licence. A marvellous spot in peaceful and tranquil
surroundings, convenient to beaches, Fota Wildlife Park,
Trabolgan Leisure Centre and Blarney Castle. No smoking in
the dining room and pets outside only.

OWNER Mrs Margaret Browne   OPEN 1 March–1 November
ROOMS 5 family (all en-suite)   TERMS B&B IR£20.00 p.p.; reduc-
tions for children; single supplement; evening meal IR£17.00

KINSALE

Murphy's Farmhouse

Kinsale, Co Cork
Tel: (021) 772229

This turn-of-the-century farmhouse is situated on 80 acres
of mixed farming, half a mile from Kinsale. The house has
been in the family for 3 generations. Mrs Murphy and her

daughter run the B&B, and her son takes care of the farm. The family have their own private quarters close by, and guests have the run of the house. The one non–en-suite bedroom has its own private bathroom one floor down. The house is warm and inviting, decorated to a high standard with pretty wallpapers. The lounge has the original fireplace, and there are antique jugs and firescreens. Tasty breakfasts are served in the dining room, which has freshly polished wooden floors. No smoking in the bedrooms. Not suitable for children; a peaceful retreat for adults. No pets in the bedrooms.

OWNER Mrs Eileen Murphy   OPEN 1 March–1 October
ROOMS 4 double (3 en-suite)   TERMS B&B IR£15.00 p.p.; single supplement

Walyunga

Sandycove, Kinsale, Co Cork
Tel: (021) 774126

A modern house on top of a hill about two miles from Kinsale, Walyunga is a kilometre from the sea and slipway where there is dinghy sailing and, for the hearty, a nice swim out to Sandycove Island! The bedrooms are comfortably furnished with quality wood furniture and orthopaedic beds. Two are attic-type rooms with skylight windows. The broad hallway has a large window at one end filled with plants, and the open-plan lounge/dining room has an upright piano. There is a patio for sitting outside.

OWNER Mrs Myrtle Levis   OPEN 1 February–5 November
ROOMS 2 triple, 1 twin, 2 double (4 en-suite)   TERMS IR£14.00–£16.00; reductions for children; single supplement

MACROOM

An Cuasan

Coolavokig, Macroom, Co Cork
Tel: (026) 40018

This small country house can be found on the main Macroom to Killarney Road, 6 miles from Macroom and 3 miles from Ballymakeera. It is in a peaceful position in lovely mature gardens. The house is comfortable and clean, and has a relaxed atmosphere. Two en-suite rooms are on the ground floor, and there is a new conservatory, which is used both as a lounge and to accommodate the overflow from the dining room. The patio is a nice spot to sit on sunny days. A good centre for visiting Killarney and the main attractions of west Cork.

OWNER Sean and Margaret Moynihan   OPEN 1 April–31 October
ROOMS 2 double, 3 twin, 1 triple (all en-suite)   TERMS IR£14.00–£15.50; reductions for children; single supplement

Findus House

Ballyvoige, Kilnamartyra, Macroom, Co Cork
Tel: (026) 40023

This poultry and dairy farm is approached down very narrow lanes in peaceful countryside. The house has been in the O'Sullivan family for some years and was built onto in 1981 to provide more accommodations. The lounge/dining room is a long, narrow room with windows all around to take advantage of the extensive views. All bedrooms are on the ground floor. Findus House was awarded the regional Farmhouse of the Year award in 1989. There are 2 ponies to ride, entertainment and singing in local pubs, and nearby is the geologically interesting area of the Gearagh – an ancient forest system on an alluvial plain with an intricate tangle of narrow channels. Findus House is midway between Cork and Killarney, signposted on the Killarney side. Visa, American Express and Access cards accepted.

OWNER The O'Sullivan family   OPEN 1 April–1 October
ROOMS 3 double, 2 twin, 1 single (4 en-suite)   TERMS B&B IR£14.75 p.p.; reductions for children; evening meal IR£13.50

The Bower

Gortanaddan, Kilnamartyra, Macroom, Co Cork
Tel: (026) 40192

The Snells, who come from America, built the Bower seven years ago specifically to do bed and breakfast. They have decorated and furnished the house in an older style, with beamed ceilings. The dining room is panelled and has small tables with cane chairs. Both breakfast and dinner are served. The sitting room is cosy and rustic-looking, with a small bar. The Bower is set in a pretty garden with peacocks and ducks.

OWNER Ted and Flurry Snell   OPEN All year   ROOMS 3 double, 1 twin, 1 single (2 en-suite)   TERMS IR£13.50–£15.00; reductions for children; single supplement; dinner IR£11.00

Bailick Cottage

Midleton, Co Cork

Tel: (021) 631244

Bailick Cottage is in a surprisingly secluded location in the town of Midleton. It was originally a cottage, but, with various additions, became quite a substantial house. The drawing room, with its grand piano and fireplace, is decorated in a strong yellow and overlooks the garden and estuary, while the dining room, which serves breakfast only, overlooks the garden. The house is comfortable and attractively furnished with spacious rooms. One twin-bedded room has French doors opening out to the garden, which is particularly pleasant and a lovely place to sit in the late afternoon sun.

OWNER Mrs Ava Glasson   OPEN All year   ROOMS 2 twin, 3 double, 1 family (all en-suite)   TERMS IR£23.00-£25.00; reductions for children

Glenview House

Ballinaclasha, Midleton, Co Cork

Tel: (021) 631680, Fax: (021) 631680

Dating from 1780, this Georgian home is in a lovely rural setting, and stands in 20 acres of grounds and gardens. It has a grass tennis court and croquet lawn. When the Sherrards bought the house 30 years ago it was derelict, with ivy growing through the floor. They added the bow-shaped end of the drawing room that faces south, and in the course of renovation and furnishing bought the contents of 16 houses, using what they needed and auctioning off the remainder. One of these acquisitions is the old bath, which has a brass surround. Evening meals are served in the attractive dining room, and there is a wide hall with a fireplace at one end. The ground-floor double bedroom has outside access and is suitable for the disabled. There are doors leading from the bar out onto the patio, which is a nice sunny spot to sit on fine days. Visitors to Glenview find it a relaxing and peaceful place, the ideal setting in which to paint or write. Access and Visa accepted.

OWNER Ken and Beth Sherrard   OPEN All year   ROOMS 2 double, 1 twin (all en-suite)   TERMS IR£25.00–£30.00; reductions for children; dinner IR£18.00

Ballymaloe House

Shanagarry, Co Cork
Tel: (021) 652531, Fax: (021) 652021

Ballymaloe House is part of an old Geraldine Castle that has
been rebuilt and modernised throughout the centuries, the
fourteenth-century keep remaining in its original form. It is
situated in the middle of a 400–acre farm, owned and run by
the Allen family. Thirteen of the 29 bedrooms are in the
main house; they vary in size and character as dictated by
the old buildings. Five new, large rooms lie on the north side,
which open onto a lawn and stream. Eleven rooms surround
the old coachyard beside the main house. Four of these are
on the ground floor, and have been designed to take wheel-
chairs. All rooms have telephones and hairdryers. Full of
character, history and charm, Ballymaloe is a place in which
to recover from the stresses of life. Dinner is a formal affair;
the food is always chosen for its quality; vegetables and
salads are picked fresh that day. Lunch is also served, and
there is a children's menu available. There is an extensive
wine list, and Ballymaloe has a full licence. Restricted
smoking in the dining room, and no pets. An excellent craft
and kitchenware shop lies on the premises, and the
Ballymaloe Cookery School is nearby. Visa and Access cards
accepted.

OWNER Myrtle and Ivan Allen OPEN All year, except Christmas
ROOMS 15 double, 13 twin, 1 single (all en-suite) TERMS B&B
IR£50.00–£65.00 p.p.; single supplement; evening meal IR£30.00

SKIBBEREEN

Bow Hall

Castletownsend, Skibbereen, Co Cork
Tel: (028) 36114

Dating from the late seventeenth century, Bow Hall is right
in the centre of the charming village of Castletownsend,
whose one steep street leads to the harbour and sea. The
Vickerys are a delightful retired couple from New York state
who have lived here for 17 years and have created a charming
home. The bedrooms are light and spacious, with some
American furniture. Breakfast is a grand affair, with home-
made sausages and pancakes a particular treat. Good home-

cooked dinners are served in the dining room and the large drawing-room-cum-library has floor-to-ceiling bookshelves at one end with a fireplace at the other; all kinds of ornaments and knick-knacks are found throughout the house. The slate-faced front of the house overlooks a very large and immaculately kept walled garden. Smoking only in the drawing room. No pets.

OWNER Richard and Barbara Vickery   OPEN All year, except Christmas   ROOMS 1 double, 2 family (3 en-suite)   TERMS B&B IR£28.00 p.p.; reductions for children; single supplement; evening meal IR£20.00

Whispering Trees

Baltimore Road, Skibbereen, Co Cork
Tel:(028) 21376

A comfortable, modern, detached house set back off the main road on the edge of town. The bedrooms are clean and comfortable, and are furnished in a modern style with fitted wardrobes; all have hairdryers and electric blankets. All rooms except one are now en-suite. The TV lounge, which has a piano, is spacious and comfortable, with fires lit on chilly days. Mrs O'Sullivan has been in business for over 8 years, and is happy to assist guests with itineraries for local sightseeing. Whispering Trees is a good base for touring, and amenities include golf, fishing, sailing and walking. Breakfasts include home-baked bread and scones. Tea- and coffee-making facilities in conservatory. No smoking in the dining room. No pets. Visa and Access cards accepted.

OWNER Michael and Kay O'Sullivan   OPEN Easter–1 October
ROOMS 3 double, 2 twin, 1 single (5 en-suite)   TERMS B&B
IR£15.00 p.p.; reductions for children; single supplement

YOUGHAL

Aherne's

163 North Main Street, Youghal, Co Cork
Tel: (024) 92424, Fax: (024) 93633

Aherne's, found in the heart of the old town of Youghal, has become an internationally known seafood restaurant and is a superbly comfortable place to stay. The Fitzgibbon family have owned Aherne's for three generations. The inn started life as the family's pub and small grocery store that made sandwiches. The present generation of the family made the transformation from sandwiches to a restaurant, and just recently built on an entire wing for accommodation in what used to be the old car park. The bedrooms are exceptionally large, with very big beds, and are beautifully decorated, comfortable and restful. The drawing room has an open fireplace, books and antique furniture, and the bright dining room in the new part is where residents are served breakfast. The seafood restaurant is decorated in warm, glowing colours, and locally caught oysters are a speciality. There are two small, cosy bars decorated with prints and pictures. A supremely comfortable place to stay on this southern part of the coast. All major credit cards accepted.

OWNER The Fitzgibbon family   OPEN All year   ROOMS 10 double/
twin (all en-suite)   TERMS IR£33.00–£45.00; dinner IR£22.00

County Kerry

Every tourist wants to visit Kerry to see for him- or herself the beauty of the landscape. The sea surrounds most of the county and it is the mixture of water and light that makes Kerry such a special place. There is an inconsistency in the weather – wind and rain from the Atlantic, misty drizzle or bright light and sunshine – making each day or part of a day different from the next and projecting a constantly changing pattern over the mountains, lakes and streams. Each type of weather brings its own peculiar beauty to the landscape.

The Killarney area is the most famous of Irish places of beauty. The town caters for large numbers of tourists and is full of hotels, yet the lakes, mountains and woods of the surrounding countryside remain unspoiled. Close to Killarney is the ruined fourteenth-century Ross Castle. From here one can hire a boat to Inisfallen Island and visit the ruins of the twelfth-century Augustinian Inisfallen Abbey. Muckross House is now a folk museum and has the most beautiful garden. From the Gap of Dunloe there is a marvellous view of the Black Valley. This is where huge torrents of water poured through the Gap at the end of the ice age.

The Ring of Kerry is a famous scenic drive around the Iveragh Peninsula. Killorglin is known for its annual horse and cattle fair, Puck Fair, held for 2 days in August, a great event with pagan origins, when a wild mountain goat is captured and enthroned in the centre of town. Waterville is the principal resort on the Ring of Kerry, and at Cahirsiveen one can see the ruins of magnificent police barracks, which were meant to have been built in the northwest frontier of India, but the plans got mixed up. At Ballinskelligs, which is an Irish-speaking area, there are the ruins of a monastery and a fine beach with wonderful views. The Skelligs are rocky islands off the extreme western part of the Ring of Kerry, which can be visited. It is a wonderful place for birds, notably kittiwakes, guillemots, petrel, shearwater and fulmar, and one can also see the ruins of the old monastery which stands 183 metres above the landing place and is approached by long flights of stone steps. There are also beehive huts, stone crosses, the Holy Well, oratories and cemetries to see. This is a beautiful, peaceful spot in fine weather, but terrifying in a storm.

The Dingle Peninsula is made up of mountains, cliffs, glacial valleys, lakes and beaches, and west of Dingle the scenery is wild and beautiful. Some 2,000 prehistoric and early Christian remains have been discovered, and a little of the old Gaelic culture can be observed at the tip of the peninsula. The little village of Ventry was the scene of a great legendary battle, and at Fahan lies the greatest collection of antiquities in Ireland: stone beehive huts, cave dwellings, standing and inscribed stones and crosses, souterrains, forts, cahers and a church. There are spectacular views around Slea Head, especially of the Blasket Islands and scattered rocks, all part of an exploded volcanic area, and it was around here that the film *Ryan's Daughter* was made. Beyond Ballyferriter, a mostly Irish-speaking village that attempts to preserve its Gaelic culture, is Gallarus, the most perfect example of early Irish building and dry-rubble masonry.

The principle town of Kerry is Tralee, a trading and industrial centre. At Ardfert, the cathedral, which was built in 1250 and has the ruins of its Franciscan Friary, is the most striking building.

ANASCAUL

Four Winds

Anascaul, Co Kerry

Tel: (066) 57168

Mrs O'Connor started doing bed and breakfast 15 years ago when a friend asked if she could help out during a busy season. She enjoyed meeting people and sharing her house and has been offering accommodations ever since. There is a view of the Anascaul Mountains from the front of the house and a clear view of Dingle Bay and Ross Beigh from the rear. The rooms are simply furnished and clean. There is an antique chaise-longue in the hallway. Located approximately midway on the Dingle/Tralee walk, 3½ miles (5 km) away from Anascaul Lake, and close to the 4-mile (6-km) long sandy Inch Beach. Drying facilities available. No pets. Five minutes' stroll to the village.

OWNER Kathleen and P. J. O'Connor OPEN 1 March–31 October ROOMS 4 double/twin (3 en-suite) TERMS B&B IR£14.00 p.p.; reductions for children; single supplement

BALLYBUNION

The Country Haven and Driving Range

Car Ferry Road, Ballybunion, Co Kerry

Tel: (068) 27103

This superb Georgian-style house is ideally situated on the

R55 road, 2 miles (3 km) from the golf course and a 10–minute drive from the Tarbert car ferry. The new driving range with 12 all-weather indoor bays will enable you to practise your golf and enjoy panoramic views of the Atlantic at the same time. Mrs Eileen Walsh is a friendly lady with a good sense of humour. The house sits on a 160–acre farm, and there are 19 acres of young forest and a 4-mile designated walk. The spacious bedrooms are of a very high standard, tastefully decorated with every comfort; all are en-suite. There is one ground-floor en-suite bedroom with a small conservatory. Honeymoon suite also available. Full Irish Breakfast with homemade scones, breads and marmalade; early breakfasts are prepared for golfers. The house has antique furniture throughout and most bedrooms have sea views. Guests will be extremely comfortable here, and have easy access to golf courses and scenic countryside.

OWNER Mrs Eileen Walsh   OPEN All year   ROOMS 1 double, 3 twin, 1 family (all en-suite)   TERMS B&B IR£15.00 p.p.; reductions for children under 12; driving range IR£3.00 per basket (discount if you mention this book!); 10% off green fees for golfers

The 19th Green

Golf Links Road, Ballybunion, Co Kerry
Tel: (068) 27592

An immaculate bungalow in a superb location overlooking the golf course, with a 2-minute walk to the first tee. The bedrooms are furnished with rich wood, pretty pastel fabrics and lace curtains, and all have hairdryers. The sitting room with TV is pleasantly furnished and has a new carpet. Breakfast is plentiful and is available as early as 4 am. Owners Mr and Mrs Beasley are a most accommodating couple who go out of their way to ensure that their guests have everything they need. Tea or coffee is offered upon arrival at no extra charge. Garden furniture is available for guests' use on nice days. All the bedrooms are en-suite. Not suitable for children. A phone is available. No pets.

OWNER Mrs Mary Beaseley   OPEN All year   ROOMS 1 double, 2 twin, 1 family (all en-suite)   TERMS B&B IR£17.00 p.p.; single supplement; reductions for golfers; golf bookings made

CAHERDANIEL

Moran Farm

Bunavalla, Caherdaniel, Co Kerry
Tel: (0667) 5208

A modern bungalow with the most spectacular views, over-
looking Derrynane and the Atlantic, and just 5 minutes' walk
down to the sea. There are two clean, sandy beaches where
guests can swim, hike, boat or just relax and enjoy the beauti-
ful scenery. The house is basic, simply furnished and has a
homely, welcoming atmosphere. All bedrooms are on the
ground floor. Moran Farm is a working farm of sheep and
cows, 8 miles (12 km) from Waterville, signposted off the
Ring of Kerry road (Waterville/Caherdaniel road). Simple,
home-cooked, wholesome evening meals are available by
prior arrangment. There is a separate guest lounge. Smoking
in the sitting room only.

OWNER Mrs Nancy Moran   OPEN All year, except Christmas
ROOMS 1 double/twin/family (all en-suite)   TERMS B&B IR£15.00
p.p.; reductions for children; single supplement; evening meal IR£12.50

The Old Forge

Rathfield, Caherdaniel, Co Kerry
Tel: (0667) 5140

The Old Forge, built in 1983, is surrounded by 30 acres of
rugged land, and offers panoramic views of the Caha Moun-
tains and Kenmare Bay. The property extends down to the
sea, where there is a rocky cove for swimming, windsurfing
and fishing. A restaurant and coffee shop are now in opera-
tion, and the Old Forge has been restored to a museum.
The Fitzmaurices share the work: Reg cooks breakfast and
Cathy cooks dinner, served in the dining room, which
overlooks the view, as does the comfortable lounge. The
rooms are clean and simply furnished, all have hairdryers
and are en-suite. There is a wine licence. Trips to the
Skelligs and fishing excursions can be arranged. Situated off
the Ring of Kerry in a remote spot, 10 miles (15 km) from
Waterville. Visa, Access and Mastercard accepted.

OWNER Reg and Catherine Fitzmaurice   OPEN All year, except
Christmas   ROOMS 3 double/twin (all en-suite)
TERMS B&B IR£15.00 p.p.; reductions for children; single
supplement; evening meal IR£6.00–12.00

64

Glenville Farmhouse

Gleesk, Kells, Cahirsiveen, Co Kerry

Tel: (066) 77625

Situated in a delightful position, midway between Glenbeigh
and Cahirsiveen on the main Ring of Kerry road, Glenville
is a spacious, new country house, with panoramic views of
Dingle Bay. The rooms are well appointed, with an attrac-
tive decor. There is a comfortable TV lounge. An enjoyable
breakfast and evening meal are served in the dining room
which overlooks the bay and the mountains. A speciality of
the house is seafood, which is served with fresh vegetables.
There is hill walking on the farm, and fishing trips on Skellig
Bay can be arranged. The famous 18-hole champion course
at Waterville is just 12 miles away.

OWNER Marion O'Grady   OPEN 1 April–31 October
ROOMS double/twin/family (all en-suite)   TERMS IR£14.50;
reductions for children; single supplement; evening meals
IR£12.00

CARAGH LAKE

Glendalough Country House

Caragh Lake, Co Kerry

Tel: (066) 69156, Fax: (066) 69156

Glendalough House is a charming residence, built 124 years
ago, just a short distance from the shores of Caragh Lake. It
is a warm country house with mature gardens and views of
the lake and Ireland's highest mountain range, the
McGillycuddy's Reeks. It is furnished with antiques and
there are several old paintings. An ideal spot for those
looking for peace and tranquillity, the house is approached
by a long, private gravel drive, bordered with trees, shrubs
and wildflowers. There is a pretty garden inhabited by a
colourful peacock and peahen. Candlelit dinners featuring
Caragh salmon and succulent mountain lamb are served in
the elegant dining room. There are 2 comfortable lounges
for guests, both with fireplaces. A conservatory has been
added to the house, and also a mews that comprises two
double en-suite bedrooms with a private living room and
south-facing terrace. Local activities include golf, salmon
and trout fishing, woodland walks and hill climbing; 5 golf

courses are within easy driving distance. Not suitable for young children. Some German spoken. Wine licence. Take the Ring of Kerry road to Caragh Lake, turn off on left after 3¹/₂ miles (5 km); signposted from the road. Visa and Mastercard accepted.

OWNER Josephine Roder   OPEN 1 January–30 November
ROOMS 3 double, 2 twin (all en-suite)   TERMS B&B IR£40.00 p.p.; single supplement; evening meal IR£23.00

CASTLEISLAND

Beech Grove Farm

Camp Road, Castleisland, Co Kerry

Tel: (066) 41217

Beech Grove is a 100–year-old farmhouse that has been tastefully modernised over the years, set on a 200–acre Hereford cattle farm. This is a wonderful place for animal lovers and families who love the outdoors. There are deer, pheasant, goats and a host of wildlife. Pony rides are available for children, as well as a play area with a tree house. The hospitality here is outstanding. There is a comfortable sitting room, with an old-fashioned marble fireplace and turf fires. Farm-fresh breakfasts are served on separate tables in the dining room, whose original cornices and ceiling rose have been restored. There is a furnished sun porch, overlooking the scenic countryside, where tea and scones are served on arrival. Guests may bring their own wine. There is plenty to see and do in this area, including visits to Crag Cave and a wide choice of sports – and where better to participate than from Beech Grove Farm with its warm atmosphere and its own ring fort? Three miles (4¹/₂ km) west of Castleisland – signposted.

OWNER The O'Mahoney family   OPEN 1 April–1 October ROOMS 2 double, 2 twin, 1 family (4 en-suite)   TERMS B&B IR£15.00–£17.00 p.p.; reductions for children; single supplement; evening meal IR£11.00

DINGLE

Ard na Greine House

Spa Road, Dingle, Co Kerry

Tel: (066) 51113 or 51898

An attractive bungalow in a quiet location, just 5 minutes'

walk from the town centre. Mary Houlihan wanted to ensure that guests had everything they could need, and she has certainly accomplished her goal. All the bedrooms, which are on the ground floor, have satellite TVs, tea-makers, electric blankets, hairdryers, irons and ironing boards, and direct dial telephones. The orthopaedic beds have Dorma-designed duvets, and the rooms are bright and attractive. There is a breakfast menu featuring smoked herring, salmon, home-baked breads, Irish cooked breakfast, etc. You certainly won't need lunch. Ard na Greine is very popular with tourists and walkers. Drying facilities are available. The house is extremely good value and the owners are most accommodating and friendly. The beautiful sham-rock/harp tapestry displayed in the dining room was hand-made by Mary's sister. No smoking in the bedrooms or in the dining room. Pets outside only. Easily located, it is the third house past Hillgrove Hotel. All major credit cards and vouchers accepted.

OWNER Mrs Mary Houlihan OPEN All year, except Christmas
ROOMS 2 double, 1 twin, 1 family (all en-suite)
TERMS B&B IR£15.00–£17.00 p.p.; reductions for children; single supplement

Devane's Farmhouse

Lisdargan, Lispole, near Dingle, Co Kerry
Tel: (066) 51418

A warm welcome awaits you at Devane's farm, a working dairy farm of 40 acres, nestled at the foot of the mountains, with beautiful views all around. It is very popular with walkers and tourists, as it is situated on the Dingle Way walk. The bedrooms are clean, if a little small, but the owners are so hospitable, offering tea, home-baked bread and cake to guests, that room size seems unimportant. Two bedrooms have en-suite facilities, and there are tea-making facilities in the TV lounge. Hairdryers, irons and a trouser press are available upon request. Dinner by advance arrangement only. Guests return here year after year, and visitors new to the property sometimes book in for a night and end up staying a week or more. Guests are welcome to enjoy the daily farm activities, watch the sheep grazing or walk in this beautiful area. The farmhouse is located on a small side road, but don't give up; just when you think you must have passed it, the farm comes into view. A peaceful, tranquil setting. Pets outside only. Cot available. No smoking in the dining room. Off the main Tralee-to-Dingle road. Horse-riding available close by.

OWNER Mary Devane   OPEN 1 April–1 November
ROOMS 1 family, 2 double (2 en-suite)   TERMS B&B IR£13.00–£14.00 p.p.; reduction for children; single supplement; evening meal IR£13.00

Duinin

Conor Pass Road, Dingle, Co Kerry
Tel: (066) 51335

Duinin, meaning 'little fort', is a friendly, modern family home with beautiful views of the sea and mountains. There is a large front garden with a manicured lawn and lots of pretty flowers and shrubs; guests enjoy tea outside on warm days, or in the conservatory that overlooks Dingle Harbour and Valley. The comfortable TV lounge has a VCR that guests may use. There is a separate lounge for reading or just relaxing in after a busy day. All of the bedrooms are on the ground floor, with modern furnishings, large, fitted wardrobes and chairs in each. The front bedrooms have lovely views. Extensive breakfast menu, with fresh-baked breads, served in the sunny dining room overlooking the harbour. Golf, fishing, boat trips, beaches, hillwalking and excellent pubs and restaurants are close by. No smoking in the bedrooms. Located on the Conor Pass Road, ¹/₂ mile from Dingle. Visa accepted.

OWNER Anne and Pat Neligan   OPEN mid March–1 November
ROOMS 3 double, 2 twin (all en-suite)   TERMS B&B IR£15.00–£16.00 p.p.; reductions for children under 10; single supplement

Greenmount House

Gortonora, Dingle, Co Kerry
Tel: (066) 51414

Greenmount House, also known as Currans' Bed and Breakfast, is a comfortable house, set in a peaceful location with lovely views, 5 minutes' stroll to town. A special feature here are the breakfasts, for which Mary Curran received the 1991 Certification of Merit award, featuring homemade muesli, breads, muffins, fresh juices, followed by a cooked breakfast, ordered from an extensive menu; vegetarians catered for. An additional bonus is that it is served in a lovely conservatory/dining room that overlooks the bay. The tastefully decorated bedrooms all have en-suite bathrooms, TVs, clock radios, telephones, hairdryers and electric blankets. Snacks are available upon request. No smoking in the dining room. No pets. On entering Dingle from Tralee/Killarney, turn right at roundabout, take first right, drive to the top of John Street; Greenmount House is the second bungalow on the left.

OWNER Mary and John Curran   OPEN All year, except Christmas
ROOMS 8 double/twin/family (all en-suite)   TERMS B&B IR£15.00–£18.00 p.p.; reductions for children; single supplement

Kavanagh's Bed and Breakfast

Garfinney, Dingle, Co Kerry
Tel: (066) 51326

An attractive, modern, split-level home with a pretty front garden, set back off the road. The bedrooms are of a good size, tastefully and individually decorated in pastel shades, and with comfortable beds. Guests' bedrooms that are not en-suite have keys to their private bathroom. A warm and welcoming atmosphere pervades here, and your hosts are enthusiastic and accommodating. The house has been open for B&B for 6 years and is a very popular stop for cyclists and tourists. There are several stairs to the approach of the house, so Kavanagh's is not suitable for disabled people. Situated in beautiful countryside, 1$^1/_2$ miles (2$^1/_2$ km) from Dingle. Visa and Access cards accepted.

OWNER Marguerite Kavanagh   OPEN Easter–31 October
ROOMS 4 double, 1 twin, 1 family (all en-suite)
TERMS B&B IR£13.00; reductions for children; single supplement; high tea IR£9.00

The Old Stone House

Cliddaun, Dingle, Co Kerry
Tel: (066) 59882, Fax: (066) 59882

The Old Stone House was built in 1864 as a gentry farmhouse by Lord Ventry. It is in a lovely position set on three acres of land, stocked with ducks and chickens that provide the free-range eggs for breakfast. It has been lovingly restored by the present owners, Becky and Michael O'Connor. The three bedrooms are upstairs; two have antique brass and iron beds, and the other an interesting old wooden cot bed. The old kitchen, which was for years the main room where family and friends gathered, is now a cosy sitting room and dining area. On cooler evenings, a fire is lit in the old-fashioned stone fireplace, and guests gather round to chat or read books selected from the bookshelves. The house is tastefully decorated and furnished with simple country antique furniture. Guests have an opportunity to sail on Michael's 41-foot cutter sailboat, the *Kimberly Laura*. No pets. No smoking.

OWNER Becky and Michael O'Connor   OPEN All year
ROOMS 3 double   TERMS B& IR£17.00 p.p.; reductions for children under 12; single supplement

KENMARE

Ardmore House

Killarney Road, Kenmare, Co Kerry
Tel: (064) 41406

Set in an attractive rose garden, this black-and-white bungalow is in a quiet cul-de-sac, less than 5 minutes' walk to the town centre. The back bedrooms overlook mountains and fields with grazing cattle. There is a well-furnished TV lounge. Golf, fishing and hill walking are available locally. Toni and Tom are a friendly, accommodating couple, always willing to assist their guests in every way. Hot drinks are available on request, and freshly prepared breakfasts include homemade brown bread. Ardmore House offers good value accommodation in a quiet location. Pets outside only. Situated ½ km from the town centre on the main Kenmare-to-Killarney road, opposite Whyte's Esso Station. Visa, Access and Mastercard accepted.

OWNER Toni and Tom Connor   OPEN 1 March–1 December
ROOMS 6 double/twin/family (all en-suite)   TERMS B&B IR£16.00 p.p.; reductions for children; single supplement

Ashgrove

Gortalinney South, Kenmare, Co Kerry
Tel: (064) 41228

A charming, new country house set in peaceful surroundings of pasture and woodland with a view of the Caha Mountains. Lynne O'Donnell is a friendly lady who welcomes guests as friends into her family home. After dinner, guests are welcome to relax in armchairs in front of the fire, or, if preferred, to join the family in their spacious and elegantly furnished TV lounge. Breakfasts are served in the Jacobean-style dining room with its exposed beams, stone fireplace and log fire. Light snacks are available and tea and coffee can be requested any time at no extra charge. There is one ground-floor en-suite room with bath and shower. Satellite TV and a VCR are available for guests' use. A hairdryer and iron are provided upon request. No smoking in the bedrooms. Two miles (3 km) from Kenmare – signposted on the Kenmare-to-Glengariff road. Pets outside only.

OWNER Mrs Lynne O'Donnell   OPEN Easter weekend; 1 May–31 October   ROOMS 2 double, 1 twin, 1 family (3 en-suite) TERMS B&B IR£16.00 p.p.; reductions for children under 10; reductions for senior citizens May, June, and September; single supplement

Ceann Mara

Kenmare, Co Kerry
Tel: (064) 41220

Ceann Mara is in a peaceful location overlooking Kenmare Bay. The views are breathtaking, and both the dining room and lounge have views of the bay. Special facilities include a grass tennis court and rowing boat for guests' use. The bedrooms all have tea-makers and electric blankets. The welcome is warm: Mrs Hayes is a helpful host, and will arrange hill walking (on offshoots of the Kerry Way) and lake fishing (at special rates) if desired. There is an intimate atmosphere here, which is enhanced by the log fires. Evening meals, by arrangement, include organically grown vegetables from the garden; vegetarians are catered for. There is a wine licence. No smoking in the dining room. Located 1 mile (1¹/₂ km) from Kenmare.

OWNER Mrs Theresa Hayes   OPEN 1 June–31 August   ROOMS 1 double, 3 twin, 1 family, 1 single (4 en-suite) TERMS B&B IR£16.00; reductions for children; single supplement ; evening meals IR£14.00; high tea IR£9.00

Muxnaw Lodge

Castletownbere Road, Kenmare, Co Kerry
Tel: (064) 41252

This interesting, eighteenth-century house stands in a lovely position set in 3¹/₂ acres of beautiful landscaped grounds, with an all-weather tennis court. The house has an informal, lived-in atmosphere, and is decorated with Laura Ashley wallpapers, a Waterford crystal chandelier, antique furnishings and many items of interest. The comfortable TV guest lounge has the original fireplace and window shutters. The spacious bedrooms, refurbished in keeping with the character of the house, have lovely views, original fireplaces and antique furniture; one bedroom has a brass bed. Telephones and hairdryers are available upon request. Evening meals, by arrangement, are available. There is no licence, but guests may bring their own wine. A peaceful and relaxing house and a wonderful base for touring this beautiful area. Pets outside only. A pleasant, 10–minute stroll into town over the bridge.

OWNER Mrs H. Boland OPEN All year, except Christmas
ROOMS 3 double, 2 twin (all en-suite) TERMS B&B IR£16.00 p.p.; single supplement; evening meal IR£13.00

Whispering Pines

Bellheight, Kenmare, Co Kerry
Tel: (064) 41194

Whispering Pines is a delightful place to stay, located just a two-minute walk from the town centre and a five-minute walk from the golf course. The house is set back off the road and has large front and back gardens where guests are welcome to sit on pleasant days. The bedrooms are attractively decorated with matching fabrics and duvets. The charming owners, John and Mary Fitzgerald, make this a wonderful place to stay; nothing is too much trouble, and they are happy to give advice on what to see and do in the area. John Fitzgerald recently retired, so he now has more time to work in his garden and assist guests. An ideal location for touring the scenic Ring of Kerry. Pets outside only. Smoking restricted. Private parking.

OWNER John and Mary Fitzgerald OPEN 1 April–1 November
ROOMS 4 double/twin (all en-suite) TERMS IR£16.00; reductions for children; single supplement

Clonalis House

Countess Road, Killarney, Co Kerry
Tel: (064) 31043, Fax: (064) 31043

A luxurious, Georgian-style residence within half a mile of the town centre. Mr O'Connor designed the house, and there are cornices, a ceiling rose and an archway made by a local craftsman. The house is spacious, well furnished and there is a lounge with TV. Plentiful breakfasts are served in the dining room at a large mahogany table overlooking the pretty garden. There is a fine display of crystal on the sideboard. Anne O'Connor takes great pride in her home and goes out of her way to ensure that her guests are comfortable and well taken care of. This is a no-smoking house. Evening meals are not served, but there is a wide choice of restaurants and pubs in the town centre. Golf, fishing and mountain climbing are available locally.

OWNER Anne O'Connor   OPEN 1 April–1 October
ROOMS 2 double, 2 twin (both en-suite)   TERMS B&B IR£16.00 p.p.; single supplement

Fair Haven

Cork Road, Killarney, Co Kerry
Tel: (064) 32542

Fair Haven is a comfortable, warm country house set in an acre of land in peaceful scenic surroundings. The bedrooms are comfortable, simply furnished and spotlessly clean. The TV lounge has open fires and tea-makers, and guests may help themselves at any time at no extra charge. There's a separate, bright dining room where freshly cooked breakfasts, with home-baking, are served. Anne Teahan is an extremely friendly lady who has been welcoming visitors since 1984. Fair Haven was named after the hometown of an American who was the first guest, and it is an apt description. For guests who would enjoy a rest from driving, Anne Teahan can arrange tours of the Ring of Kerry and Dingle Bay at a cost of IR£10.00 p.p. Buses collect guests at the door. Reservations can also be made in advance for the Killarney Manor House Banquet, which started in 1990 – an excellent evening of food and entertainment. Located on the Cork road. 1½ miles (2½ km) from town and 1 mile (1½ km)

from the roundabout near the Shell station. No pets.
Smoking in the lounge only.

OWNER Mrs Anne Teahan   OPEN 1 May–mid-October
ROOMS 3 double, 1 twin, 1 family (5 en-suite)
TERMS B&B IR£15.00 p.p.; reductions for children; single supplement

Kathleen's Country House

Tralee Road, Killarney, Co Kerry
Tel: (064) 32810, Fax: (064) 32340

Kathleen's Country House is a delightful, family-run guest
house where traditional hospitality and courteous personal
attention are assured. The house is extremely well
maintained and was refurbished in 1993. It is decorated
with a fine display of original oil and watercolour paintings.
The well-appointed en-suite bedrooms have individually
controlled central heating, radio/clock alarms, TVs and tea-
makers. Breakfasts and evening meals are served in the
spacious dining room, with the emphasis on traditional,
wholesome dishes, using fresh garden produce in season.
There is a wine licence, enabling guests to enjoy a glass of
wine with dinner. Kathleen's combines the facilities of a
first-class hotel with the comforts and warmth of an Irish
home. The house motto is 'Easy to get to, hard to leave!',
endorsed by the many visitors who return again and again.
There are three 18-hole golf courses, plus two 9-hole
courses within a 5-minute drive, and fishing, lovely country
walks, cycling and swimming are all available close by. No
pets. Special group rates upon request. Visa accepted.
Awarded RAC Small Hotel/Guest house of the year.

OWNER Kathleen O'Regan Sheppard   OPEN 1 March–30
November   ROOMS 5 double, 9 twin, 2 family (all en-suite)
TERMS B&B IR£25.00–£35.00 p.p.; reductions for children; single
supplement; evening meal IR£15.50 p.p.

Knockcullen

New Road, Killarney, Co Kerry
Tel: (064) 33915

Knockcullen, which means 'hill on top', is an immaculate
family home in a private location off the main road, situated
2 minutes' walk from town and the National Park. Marie

O'Brien has been in business for 18 years; she started when her family had grown and she needed to do something to fill her time and her home. It has become a popular venue, many guests returning often for her special hospitality and the warm and welcoming atmosphere. The house is an ideal base for touring this scenic area. There's a pleasant lounge with a TV, where guests can relax after a busy day and enjoy a cup of tea or coffee. Breakfasts only are served, but there are lots of good restaurants and pubs close by. Marie is interested in walking and mountain climbing and is pleased to assist guests with information and/or planned itineraries. No pets. No smoking in the dining room.

OWNER Mrs Marie O'Brien   OPEN 1 March–31 November
ROOMS 3 double, 1 twin (4 en-suite)   TERMS B&B IR£13.50 p.p.;
reductions for children; single supplement

Linn Dubh

Aghadoe Heights, Killarney, Co Kerry
Tel: (064) 33828

A dormer bungalow surrounded by scenic countryside, overlooking Killarney's lakes and mountains. The bedrooms are nicely decorated, all with pine orthopaedic beds. There are tea-making facilities on the landing. Carmella Sheehy is an enthusiastic lady who decided to open up her home to guests when her children were young; B&B meant that she could stay at home with her children and still have the opportunity to meet people. There's a comfortable lounge with a TV, a large, furnished patio area and a spacious garden for guests' use. Breakfasts and dinners (if prearranged) are served in the pleasant, bright dining room. A telephone is available. Situated on the Dingle Road, signposted from there. No pets. Smoking in the lounge only. Three minute drive from Killarney Golf Club.

OWNER Carmella Sheehy   OPEN 1 March–1 November   ROOMS 2
double, 1 twin, 2 family (4 en-suite)   TERMS B&B IR£15.00 p.p.;
reductions for children; single supplement (high season); evening
meal IR£11.00

Montrose

Cork Road, Killarney, Co Kerry
Tel: (064) 31378

A modern, two-storey house set back off the road within walking distance of the town, bus and train station. Guests are encouraged to leave the car at the house, thus avoiding parking problems. The house has been well maintained, the bedrooms are colour-coordinated and have orthopaedic beds. The one non–en-suite bedroom does have its own bathroom. Breakfast only is served in the spotless dining room, which has pretty lace tablecloths. Mrs Sayers has been doing bed and breakfast most of her life, starting as a young girl. She loves her vocation, and guests return here often. Local tours can be arranged, and the bus picks up visitors right at the door. No smoking in the dining room. There is also a 4-bedroom self-catering unit available.

OWNER The Sayers family   OPEN Easter –October
ROOMS 1 double, 1 twin, 2 family (2 en-suite)
TERMS B&B IR£15.00–£17.00 p.p.; reductions for children under 12; single supplement

Park Lodge Guesthouse

Cork Road, Killarney, Co Kerry

Tel: (064) 31539, Fax: (064) 34892

This attractive guest house, on the main road, is set on 3 hectares of grounds, with horses grazing in the fields. The rooms are attractively decorated, colour-coordinated with nice furnishings, and all have direct-dial telephones and TVs. Hairdryers on request. There are several ground-floor rooms. Varied breakfasts are ordered off the menu and are served in the bright dining room. The guest lounge has an open fire, and there is a beautiful piano. No pets. Situated next to the Ryan Hotel, 1/2 mile from Killarney.

OWNER Todd & Mary Falvey   OPEN 1 February–30 November
ROOMS 22 double/twin/family (all en-suite)   TERMS B&B
IR£17.50–£22.50 p.p.; single supplement off season only

The 19th Green

Fossa, near Killarney, Co Kerry

Tel: (064) 32868, Fax: (064) 32637

The 19th Green is an immaculate, well-maintained property situated in quiet and peaceful countryside, yet only a 5-minute drive from Killarney on the Killorglin Ring of Kerry road, close to the entrance to the Killarney Golf Club. High standards prevail here. The house is efficiently run, and the large bedrooms are tastefully decorated with comfortable, firm beds, TVs and telephones. There is a large, well-furnished TV lounge, which overlooks the mountains. Situated across the road from Killarney's two 18-hole championship courses, sited in mature woodlands. Tours can be arranged for the Ring of Kerry, Dingle Peninsula, Blarney Castle, etc. Timothy and Bridget Foley are proud of the personal attention guests receive here, and they make every effort to ensure that guests feel welcome and comfortable. An excellent base from which to play golf and tour this scenic area. Credit cards accepted.

OWNER Timothy and Bridget Foley   OPEN 1 January–20 December   ROOMS 3 double, 5 twin, 5 family (13 en-suite   TERMS B&B IR£17.50–£22.00; reductions for children; single supplement

Villa Marias

Aghadoe, Killarney, Co Kerry

Tel: (064) 32307

A dormer bungalow in a peaceful and quiet location, 2$\frac{1}{2}$ miles (4 km) from Killarney. The house is immaculate, the bedrooms well appointed and comfortable. There is a separate dining room and a TV lounge with an open fireplace, over which is displayed a fine Waterford Crystal sword. Mary Counihan has been established for 10 years, prior to which she was in the catering industry. She went into the B&B business in order to maintain her contact with people. Mary's first criterion is her guests' comfort, and a warm, friendly welcome is extended to everyone. Guests are greeted with a cup of tea or coffee and biscuits upon arrival. There are two en-suite bedrooms, and 2 bathrooms exclusively for guests' use. Located 1 mile (1$\frac{1}{2}$ km) from the golf course, signposted on the Tralee Road from Killarney.

OWNER Mrs Mary Counihan   OPEN 1 March–1 October   ROOMS 3 double, 1 twin   TERMS B&B IR£15.00; reductions for children; single supplement

SNEEM

Avonlea House

Sneem, Co Kerry

Tel: (064) 45221

An immaculate, luxurious house set in scenic, rural

surroundings. Mrs Hussey began her bed-and-breakfast business after a friend asked her to take her overflow of guests during high season. Mrs Hussey enjoyed the guests so much that she decided to do it full-time. A most accommodating host, she is assisted by her children during the summer holidays. The modern bedrooms are all en-suite, and are warm and comfortable. The TV lounge, with a real fire, has a piano that guests may play. There are two ground-floor bedrooms. Hairdryers are available. Tea and coffee are provided upon request. Situated just one minute from the village, which has several good restaurants and local pubs with entertainment during the season. Advance reservations recommended during high season. No smoking in the dining room. Signposted from Sneem. Visa accepted.

OWNER Mrs Maura Hussey   OPEN Easter–November   ROOMS 3 double/twin (3 en-suite)   TERMS B&B IR£13.50–£14.50 p.p.; reductions for children; single supplement; evening meal IR£13.50

Derry East Farmhouse

Sneem, Co Kerry

Tel: (064) 45193

Derry East is a working beef-suckling farm, situated 1 mile from Sneem on the Ring of Kerry road on the Waterille side. This is a botanist's paradise, with its wild mountain landscape background. Derry East has its own hard tennis court, a private fish pond stocked with trout, and farm walks, and guests are welcome to use these facilities. The bedrooms are warm and comfortable, and there is a bright, colourful dining room. Turf fires glow brightly on chilly days. Evening meals are available, and feature home-grown vegetables, with vegetarian and special diets catered for. An ideal spot for a quiet and relaxing holiday. Mrs Teahan is a caring and considerate host offering guests a truly warm welcome, and is ably assisted during the summer holidays by her children, who are happy to play Irish music for guests. No pets. No smoking in the dining room. One mile from Sneem, on the Waterville side, on the N70.

OWNER Mrs Mary Teahan OPEN Easter–October   ROOMS 1 double, 3 twin (3 en-suite)   TERMS B&B IR£15.00–£18.00 p.p.; reductions for children; single supplement; evening meal IR£12.00

Hillside Haven

Tahilla, Sneem, Co Kerry
Tel: (064) 82065

Hillside Haven is a country house set in mature gardens
with magnificent views of the sea, mountains and glorious
countryside. There is a separate lounge and cosy dining
room. The 4 bedrooms, all on the ground floor, are spot-
lessly clean and comfortable. Tasty evening meals are served
(if prearranged): traditional dishes, Irish stew, bacon and
cabbage, home-baked breads and desserts; vegetarians are
catered for. Breakfasts are served either in the dining room
or, if the guests prefer, outside, in good weather. Helen
Foley is an accommodating host; walking is one of her
hobbies, and she would be pleased to arrange walking
holidays for small groups. Tea or coffee is available at any
time. Smoking in the lounge only. No pets. Located on
route from Killarney into Kenmare; take Sneem road 2^1/$_2$
miles (4 km) past the Blackwater Bridge. The house is easily
located on the right-hand side.

OWNER Mrs Helen Foley OPEN 1 April–30 October ROOMS 2
double/family (all en-suite) TERMS B&B IR£15.00 p.p.; reduc-
tions for children; single supplement; evening meal IR£12.50,
packed lunch IR£5.00

Woodvale House

Pier Road, Sneem, Co Kerry
Tel: (064) 45181

Full of old-world atmosphere, Woodvale House is set in its
own grounds on the estuary of a river, in the charmingly
situated village of Sneem in the Ring of Kerry. In the middle
of the last century, the house was built as a convent for the
presentation nuns, who taught in the local school until
1891. Since that time, it has been in the hands of the
O'Sullivan family, who have been careful to preserve the
house's character, while offering all modern comforts. There
are 2 lounges, one for reading or chatting to other guests,
and a very spacious TV lounge. A large sun lounge has also
been added. There is access to the river, and fishing enthusi-
asts may take trips out on the bay from Oysterbed Pier. Just
a pleasant 3-minute stroll into Sneem, with its gaily painted
houses and landscaped greens. Mrs O'Sullivan is an enthusi-
astic walker and is happy to assist with walking itineraries.

Smoking in the lounge only. Pets outside only. Situated on the road to the pier from Sneem.

OWNER Mrs Alice O'Sullivan   OPEN All year, except Christmas
ROOMS 2 double, 1 twin, 3 treble (all en-suite)   TERMS B&B
IR£15.00 p.p.; reduction for children; single supplement; evening meal IR£13.00

TRALEE

Brianville

Clogherbrien, Fenit Road, Tralee, Co Kerry
Tel: (066) 26645

A luxurious, modern bungalow bordered by flowers, with a scenic view of the mountains. The well-furnished lounge has a fireplace, TV and piano. The rooms have all been refurbished, and each bedroom has a hairdryer and tea- and coffee-making facilities. There is a lovely antique grandfather clock in the hallway. This is very much a family-run establishment, with Mrs Smith's daughter helping out during school holidays. All rooms are on the ground floor. There are some excellent seafood restaurants close by. Golf, fishing and sailing all nearby. No pets. Visa and Access cards accepted.

OWNER Mrs Joan Smith   OPEN All year, except Christmas
ROOMS 3 double, 2 twin, 1 treble (all en-suite)   TERMS B&B
IR£18.00 p.p.; reductions for children; single supplement

Gleann Cuilinn House

Tralee Road, Cleeney, Tralee, Co Kerry
Tel: (064) 32101

Gleann Cuilinn means Holly Glen, and the house is named after the area on the Wicklow border where Anne O'Connor is from. Anne started her B&B in 1973 when she was asked to help out during the Killarney races. Anne and her husband are warm, friendly, outgoing people who really enjoy their guests and are happy to assist in planning what to see and do in the area. Tea is offered upon arrival. Mr O'Connor is retired, and enjoys tending the beautiful gardens, which feature an old cast-iron crane and skillet. The bedrooms are airy and clean, all on the ground floor. A half-mile from Killarney. Not suitable for small children. No smoking in the dining room.

OWNER Mrs Anne O'Connor OPEN 1 January–20 December
ROOMS 2 double, 1 twin (1 en-suite)   TERMS B&B IR£14.00–
£15.00 p.p.; reductions for children; single supplement

The Fairways

Kerries, Fenit Road, Tralee, Co Kerry

Tel: (066) 27691

The Fairways is in a tranquil position overlooking Tralee
Bay, Slieve Mish Mountains, a new 9-hole golf course and
cattle-grazing pastures. This light and airy new country
house is impeccably maintained and well appointed. The
bedrooms are large and tastefully decorated. Two are on the
ground floor. Breakfasts are excellent; guests can have just
about anything they like, including yoghurts, fruits, cereals,
homemade brown bread and/or a traditional full cooked
breakfast. The dining and guest lounge, with TVs, have
excellent views. Evening meals are not available, but there
are some excellent restaurants in Tralee. No pets. Smoking
allowed.

OWNER Marion Barry OPEN January–November   ROOMS 4 double/
twin/family (all en-suite)   TERMS IR£15.50 p.p.; reductions for
children under 12; single supplement

WATERVILLE

Benmore Farmhouse

Oughtive, Waterville, Co Kerry

Tel: (066) 74207

A 200–year-old farmhouse on a 250–acre working sheep
farm, situated in a remote area with spectacular mountain
views. The farmhouse itself is quite basic, but the O'Sheas
extend a five-star welcome. This is a popular property and
advance reservations are highly recommended. Two of the
bedrooms are in an annex, with their own entrance. They
share one bathroom. There are hairdryers in all rooms.
There's a comfortable lounge where musical evenings are a
regular occurrence, as well as a slide show presented around
the fire by Mr O'Shea, whose interest is local history,
legends and archaeology. Fresh farm-style dinners are
served, if prearranged, using home-grown produce, with
delicious home-baking and desserts. Some people come just
for the raisin bread. A sixth-century souterrain and old
village ruins lie on the farm. There are private walks and

spectacular mountain climbs close by. No pets. Signposted from Waterville.

OWNER The O'Shea family OPEN 1 April–1 November
ROOMS 2 double, 2 twin, 1 family (1 en-suite)
TERMS B&B IR£14.00–£16.00 p.p.; reductions for children; single supplement; evening meal IR£13.00

Sunset House

Waterville, Co Kerry
Tel: (066) 74258

An attractive bungalow overlooking Ballinskelligs Bay on the edge of town. The house is clean and pleasantly furnished, with a large, spacious dining room and a lounge with a TV and piano. There is a pretty, furnished patio for guests' use. Mrs Fitzgerald began offering bed and breakfast over 16 years ago, adding more rooms for the many guests looking for accommodation. However, she still has to turn people away, so advance reservations are recommended, particularly during high-season. Four rooms now have en-suite facilities, and there are ample bathrooms for the other bedrooms. Evening meals are not available, but Mrs Fitzgerald would be happy to recommend local eating places serving good food at reasonable prices. Pets welcome by arrangement. Situated on the Ring of Kerry road, 3 minutes' walk to town. Private parking to rear.

OWNER Mrs Patricia Fitzgerald OPEN All year ROOMS 5 double, 7 twin, 1 single, 1 family (4 en-suite) TERMS B&B IR£14.00–£26.00 p.p.; reductions for children; single supplement

County Waterford

Waterford is probably best known for its crystal factory, which has regular hours for visits. Situated in the southeast of the country, it is reputedly one of the sunniest spots in Ireland. Waterford has a pretty coastline and a more rugged interior, with good farmland. The Nire Valley is good for walking and pony trekking, and has wonderful views.

Waterford city has much of interest to visit. Reginald's Tower, a massive circular fortress, is now the civic museum. Christ Church Cathedral, built in 1779; the French church; the Chamber of Commerce, a lovely Georgian building; and the City Hall, which houses two old theatres, are all worth seeing. The International Festival of Light Opera is held in Waterford in September.

Dunmore East, Tramore, Annestown and Dungevan are all pleasant seaside spots, particularly Dunmore East, which resembles a Devon fishing village. Further south is the Irish-speaking village of Ring, where Irish scholars go to study.

St Declan's Oratory, built in the ninth century, and St Declan's Well and Temple Disert can be found at Ardmore. The cathedral, which dates back to the twelfth century, is known for its sculptured figures.

Four miles from Cappoquin is the Cistercian Abbey of Mount Melleray. The Abbey maintains the old rule of monastic hospitality, so it is quite in order to accept a meal if it is offered to you.

Lismore, which was at one time a great centre of learning, has one of Ireland's finest castles, built by King John in 1185 and at one time belonging to Sir Walter Raleigh. The gardens are open to the public. The medieval Cathedral of St Carthach is most attractive, and was restored in 1633.

ARDMORE

Newtown View Grange

Ardmore, Co Waterford

Tel: (024) 94143, Fax: (024) 94143

A 100–acre dairy farm in idyllic surroundings, with a lovely garden and views of sea and hills. The bedrooms are furnished simply and all have TVs and tea-making facilities. Mrs O'Connor, a friendly, cheerful lady, has won several cooking awards, including Gourmet Queen, and a special award for seafood preparation. Excellent evening meals are served in the newly added dining room, with its attractive pine wood ceiling. There is a cosy TV lounge, and a hard tennis court. Close by is a sandy beach, deep-sea fishing, golf, horse-riding and a local swimming pool. Located off the Youghal/Dungarvan road. Visa and Access cards accepted. No smoking.

OWNER Mrs Teresa O'Connor   OPEN 1 March–mid October
ROOMS 1 double, 3 twin, 2 family (all en-suite)
TERMS B&B IR£14.00–£15.00 p.p.; reductions for children; single supplement; evening meal IR£11.00

Nire Valley Farmhouse

Ballymacarbry, Co Waterford

Tel: (052) 36149

Easy to find, Nire Valley Farmhouse stands in the centre of Ballymacarbry beside a petrol station, which, together with a small shop, is also run by the Doocey family. This square, whitewashed house at the foot of Deerpark Hill is part of a sheep and cattle farm. There is one ground-floor en-suite room, and the dining room has windows all along the back, opening out onto the patio. Smoking in the lounge only and no pets.

OWNER The Doocey family   OPEN 1 May–1 October   ROOMS 1 double, 1 family, 1 twin, 1 single (3 en-suite)   TERMS B&B IR£15.00 p.p.; reductions for children; single supplement

CAPPOQUIN

Aglish House

Cappoquin, Co Waterford

Tel: (024) 96181, Fax: (024) 96482

A period house on a working dairy farm in the Blackwater Valley lying between the Knockmealdown Mountains and the sea. Aglish House is very much a family home, with 6 children and 5 dogs, and has a relaxed atmosphere, with very friendly hosts. The dining room has been recently refurbished. All bedrooms have phones, TVs and hairdryers, and there is a wine licence. Golf, deep-sea fishing, pony trekking and bike hire can be arranged locally. No smoking in the bedrooms.

OWNER Tom and Terry Moore   OPEN All year   ROOMS 2 double, 2 family (all en-suite)   TERMS B&B from IR£18.00 p.p.; reductions for children; single supplement; evening meal IR£16.00; lunch IR£10.00, afternoon tea IR£3.00

Richmond House

Cappoquin, Co Waterford

Tel: (058) 54278, Fax: (058) 54988

Half a mile from Cappoquin, Richmond House, a substantial eighteenth-century residence, stands in well-maintained parkland. It is a peaceful, comfortable country house, beautifully maintained, with spacious, bright rooms. Paul Deevy trained as a chef at Ballymaloe, and both he and his wife, Jean, trained in hotel management. There are two dining rooms, and non-residents are also catered for. Guests have use of a small sitting room with a lovely marble fireplace and a conservatory overlooking the garden. Access, Visa and Diners cards accepted.

OWNER Jean Deevy   OPEN 1 February–31 July   ROOMS 5 double, 5 twin (all en-suite)   TERMS IR£20.00–£28.00; reductions for children; no single supplement; dinner IR£22.00

CHEEKPOINT

Three Rivers Guesthouse

Cheekpoint, Co Waterford

Tel: (051) 382520, Fax: (051) 382542

Built only three years ago, the Three Rivers Guesthouse is in a superb position at the end of a promontory overlooking the three rivers – the Suir, the Barrow and the Nore. The present, very helpful, owners only took over the guest house in 1994, and their previous hotel management experience means that you can be assured of professional and attentive service. All the bedrooms have telephones and bathrooms, and most have a sea view. The lounge, furnished with wicker chairs, has a bay window to take advantage of the view, and the restaurant is light and bright and overlooks the estuary. Nearby is a championship golf course. It is an excellent area for swimming, fishing, sailing, horse-riding and walking. Major credit cards accepted.

OWNER Stan and Mailo Power   OPEN All year   ROOMS 8 double, 4 twin, 2 single (all en-suite)   TERMS IR£20.00–£30.00; reductions for children under 14 yrs; single supplement

DUNGARVAN

Ballyguiry Farm

Dungarvan, Co Waterford

Tel: (058) 41194

The Kiely family bought this property in 1940 for £1,200. The original house is 300 years old, and the front facade dates from the late Georgian period. Ballyguiry stands in a wonderful position, with superb views, on a mixed farm, the farm buildings being to the rear of the property. Mrs Kiely has recently done up virtually the whole house, installing quite a lot of reproduction plasterwork. An immaculately clean home, Ballyguiry Farm caters predominantly for families. It is signposted south of Dungarvan. No smoking.

OWNER Kathleen Kiely   OPEN 1 April–31 October   ROOMS 2 double, 1 twin, 2 family (3 en-suite)   TERMS B&B IR£15.00–£16.00 p.p.; reductions for children; single supplement; evening meal IR£12.50

DUNMORE EAST

Church Villa

Dunmore East, Co Waterford

Tel: (051) 83390

A whitewashed period house, one of a row of cottages opposite the Church of Ireland and adjacent to the Ship bar and restaurant right in the centre of the attractive village of Dunmore East. The small, cosy bedrooms are individually decorated, some with the original fireplaces. The light fixtures are Waterford crystal. There is a guest lounge with TV. Breakfasts only are served in the dining room, which leads onto the patio. Lucy Butler is a friendly, outgoing lady who wants her guests to feel relaxed and very much at home. Evening meals are available at the adjacent restaurant. There are several other eating establishments close by. Minutes from the beach and fishing harbour and close to the park, for those interested in exploring the many caves there. No pets. No smoking in dining room.

OWNER Mrs Lucy Butler   OPEN All year   ROOMS 4 double, 2 twin, 3 single (8 with showers)   TERMS B&B IR£15.00 p.p.; reductions for children; single supplement

Dunmore Lodge

Dunmore East, Co Waterford

Tel: (051) 83454

Formerly called the Cottage, this is one of the oldest houses in Dunmore East. Extremely attractive, it is located right in the centre of town yet is protected by its own grounds, with a pretty, half-circular front garden and some outbuildings to the back. Dunmore Lodge is a low stone building with a porch and 20 very pronounced bow windows, with wonderful views over the water. The front-facing sitting room is comfortable and tastefully decorated. A long hallway stretches to the back of the house, ending with the old kitchen, beyond which is a small patio for sitting outdoors on fine days. The rooms are off to each side. Pets outside only. Smoking in lounge only.

OWNER Zoe Coffey   OPEN 1 March–1 November   ROOMS 3 double, 1 twin, (3 en-suite)   TERMS B&B IR£16.00–£18.00 p.p.; single supplement

MILLSTREET

Castle Farm

Millstreet, Cappagh, Co Waterford

Tel: (058) 68049, Fax: (058) 68049

Mountain Castle was the principal seat of the McGraths of Sliabh gCua, one of the two Gaelic families that owned land in this county before the arrival of Cromwell. The accommodation is in a restored wing of the fifteenth-century castle. The oldest section, with the original archway, contains the long, narrow dining room with its 4-foot-thick stone walls. The rooms are decorated with attractive furnishings. Castle Farm, which won the Agri-Tourism award in 1991, stands in lovely countryside with fine views and can be found down a lane beside the pub in Millstreet. There is a wine licence, and dinner is available, featuring organically grown vegetables. At breakfast, guests are served milk from the farm and homemade jam. Guests can help themselves to tea or coffee in the kitchen. Smoking confined to one room. Pets outside only. Signposted from the Dungarven to Killarney road.

OWNER Mrs Joan Nugent   OPEN 1 March–1 November ROOMS 2 double, 2 twin, 1 family (all en-suite) TERMS B&B IR£17.00 p.p.; reductions for children; single supplement; evening meal IR£13.00

NIRE VALLEY

Hanora's Country Cottage

Nire Valley, via Clonmel, Co Waterford

Tel: (052) 36134, Fax: (052) 36540

An absolute haven of peace and tranquillity, Hanora's Cottage, a converted ancestral home, nestles at the foot of the Comeragh Mountains, beside the Nire Church and old schoolhouse. The Nire River runs alongside. The cottage was recently refurbished, and the bedrooms are now individually and tastefully decorated and have TVs, telephones, hairdryers and tea- and coffee-making facilities. One room also has a Jacuzzi bath. There is a sitting area with TV. Sumptuous breakfasts include freshly baked scones, homemade jams and muesli. Dinners must be prearranged. Meals are served in the cosy dining room, where the fireplace has a 100–year-old "wheel" – a device for getting the fire going – or in the new conservatory. Eoin, the son and also the chef, completed his training under Darina Allen at Ballymaloe Cookery School. Seamus Wall is past captain of Clonmel Golf Club and would be happy to make all golfing arrangements. A paradise for walkers and nature lovers, where guests return often to relax and unwind in the beautiful surroundings. Maps and itineraries are provided. Smoking in lounge only. Not suitable for children. Twenty minutes' drive from Clonmel or Dungarvan.

OWNER Seamus and Mary Wall OPEN All year, except Christmas week ROOMS 2 double, 6 twin (all en-suite) TERMS B&B IR£22.00–£25.00 p.p.; single supplement; reductions for children; evening meals à la carte

ROSSDUFF

Elton Lodge

Rossduff, Co Waterford

Tel: (051) 382117

A 200–year-old farmhouse, Elton Lodge has been in the Richardson family for some 80 years. There are pleasant gardens to the front, and at the back of the house is the farmyard for the dairy farm, which is run by Mr Richardson and his son. The rooms have recently been redecorated and furnished, and there is one twin en-suite room off the sitting room. Eileen Richardson is a very friendly lady with 6 children. The house is located on the main Dunmore East-to-Waterford road, 6 miles from Waterford.

OWNER Mrs Eileen Richardson OPEN 1 June–1 November ROOMS 2 double, 2 twin, 1 family (all en-suite) TERMS B&B from IR£15.50; reductions for children; single supplement

Cliff House

Cliff Road, Tramore, Co Waterford
Tel: (051) 381497

This house, built 13 years ago by the owners, stands in its own landscaped gardens overlooking the sea. The bedrooms, 2 of which are on the ground floor, are well appointed and spotlessly clean, with attractive pastel print duvets. All bedrooms now have their own bathrooms and most overlook Tramore Bay. There are tea- and coffee-making facilities, and an extensive breakfast menu. A thoroughly enjoyable place to stay: friendly people, a family atmosphere and, an added bonus, panoramic views. Within walking distance of town centre and adjacent to new leisure centre. Secure parking. No smoking in the bedrooms. No pets. Ten minutes to Waterford Glass Factory. The house is on the coast road. Visa and Mastercard accepted.

OWNER Mrs Hilary O'Sullivan   OPEN 1 March–1 November
ROOMS 3 double, 2 twin, 1 family (all en-suite)
TERMS B&B IR£14.00–£16.00 p.p.; reductions for children; single supplement

Mountain View

Fenor, Tramore, Co Waterford
Tel: (051) 396107

Mountain View, an idyllic thatched cottage, dates from the 1700s. The owners have lovingly restored the farmhouse to a most delightful and charming property, furnished with traditional and period pieces, chintzy decor and satin bedspreads. One family room is very large indeed, combining 2 bedrooms, bathroom and sitting room. Ideal for families or people wanting a little extra privacy. There is a colourful TV lounge, with an additional sitting room where sing-alongs take place in the evening. When wandering about please be careful: this is a "mind your head" house, thanks to the low beams! Fresh, home-style three-course meals are served in the cosy dining room. All rooms are on the ground floor. Four miles (8 km) from Tramore, 1¹/₂ miles (2 km) to beaches. All major credit cards accepted.

OWNER Mrs E. Rockett   OPEN late March–1 October
ROOMS 4 double, 3 twin, 1 single, 2 family (7 en-suite)

TERMS B&B IR£13.50–£15.50 p.p.; reductions for children; single supplement; evening meal IR£12.00

Rushmere House

Branch Road, Tramore, Co Waterford
Tel: (051) 381041

A Georgian-style house built in the late 1800s, overlooking Tramore Bay and beside the Majestic Hotel. The rooms vary in size from small to spacious, the front rooms having views of the bay. Teddy and Rita McGivney purchased the house 16 years ago with the intention of starting a bed and breakfast. It is an ideal location, and they have been busy with guests from the beginning. The TV lounge is small and cosy, and the house is minutes from the beach and all amenities. Lots of good eating establishments close by. There are tea-making facilities in all the bedrooms. Ample parking across the street. No smoking in the dining room. No pets. Major credit cards accepted.

OWNER Rita McGivney OPEN All year, except Christmas
ROOMS 2 double, 3 twin, 1 family (3 en-suite)
TERMS B&B IR£14.00–£16.00 p.p.; reductions for children; single supplement

Venezia

Church Road Grove, Tramore, Co Waterford
Tel: (051) 381412

A well-maintained and comfortable bungalow on a quiet residential street, with a landscaped garden and car park to the front of the house. The bedrooms are a good size, individually decorated in blue, pink, green or peach, with modern, comfortable furnishings and fitted wardrobes. Excellent breakfasts are served in the bright dining room, which is nicely decorated with quality wallpapers. The lounge/dining room has a cosy gas fire and a Kilkenny marble fireplace. Mrs St John is a charming host, trained in hotel management. The house is within walking distance of the beach and 10 minutes' drive to Waterford. No smoking and no pets. All bedrooms on the ground floor.

OWNER Josephine St John OPEN 1 April–1 October
ROOMS 1 double, 1 twin, 2 family (3 en-suite)
TERMS B&B IR£16.00 p.p.; reductions for children; single supplement

90

Blenheim House

Blenheim Heights, Waterford, Co Waterford
Tel: (051) 74115

Blenheim House was built in 1763 and stands in 4 acres of grounds. There is a small deer park and a children's play area. The bedrooms are spacious and comfortable, most of them with original Georgian fireplaces. The large lounge, with an open fire, overlooks the grounds and is a peaceful spot to unwind in. The house derives its name from the Battle of Blenheim. The Waterford Glass factory is close by. Other local activities include golf, fine beaches and swimming. Horse-riding can be arranged. Situated 3^1/$_2$ miles (5 km) from Waterford city on the Passage East Road, just 7 minutes' drive from the Passage East car ferry.

OWNER Mrs Claire Fitzmaurice   OPEN All year, except Christmas   ROOMS 6 rooms (all en-suite)   TERMS B&B IR£15.50 p.p.; reductions for children

Diamond Hill Guest House

Slieverue, Waterford, Co Waterford
Tel: (051) 32855 or 32254

A well-appointed and comfortable guest house in an elevated position in a quiet part of Waterford, situated in award-winning gardens. The modern bedrooms are well furnished, immaculately clean and a good size. The upstairs bedrooms overlook the gardens, peaceful countryside and grazing cattle. There are two lounges; one has a TV. There is a menu for breakfast. Diamond Hill is run by the Malone family, who skilfully combine personal service with efficiency. Two miles (3 km) from Waterford, with golf, horse-riding, fishing and sandy beaches nearby. No smoking in the dining room and no pets. Visa and Access cards accepted.

OWNER John and Mary Malone   OPEN All year   ROOMS 5 double, 2 twin, 1 single, 2 family (all en-suite)   TERMS B&B IR£16.50–£17.50 p.p.; reductions for children; single supplement; dinner à la carte

Foxmount Farm

Passage East Road, Waterford, Co Waterford
Tel: (051) 74308

A lovely seventeenth-century house in attractive countryside down a lane surrounded by a 250–acre farm, which is managed by Mr Kent and one of his sons. The Kents are a most welcoming, friendly couple and have been many years in the bed-and-breakfast business. In 1991, they were the winners of the Galtee National award. The drawing room is most attractive and has an open fireplace; the dining room has separate tables and a piano. The 2 front family rooms are very large and offer lovely rural views. The whole house has recently been redecorated; 2 of the bedrooms have been extended and all now have en-suite facilities. The evenings have a party-like atmosphere, with excellent home-cooked meals using fresh, local produce; afterwards it is but a short walk to the pub. Amenities include a hard tennis court, table tennis, snooker and ponies to ride on – on leading rein only. The house is signposted at the Maxol garage.

OWNER Mrs Margaret Kent OPEN 1 March–1 November
ROOMS 1 double, 2 twin, 3 family (all en-suite) TERMS B&B
from IR£20.00; reductions for children; single supplement;
evening meal IR£15.00

Lakefield House

Rossduff, Dunmore Road, Waterford, Co Waterford
Tel: (051) 382582

A large, modern house set in its own grounds about 200 yards off the Dunmore East-to-Waterford road. Lakefield overlooks Bellake, below the house, and there are views to the coast at Woodstown beach about 2 miles (3 km) away. The surrounding farmland is mostly tillage, but there are a few goats, sheep, chickens and ducks, as well as 2 ponies and a donkey. Most of the rooms have a view, and there is a patio outside the drawing room. Mrs Carney is a friendly lady who was previously in the hotel and restaurant management business. No smoking in the dining room. Major credit cards accepted.

OWNER Cally Carney OPEN 1 February–1 December ROOMS 3
double, 1 twin, 1 family (all en-suite) TERMS B&B IR£16.50–
£17.00; reductions for children; single supplement; evening meal
IR£13.50

County Wexford

The most southeasterly county and one of the main gateways, through the port of Rosslare, it is also the driest and warmest part of the whole country, an area of gentle hills, fertile farmland and a coastline of sandy beaches. Much of Wexford history is associated with the Norman invasion and the 1798 rebellion.

The Wexford Opera Festival, which takes place every October, is world-renowned and features top international singers. The town throbs with an influx of opera lovers, and many fringe events take place during the festival. It is an attractive town with narrow, winding streets, and the Maritime Museum and the twelfth-century ruins of Selskar Abbey are of particular interest.

The castle at the attractive market town of Enniscorthy now houses the county museum, with an interesting folk section. Worth a visit are the thirteenth-century castle at Ferns, the old town of New Ross, and Dunrody Abbey, dating from 1182, near Campile. Nearby at Dunganstown is the Kennedy ancestral home.

BUNCLODY

Clohamon House

Bunclody, Co Wexford

Tel: (054) 77253, Fax: (054) 77956

Clohamon is a delightful eighteenth-century house on 180 acres, surrounded by beech woods and gardens that contain many rare trees and plants. There are garden walks, and the fields in front run down a gentle hill to the River Slaney, where, by special arrangement, guests can fish for salmon and trout in season. The land is farmed as a dairy farm and is also home to internationally renowned Connemara ponies. The bedrooms are tastefully decorated, with four-poster beds (including the single), all with matching fabrics. Each bedroom has a hairdryer and tea- and coffee-making facilities. The annex is more basic, but ideal for someone who wants a little privacy. The study has a TV and telephone for guests' use. Organically grown vegetables are used in the excellent five-course meals, which are served by prior arrangement. The atmosphere here is informal; guests are treated like personal friends. Pets outside by arrangement. No smoking in the bedrooms. The house is signposted from Bunclody. Visa and Access cards accepted.

OWNER Sir Richard and Lady Levinge   OPEN 1 March–mid
November   ROOMS 2 double, 1 twin, 1 single (all en-suite)
TERMS B&B IR£42.00 p.p.; reductions for children; single supple-
ment; dinner IR£22.50

CAMPILE

Park View Deer Farm

Campile, Co Wexford

Tel: (051) 388178

This 200-year-old house is set in 50 acres of deer farm.
Mike and Barbara Barrett are attentive and amusing hosts
who enjoy the company of their guests. The furnishings in
the lounge, dining room and three bedrooms reflect the '60s
era. All bedrooms have tea-making facilities, hairdryers and
electric blankets. Park View is a good location for cycling
holidays, is close to sandy beaches and is beside the John F.
Kennedy Park, renowned for its collection of trees and
shrubs. No smoking.

OWNER Mike and Barbara Barrett   OPEN May–October
ROOMS 1 double (ground floor), 2 twin (all en-suite)
TERMS IR£17.50; single supplement

ENNISCORTHY

Ballinkeel House

Ballymurn, Enniscorthy, Co Wexford

Tel: (053) 38105

Built in 1840, this impressive country house still belongs to
the Maher family 4 generations later. It is approached up a
sweeping avenue and is set in 350 acres of farmland. Apart
from the addition of such modern conveniences as bath-
rooms and heating, it remains much as it was built, with a
distinctively Victorian flavour. The Mahers are a friendly
couple, and Margaret produces delicious dinners and an
enormous breakfast, which can include hot pancakes and
homemade jams. The master bedroom, which has a four-
poster bed, is the same shape as the drawing room below,
and the formal dining room has one large table. Guests have
use of the billiard room, hard tennis court and are welcome
to walk around the estate. No smoking in the bedrooms, and
pets outside only. Visa and Access accepted.

OWNER John and Margaret Maher   OPEN 1 March–mid November

ROOMS 3 double, 2 twin (all en-suite) TERMS B&B IR£30.00–£35.00 p.p.; reductions for children; single supplement; evening meal IR£18.00

Clone House

Ferns, Enniscorthy, Co Wexford
Tel: (054) 66113

This attractive, creeper-covered 300-year-old farm house is in a quiet location on nearly 300 acres of mixed farmland. Guests can fish on the Bann river, which runs through the property, feed the lambs, see calves born or just go for wonderful walks. The Breens bought the property about 40 years ago, and gradually did it up. Betty is particularly gifted at landscaping and has created a lovely garden. Guests here are treated as friends and enjoy such luxuries as breakfast in bed, served at any time, and delicious home-cooked food, using homegrown or -reared produce. The house is very comfortable and has been attractively furnished. One of the ground-floor rooms is suitable for the disabled. There is a comfortable sitting room and dining room. There is a pony for children to ride, and baby sitting is available. Many guests come to buy horses, others to visit a local herbalist, others to hunt, and others just to relax.

OWNER Tom and Betty Breen OPEN 1 March–1 November
ROOMS 5 twin/double (4 en-suite) TERMS IR£16.00–£18.00; reductions for children; single supplement; dinner IR£14.00

Oakville Lodge

Ballycarney, Enniscorthy, Co Wexford
Tel: (054) 88626

A friendly, welcoming family home set in a $^3/_4$-acre garden in a quiet, peaceful location. The gardens are landscaped with heathers, flowering shrubs and ornamental trees, with a background of beech, oak and holly trees. There is a conservatory for guests' use. Three of the comfortable bedrooms have their own individual porches. There are several stairs to the approach of the house, though these can be avoided by entering through a side door. All rooms are on the ground floor. No smoking in the dining room. Located off the N80 road to Enniscorthy. Visa and Access accepted. No pets.

OWNER Mrs Attracta Doyle   OPEN 1 March–1 November
ROOMS 2 double, 1 twin, 1 family (2 en-suite) TERMS B&B
IR£14.00–IR£16.00; reductions for children; single supplement

Woodville Farm House

Ballyhogue, Enniscorthy, Co Wexford
Tel: (054) 47810

A wisteria-covered, 70-year-old farmhouse in a tranquil
setting. There is a wonderfully informal atmosphere, and
guests are treated as friends. The bedrooms are comfortable,
one with a marble washstand. The family room is very large
and there is a cot for a small child. Although there is a guest
lounge, Mrs Doyle welcomes guests into the family lounge,
offering tea or coffee and delicious homemade scones. The
guest lounge has a wooden ceiling and a fine display of
silver. Both Mr and Mrs Doyle enjoy chatting to their guests
and are a most accommodating, helpful couple. They won
the South-East Farm Family Award for 1994–5. Excellent
home-cooked dinners are served, with large portions, fresh
vegetables and tasty desserts. Smoking in the family lounge
only. Pets outside only. Forty minutes' drive to Rosslare.
Woodville Farm House is signposted on N11, between
Enniscorthy and Wexford.

OWNER Mrs Ann Doyle OPEN 1 March–1 November
ROOMS 1 double, 2 twin, 1 single, 1 family (all en-suite)
TERMS B&B IR£16.00 p.p.; reductions for children; evening meal
IR£11.00, high tea IR£6.00

FOULKESMILLS

Horetown House

Foulkesmills, Co Wexford
Tel: (051) 565771, Fax: (051) 565633

Horetown House is a lovely, seventeenth-century Georgian
manor house situated in beautiful parklands and tranquil
countryside, amidst 250 acres of mixed farming. All of the
rooms are fairly spacious and comfortable, with old-fash-
ioned furnishings. Upon arrival guests are offered tea or
coffee in the drawing room, where they can relax around
the log fire. There's a separate TV room. The Cellar Restau-
rant has received several international awards and recom-
mendations, including Egon Ronay Recommendations in
1994 and 1995; reservations are required (children's meals

96

available). An equestrian centre includes 2 large, all-weather indoor arenas and offers riding instruction for the beginner and the competent rider. No pets. Located 1¹/₂ miles (2¹/₂ km) east of Foulkesmill. Visa, Diners Club International and Mastercard accepted.

OWNER The Young family   OPEN All year, accept Christmas
ROOMS 6 family, 6 double (4 en-suite)   TERMS B&B IR£22.00;
reductions for children; single supplement; dinner IR£16.50–
£22.50; lunch IR£10.00

NEW ROSS

Creacon Lodge

Creacon, New Ross, Co Wexford

Tel: (051) 21897, Fax: (051) 22560

A charming, long, low whitewashed house covered with climbing plants and set in a very pretty, sheltered garden. Josephine Flood is a most imaginative and attentive host. There is a comfortable drawing room with an open fire and two dining areas, one with pine furniture, in what was the old kitchen. Some of the attractive bedrooms are in the main house, three are in the old byre and a recent conversion has transformed the former greenhouse into two further bedrooms. Evening meals are available if arranged in advance. The J. F. Kennedy Memorial Park is a 10-minute drive away, and nearby is the Hook Peninsula, with secluded beaches and coves and the oldest lighthouse in Europe.

OWNER Josephine Flood   OPEN All year   ROOMS 9 double/twin (all en-suite)   TERMS IR£20.00–£25.00; reductions for children; single supplement; dinner IR£15.00

Riversdale House

Lower William Street, New Ross, Co Wexford

Tel: (051) 22515

This large, modern house is just 3 minutes from the town centre. It was built by the Foleys four years ago and is surrounded by half an acre of gardens. Riversdale has lovely views over the town and the River Barrow and from the back it is particularly attractive at night, when the church is floodlit. This is a comfortable house with an upstairs lounge, and the dining room on the ground floor. Mrs Foley is a friendly, chatty lady who teaches cookery classes and has won the National Housewife of the Year award. No smoking in the dining room and pets outside only.

OWNER Mrs Ann Foley   OPEN 1 March–1 November   ROOMS 4 family (all en-suite)   TERMS B&B IR£16.00 p.p.; reductions for children; single supplement

Robinstown Farmhouse

New Ross, Co Wexford

Tel: (051) 28337

This 250-year-old farmhouse, set in 20 acres, makes a perfect base from which to explore the many places of interest close by. The house has been the family home since it was built. The grounds are lovely, and there is a peaceful and friendly atmosphere. The lounge is spacious and very comfortable, and there is an alcove with an interesting wooden ceiling and an antique chaise-longue and chair. Light snacks are available. There are plans to have some bedrooms with en-suite facilities. Locally, there are lovely walks and fishing. Mrs O'Keeffe is pleased to recommend local eating establishments. No smoking in the bedrooms. Located 4 miles (6 km) south of Rosslare, off the Wexford Road at Ballinaboola.

OWNER Mrs G. O'Keeffe   OPEN 1 April–1 September ROOMS 2 double, 2 twin, 2 family   TERMS B&B IR£14.00 p.p.; reductions for children; single supplement

ROSSLARE

Ballybro Lodge

Rosslare, Co Wexford

Tel: (053) 32333

The Doyles bought the land surrounding Ballybro Lodge, which once was an old stone quarry, while they were living in England. They filled in enough of the quarry to build the house, and now the garden gets bigger every year as they fill in more. The house, which is down a quiet country lane, is very accessible to Rosslare, about $2^1/_2$ miles (4 km) away. All except one of the bedrooms have both a double and single bed, and all are en-suite and offer tea- and coffee-making facilities. There is also a bathroom for guests' use. The lounge and dining room overlook the garden and small stream which borders the property. Pets outside only.

The house is signposted off the main Rosslare to Wexford road.

OWNER Mrs L. Doyle   OPEN All year, except Christmas
ROOMS 5 double/twin/family (all en-suite)   TERMS B&B from
IR£16.50 p.p.; reductions for children; single supplement

Churchtown House

Tagoat, Rosslare, Co Wexford
Tel: (053) 32555, Fax: (053) 32555

Set in 8$^{1}/_{2}$ acres of park-like grounds with a croquet lawn, this attractive house dates from 1703. The Codys only opened for guests in 1993. They have tastefully decorated and furnished the house, which has spacious rooms. There are two comfortable drawing rooms, and five ground-floor bedrooms, one suitable for wheelchairs. Evening meals available on request. Churchtown House is half a kilometre off the main Rosslare-to-Wexford road, and four kilometres from the ferryport. Activities such as birdwatching, golf, fishing, swimming, walking and horse-riding are available locally. Dogs welcome.

OWNER Patricia and Austin Cody   OPEN mid-March–mid-
November   ROOMS 5 double, 4 twin, 2 family, 1 suite (all en-
suite)   TERMS IR£23.50; single supplement

Laurel Lodge

Rosslare Harbour, Co Wexford
Tel: (053) 33291

An attractive, low, modern house down a quiet country lane in the village of Kilrane, just a couple of kilometres from Rosslare Harbour. The rooms are clean and comfortable and all are en-suite. There is a guest lounge; the dining room, where breakfast only is served, overlooks a small patio at the back of the house. Complimentary tea or coffee on request. Smoking only in the lounge. Laurel Lodge is signposted off the main Rosslare-to-Wexford road. Major credit cards accepted.

OWNER Mr & Mrs D. O'Donoghue   OPEN 1 March–1 December
ROOMS 3 double, 2 twin (all en-suite)   TERMS B&B IR£14.00 p.p.;
reductions for children; single supplement

TACUMSHANE

Furziestown House

Tacumshane, Co Wexford

Tel: (053) 31376

A small, peaceful farmhouse in rural surroundings with easy access to Rosslare and Wexford. The whitewashed farm buildings form an attractive courtyard behind the house, and the two acres support free-range chickens and organically grown vegetables. Yvonne Pim produces delicious breakfasts. The house is comfortable and has a welcoming, friendly atmosphere. Two of the bedrooms are on the ground floor, with a separate entrance, making them ideal for families. The upstairs twin-bedded room has pretty stencilling. The house is only one mile from the sea and Wexford can be reached by a coastal path.

OWNER Yvonne Pim   OPEN All year   ROOMS 1 double, 1 twin, 1 single (all en-suite)   TERMS IR£16.00; reductions for children

WEXFORD

Ardruadh

Spawell Road, Wexford, Co Wexford

Tel: (053) 23194

Ardruadh, meaning "high red house", is an elegant Gothic-style residence built in 1892, set in ³/₄ acre of landscaped gardens. Peter and Nora Corish are a friendly couple and guests are assured of genuine old-fashioned hospitality. The house is full of character, with the original pitch pine and wrought-iron staircase. The beautifully appointed bedrooms are individually furnished and decorated, and all have clock radios, TVS, hairdryers and tea- and coffee-making facilities. The front bedroom overlooks the River Slaney and is often used as a bridal suite. There are several antique furnishings about, including an ornate Italian 3-piece suite in the spacious lounge. Peter and Nora have been here just over 5 years and have done a splendid job in restoring the house to its original splendour. Five minutes' walk to town centre and to the bus and train station. No smoking in the dining room. No pets. Visa and Mastercard accepted.

OWNER Peter and Nora Corish   OPEN All year, except Christmas   ROOMS 3 double, 2 twin/family (all en-suite)   TERMS B&B IR£15.00 p.p.; reductions for children; single supplement

100

Clonard House

Clonard Great, Wexford, Co Wexford
Tel: (053) 43141 or 47337, Fax: (053) 43141

John and Kathleen Hayes and their family own and run this
Georgian farmhouse. The 120-acre dairy farm is set in
idyllic surroundings with a clear view of Wexford Harbour.
Clonard House was completely renovated in 1986, but
many of the original fixtures remain, such as cornices,
ceiling roses and the dining room fireplace. Since then, the
house has been redecorated, maintaining its already-high
standard. The spacious rooms are extremely attractive, with
traditional and antique furnishings, and have TVs, hairdryers
and some have four-poster beds. The well-appointed lounge
is the perfect spot to relax in after a busy day sightseeing.
There is a games room in the basement for guests. This is a
lovely, peaceful house with a lot of character (and a stairway
to nowhere!). Evening meals by arrangement. There is a
wine licence. No smoking in the bedrooms, and no pets. A
half-mile off the ring road – signposted.

OWNER John and Kathleen Hayes   OPEN Easter–mid November
ROOMS 4 double, 1 twin, 4 family (all en-suite)
TERMS B&B IR£16.00 p.p.; reductions for children; single supple-
ment; evening meal IR£13.00

Killiane Castle

Drinagh, Wexford, Co Wexford

Tel: (053) 58885 or 58898, Fax: (053) 58885

An eighteenth-century house attached to the tower of a fourteenth-century castle on a dairy farm, down a quiet country lane. Killiane Castle is very handy for the Rosslare ferry, which is only 10 minutes away, and early breakfasts are provided. The house has been attractively decorated and furnished, in particular the dining room. The bedrooms on the first floor are large and those on the second floor have recently been decorated most attractively and have good bathrooms. There is a hard tennis court and 4 self-catering apartments at the back of the house. No smoking in the dining room. No pets.

OWNER Jack and Kathleen Mernagh   OPEN 1 March–1 December ROOMS 8 double/twin, 2 family (all en-suite) TERMS B&B IR£16.00 p.p.; reductions for children; single supplement; evening meal IR£13.00

Newbay Country House

Wexford, Co Wexford

Tel: (053) 42779, Fax: (053) 46318

Newbay Country House is a family-run house where the emphasis is on good food, a warm welcome and comfort in a relaxed, tranquil atmosphere. The house was built in 1822 and incorporates in its outbuildings a fourteenth-century castle and a seventeenth-century farmhouse. The house is set in 30 acres of park garden and woodland. Open peat and log fires welcome guests, and the house has stripped pine furniture, which Paul Drum restores, including the four poster beds for which his wife, Mientje, makes the patch-work covers. The bow-ended drawing room and elegant dining room have kept their long sash windows and original shutters. Paul's collection of top hats, solar topis and plumed helmets is on the top of a carved Austrian tallboy in the drawing room. A still-working symphonium stands in the hall. There is a pond with wild ducks, moorhens and a peacock. Paul and Mientje are both excellent cooks, and you will be well cared for at Newbay House. Early reservations highly recommended. The house has a wine licence. No pets. Visa and Access cards accepted.

OWNER Paul and Mientje Drum   OPEN January–end November
ROOMS 5 double, 1 twin (all en-suite)   TERMS B&B IR£29.00 p.p;
reductions for children; single supplement; evening meal IR£25.00

The West and Northwest

County Clare

Two hundred castles and 2,300 stone forts going back to pre-Celtic times testify to County Clare's turbulent past. Although Shannon airport lies on the southern border, most of the county is underpopulated by tourists. The scenery varies from the barren terrain of the Barony of Burren, which, in spring, is covered in a profusion of northern and southern plants, to the scenic lakes and hills of Slieve Bernagh, wonderful walking country, and the towering Cliffs of Moher. Water plays an important role, the sea bordering the west, and the Shannon Estuary the south and east.

The Franciscan Ennis Friary, noted for its sculptures and decorated tombs, is one of the principal sights of the county capital, Ennis, which is situated on a bend of the River Fergus.

A bridge crosses the Shannon at Killaloe. Nearby is a twelfth-century cathedral built on the site of an earlier church. It has a magnificent door and the views from the top of the square tower are splendid. Across the Shannon lies Bunratty Castle, well known now for its medieval banquets. It dates from 1460 and was at one time occupied by Admiral Penn, the father of William Penn, founder of Pennsylvania. A Folk Park is to be found in the castle grounds, with examples of houses from the Shannon area.

The island of Iniscealtra on Lough Derg can be reached by boat from the attractive village of Mountshannon. There are 5 old churches, a round tower, saints' graveyard, hermit's cell and a holy well.

Moohaun Fort, one of the largest Iron Age hill forts in Europe, is to be found at Newmarket on Fergus. Knappogue Castle, another venue for medieval banquets, and Quinn Abbey are close to Craggaunowen.

Of special interest to both botanists and historians is the Burren. Once densely populated, this savagely rocky area is rich in prehistoric and historic monuments. Look closely at its limestone and discover a wealth of exquisite, delicate plant life thriving in a myriad of tiny crevices. The Burren Display Centre explains the fauna and flora of the 200 square miles of the Burren and its remains of ancient civilisation. The ruined Leamaneh Castle is near Kilfenora, which is on the edge of the Burren. Between Kilfenora and Ballyvaughan is Ballykinvarraga, one of Ireland's finest stone forts, and south east of Ballyvaughan is Aillwee Cave, which dates back to 2 million BC.

The road from Lisdoonvarna, Ireland's foremost spa town, leads to the impressive Cliffs of Moher, which stretch for nearly 5 miles (7½ km). Liscannor is famous for the Holy Well of St Brigid, which is an important place of pilgrimage.

Lahinch, a small seaside resort, is best known for its championship golf course and to the south is Spanish Point, where many ships of the Spanish Armada were wrecked.

Around the village of Quilty, seaweed can be seen drying on the stone walls. The coast south of Kilkee is every bit as spectacular as the Cliffs of Moher, with caverns and strange rock formations.

BELL HARBOUR

Bell Harbour House

Bell Harbour, Co Clare
Tel: (065) 78004

A traditional farmhouse built in 1796, Bell Harbour House stands in 75 acres of lush pastures and 45 acres of mountain grazing, with views of the sea and the remains of an old castle. The spacious bedrooms, one of which is on the ground floor, have solid, old-fashioned furniture. Only breakfast is served, but there are plenty of places for other meals close by. Mr Droney is an interesting and humorous gentleman; he is an excellent concertina player and has toured extensively in England, America, Canada and has even played for the Emperor of Japan! If there is a musical event happening in the area, he is happy to take interested guests along. This is a musical family, as is evidenced by the many trophies and medals on display. There is a piano in the lounge, a great place to congregate with other guests. Guests are warmly greeted with homemade scones and a hot drink. Non-smokers preferred. Electric blankets provided. Pets outside only.

OWNER Mrs Margaret Droney OPEN Easter–31 October
ROOMS 4 TERMS B&B IR£13.00 p.p.; reductions for children under 10; single supplement

BUNRATTY

Bunratty Hillside

Clonmoney North, Bunratty, Co Clare
Tel: (061) 364330, Fax: (061) 362024

A pleasant, warm and relaxing family home 4 miles from Bunratty Castle. There are 6 comfortable bedrooms, a lounge with TV and a separate dining room. Breakfasts only are served, but the famous pub Durty Nelly's, serving lunch and dinner, is only 1 mile (1¹/₂ km) away. The McCabes are a friendly family, the atmosphere is warm and welcoming and a hot drink is offered in the morning or evening at no extra charge. The Medieval Banquet at nearby Bunratty Castle can be prebooked upon request. Local activities include golf and horse-riding. No pets. Four miles (6 km) to Shannon Airport. Turn off at Sixmilebridge; signposted from there. American Express accepted.

OWNER Mrs Maureen McCabe   OPEN 1 January–20 December
ROOMS 2 double/twin/family (4 en-suite)   TERMS B&B IR£15.00 p.p.; reductions for children; single supplement

Bunratty View

(formerly Brooklawn), Cratloe, near Bunratty, Co Clare
Tel: (061) 87352, Fax: (061) 357352

Bunratty View, formerly known as Brooklawn, is a purpose-built bed-and-breakfast establishment. The bedrooms are large, with good-sized en-suite facilities, dressing tables and hairdryers. Breakfasts are served in the bright dining room, which has a conservatory effect due to its large windows that overlook scenic countryside. The house is exceptionally well maintained, and there are quality carpets throughout. All of the rooms are on the ground floor, and one is suitable for wheelchair access. There are views of floodlit Bunratty Castle at night, and free transportation to the castle is available. Guests may enjoy dinner and light snacks, if prearranged. There is a guest lounge. Smoking is not permitted in the dining room, and there are 2 bedrooms reserved for nonsmokers. No pets. Located only 10 minutes from Shannon airport; take first left beyond Bunratty Castle on route to Limerick.

OWNER Joe and Maura Brodie   OPEN All year   ROOMS 2 double, 2 twin, 3 family (all en-suite)   TERMS B&B IR£15.00 p.p.; reductions for children; single supplement; evening meal IR£11.00

Rockfield House

Hill Road, Bunratty, Co Clare
Tel: (061) 364391, Fax: (061) 364391

Two minutes' walk from Bunratty Castle and the famous

pub/restaurant Durty Nelly's, you will find Rockfield House, an attractive home in a peaceful setting overlooking the Shannon River. Margaret Garry is an accommodating host, dedicated to ensuring her guests receive a warm welcome. There is a TV lounge, where tea or coffee is served upon request. All of the bedrooms have TVs, private bathrooms and lovely warm duvets. There is a no-smoking area in the house. Margaret is happy to prebook the Bunratty Castle banquet. No pets. An easy drive from here to Shannon airport.

OWNER Mrs Margaret Garry   OPEN All year   ROOMS 2 double, 3 twin, 1 family (all en-suite)   TERMS B&B IR£15.00 p.p.; single supplement

DOOLIN

Atlantic Sunset House

Cliffs of Moher Road, Doolin, Co Clare

Tel: (065) 74080

Atlantic Sunset House is in an excellent location, one mile from the village and four miles from the Cliffs of Moher. The bedrooms, two of which are on the ground floor, are a good size, with built in wardrobes and en-suite facilities. Substantial breakfasts are served in the dining room, the floor of which is flagged with stone from the Cliffs of Moher. Decorating the window are several old carpenter tools that belonged to the owner's grandfather. Evening meals must be arranged in advance, there is no wine licence, but guests may bring their own wine. No pets. Smoking in the lounge only. Small golf groups can be accommodated. Self-catering also available.

OWNER Val and Brid Egan   OPEN All year except Christmas ROOMS 4 twin, 2 family (all en-suite)   TERMS B&B IR£14.50 p.p.; reductions for children; single supplement; evening meal IR£11.50

ENNIS

Ardlea House

Clare Road, Ennis, Co Clare

Tel: (065) 20256, Fax: (065) 29794

Ella Leyden is a congenial host who has been successfully running her bed and breakfast for just over 8 years. Ardlea House is a detached corner house on the edge of town, 200 yards to all amenities. There are TVs, tea- and coffee-making facilities and hairdryers in the bedrooms, and electric blankets are provided upon request. There are 3 ground-floor rooms. Excellent breakfasts, featuring homemade breads, are served in the bright and sunny dining room. A good location for exploring the Cliffs of Moher and Bunratty Castle, and within easy driving distance to Shannon. No smoking in the dining room or bedrooms. On the N18 main Shannon airport road. Access and Visa cards accepted.

OWNER Ella Leyden   OPEN All year, except 22–30 December
ROOMS 2 double, 1 twin, 1 family (3 en-suite)
TERMS IR£15.00 p.p.; reductions for children; single supplement

Carbery House

Kilrush Road, Ennis, Co Clare
Tel: (065) 24046

This house, built in 1964, is very well maintained, and stands in its own grounds on the edge of town, in a quiet location. Mrs Roberts has been offering her special brand of hospitality for over 27 years, and hers was one of the first B&Bs in the area. The motto here is: "There are no strangers here, only friends we have not met." The bedrooms are average in size, all with orthopaedic beds and electric blankets. There are tea- and coffee-making facilities in the bedrooms, and hairdryers. Tasty, fresh-cooked breakfasts are served in the bright, sunny dining room. Very popular with tourists and businesspeople in the winter; advance reservations are recommended. Situated on the road to the car ferry, and within easy driving distance of Shannon and Bunratty. No smoking. Visa, Mastercard and Access accepted.

OWNER T. J. and Pauline Roberts   OPEN 1 March–30 November
ROOMS 1 double, 4 twin (4 en-suite)   TERMS B&B IR£14.00 p.p.;
reductions for children; single supplement

Massabielle

Off Quinn Road, Ennis, Co Clare
Tel: (065) 29363

The standard of maintenance and decor is exceptionally high throughout this house. The bedrooms are beautifully furnished and individually decorated with warm duvets and restful, colour-coordinated fabrics. The large, bright lounge features a carved, inlaid mahogany sideboard with a fine display of Waterford crystal. There is a TV, and guests can also enjoy fireside conversation with the family. Massabielle is set in a beautiful landscaped garden, surrounded by trees, with a stream running by the house. There is a hard tennis court for guests' use. Pets outside only. Smoking permitted only in the lounge. From Ennis, turn left at Old Ground Hotel and drive straight for 1^1/$_2$ miles (2^1/$_2$ km); signposted from there. Located one mile (1^1/$_2$ km) from the CIE railway station, signposted on the Quinn Road.

OWNER Mrs Monica O'Loughlin OPEN 1 May–15 October
ROOMS 1 double, 2 twin, 3 treble (4 en-suite) TERMS
B&B IR£14.00–£16.00 p.p.; reductions for children; single supplement

Newpark House

Tulla Road, Ennis, Co Clare
Tel: (065) 21233

A 300-year-old country residence with an old-world atmosphere, set in 85 acres of pasture and woodland. The bedrooms are a good size, all have tea-making facilities, most have pastoral views. Breakfasts and dinners are served, wholesome home-cooked meals featuring fresh produce when the season allows. Mrs Barron is a congenial host, happy to give advice on local activities. A babysitting service is available. There are 2 sitting rooms for guests and 2 dining rooms. Pets by arrangement. Guests may bring their own wine. Take the Tulla Road from Ennis, turn right at the Roselevan Arms – Newpark House is around the corner.

OWNER Mrs Bernadette Barron OPEN 1 March–1 November
ROOMS 6 family rooms (all en-suite) TERMS B&B IR£16.00–£20.00 p.p.; reductions for children; single supplement; evening meal IR£12.50

ENNISTYMON

Station House

Ennis Road, Ennistymon, Co Clare
Tel: (065) 71149, Fax: (065) 71709

Station House offers what must be just about the best value in the area. Originally built in 1870 as a station master's home, it was extensively remodelled 5 years ago, another floor being added to accommodate additional bedrooms. All of the rooms are spacious, with standard decor. The large bedrooms have TVs, direct-dial telephones, tea-makers, orthopaedic beds and good-sized bathrooms with plenty of hot water. Adjacent to the east side of the house is the original stone building that was the Co Clare railway shop, made famous by the Percy French song "Are you right there Michael are you right". Perhaps the Station House has lost some of the intimacy of a small B&B, but the proprietors and staff are extremely helpful. Two miles (3 km) to Lahinch, a great area for golf, and beautiful scenery. No pets. No smoking in the dining room. Advance reservations highly recommended. Visa accepted.

OWNER Mrs Kathleen Cahill   OPEN All year, except Christmas
ROOMS 2 double/twin/family (all en-suite)   TERMS B&B IR£14.00 p.p.; single supplement

Tullamore Farmhouse

Kilshanny, via Ennistymon, Co Clare
Tel: (065) 71187

This award-winning farmhouse is also a working farm of 103 acres of suckler herd, situated in a picturesque location, with panoramic views and a river running through the property. The house was built over 100 years ago and has been added onto and modernised over the years. The house is in good decorative order, the bedrooms clean and comfortable. There is a tastefully furnished sun porch with magnificent views, which guests may use. Guests are assured of a warm welcome by the Carroll family – a cup of tea is offered upon arrival, at no extra charge. An excellent base from which to explore this area, Kilshanny is only 4 miles (6 km) away from Lahinch, and the Cliffs of Moher are only a 20-minute drive away. Fishing is available in the nearby river, and traditional Irish music can be heard nightly in Liscannor's famous McHugh's pub. Hairdryers are provided in the bedrooms. No pets. From Ennistymon to Lisdoonvarna, turn left at Kilshanny – the farmhouse is signposted from there.

OWNER Mrs Eileen Carroll   OPEN 1 March–1 October
ROOMS 1 double, 2 twin, 1 family (3 en-suite)   TERMS B&B IR£15.00–£16.50 p.p.; reductions for children; single supplement; light meals IR£6.00–£8.00; dinner IR£12.50

Cois Fharraige

Cregg, Lahinch, Co Clare
Tel: (065) 81580

Cois Fharraige, whose name means "seaside", is a modest bungalow in a quiet location on the coast road. The lounge has ocean views, is comfortably furnished and has an open fire. Rosemarie Donohue is a friendly lady, who has been offering bed and breakfast for 6 years; breakfasts are plentiful and include homemade bread. Tea and coffee are available just about any time, upon request. The house is adjacent to a pitch and putt and Lahinch Golf Course is close by. Smoking permitted in the lounge only. No pets.

OWNER Mrs Rosemary Donohue   OPEN 17 March–31 October
ROOMS 1 double, 1 twin, 1 family (2 en-suite)
TERMS B&B IR£13.50–£14.50 p.p.; children under 4 free; reductions for children for children under 12; single supplement; special off-season rates upon request

Lehinchy House

Dough, Lahinch, Co Clare
Tel: (065) 81512

Lehinchy House is situated in a quiet, peaceful location surrounded by open rolling countryside with views, on clear days, of the Cliffs of Moher. This is a serene and tranquil place with some lovely walks in the area, and is just minutes from the golf course. The rooms are fresh, clean and comfortable, with semi-orthopaedic beds, hair dryers and tea- and coffee-making facilities. There is a doll collection in the TV lounge, which has been added onto over the years by happy guests as far away as South Africa. Breakfast only is served but there are lots of pubs and restaurants in Lahinch with a wide choice of evening meals. Pets by arrangement. Take the hospital road halfway betwen Ennistymon and Lahinch, turn left at the T-junction – Lahinch House is the first house on the right.

OWNER Dympna Armstead   OPEN 1 April–30 September
ROOMS 1 double/twin/family (all en-suite)   TERMS B&B IR£13.50 p.p.; reductions for children for children; single supplement; special off-season rates upon request

Nazira

School Road, Lahinch, Co Clare
Tel: (065) 81362

Nazira is a friendly, comfortable house in an elevated position, with magnificent views of the bay and the beautiful, scenic countryside. As one guest commented, "It's like looking down on creation." The house was named after Mr Sarma's home in India, and was for many years the family holiday home. In 1989, an extension was added, including a dining room and lounge that overlook the bay. The well-furnished bedrooms are airy and bright. The en-suite family room has one double and an adjoining twin room, ideal for two couples or a family. A wonderful spot for golfers, just minutes from the golf course. Mrs Sarma is a very congenial host who takes excellent care of her guests. No pets. Located approximately 850 metres off the main Lahinch/Milltown Malbray ferry road. Private car park.

OWNER Frances Sarma   OPEN 1 April–31 October
ROOMS 2 double, 1 twin, 1 family (all en-suite)
TERMS B&B IR£16.00 p.p.; reductions for children; single supplement

Seafield Lodge

Ennistymon Road, Lahinch, Co Clare
Tel: (065) 81594

A double-glazed bungalow on the edge of Lahinch, 5 minutes' walk away from the town, golf courses and beaches. From the lounge and front bedrooms there are views of the lovely countryside and the ruin of one of the O'Brien castles. The bedrooms are clean and comfortable, all with their own bathrooms, TVs, hairdryers and electric blankets. The bungalow also overlooks a fairy fort (obscured somewhat by new construction), treated with great respect by the local farmers, who are careful to farm around it. There are 3 ground-floor rooms. Breakfast is served in the pretty dining room with lace tablecloths and fine china. Smoking in the bedrooms only. No pets. Situated on the main road approaching Lahinch from Shannon.

OWNER Joseph and Ita Slattery   OPEN Easter–30 November
ROOMS 2 double/family (4 en-suite)   TERMS B&B IR£15.00 p.p.; reductions for children; single supplement

Ore a Tava House

Lisdoonvarna, Co Clare
Tel: (065) 74086, Fax: (065) 74547

A pleasant, modern bungalow in a quiet area, 1 mile (1¹/₂ km) from Lisdoonvarna. The bedrooms, with pretty duvets, have en-suite facilities, direct-dial telephones, TVs and hair dryers. The dining room and lounge both have fireplaces. The owners live in a separate unit, so residents have the run of the house. There is a patio for guests' use, overlooking scenic countryside. This is an ideal base for touring the Burren, Cliffs of Moher and the well-known health spa in Lisdoonvarna. There is horse-riding close by. No pets. Drive through Lisdoonvarna on Galway road 1 mile (1¹/₂ km); turn left at the pump – Ore a Tava is the third house on the left.

OWNER Mrs Helen Stack   OPEN 1 March–31 October
ROOMS 4 double, 2 twin (all en-suite)   TERMS B&B IR£15.00 p.p.; reductions for children; single supplement; dinner IR£12.00

MILLTOWN MALBAY

Leagard House

Mullagh Road, Milltown Malbay, Co Clare
Tel: (065) 84324

Situated in its own grounds in a peaceful location, this comfortable house offers a home-away-from-home atmosphere. The lounge has a TV and video. The dining room, where breakfasts and dinners are served, leads out onto a verandah. Evening meals include a choice of starters and desserts, all made fresh daily. The bedrooms are furnished with a mixture of modern and old-fashioned furniture, and the ground floors are large enough for wheelchair access. There is a 9-hole golf course at Spanish Point is half a mile away. Pets outside only. Situated on the Mullagh Road, 400 yards from town.

OWNER John and Suzanne Hannon   OPEN April–October
ROOMS 2 double/twin/family (2 en-suite)   TERMS B&B IR£14.00 p.p.; reductions for children under 10; single supplement; evening meal IR£12.50, high tea IR£7.00

Beechgrove Farmhouse

Shannon-Ennis Road, Knocknagun, Newmarket on Fergus,
Co Clare

Tel: (061) 368140

Just 3 miles (4½ km) from Shannon airport is this modern
bungalow on a 100-acre cattle and sheep farm. A tranquil
location, with views of the River Shannon and rolling farm-
land. Mrs Conheady is proud of the personal attention given
to guests, and nothing is too much trouble to ensure they
have a comfortable and enjoyable stay at the farm. There is
one ground-floor en-suite bedroom, and the family room
has a king-sized bed plus 2 more beds. The TV lounge has a
fireplace and is shared with the family. Mr Conheady used
to train racehorses, and there are two riding stables within
1½ miles (2½ km). There are free pony rides on the farm
for children. Evening meals feature home-baking, and, when
possible, fresh home-grown vegetables. Smoking in the
lounge only. Follow the main Galway to Ennis road; Beech-
grove is 4 miles (6 km) from Bunratty.

OWNER Mr and Mrs Conheady   OPEN 1 March–1 November
ROOMS 2 double, 1 twin, 2 family (2 en-suite)   TERMS B&B
IR£15.00 p.p.; reductions for children; single supplement; evening
meal IR£11.50, high tea IR£8.00

County Donegal

County Donegal is a large county with a spectacular variety
of scenery and an indented coastline of bays, beaches, cliffs
and peninsulas set against a backdrop of mountains, moors
and lakes. It has many archaeological sites and much evi-
dence of the old Irish culture and traditions. The Irish
language is still spoken in areas north and west of Killybegs,
an important fishing port.

Donegal gets its name from the fort the Vikings estab-
lished – Dun na nGall, the Fort of the Foreigners. The town
built by Sir Basil Brooke is on the estuary of the River Eske,
a busy place that is good for buying tweeds. The castle with
its great square tower, once the stronghold of the
O'Donnells, was refurbished by Brooke in 1610.

Bundoran is one of Ireland's best-known seaside resorts
with a good golf course and famous beaches. Further north
is Ballyshannon, long a centre of importance because of its
river; the town winds up a steep hill above the River Erne.

Rossnowlagh's beach stretches for some 2¹/₂ miles (4 km).

Beyond Killybegs, the coastal scenery becomes wild and spectacular. Kilcar is a centre for the handwoven tweed industry, as is Ardara. The scenery at Glencolumbkille is magnificent, with its blend of hills and sea. Here, the late Father MacDyer organised a cooperative movement to try to keep young people from emigrating, and also established a folk museum. Portnoo and Narin are other popular seaside towns for holidaymakers.

Letterkenny is the largest town in Donegal, dominated by St Eunan's Cathedral, built in the modern Gothic style between 1890 and 1900. The winding road approaching Doocharry from Fintown is known as the 'corkscrew' and brings you through the Gweebarra Glen to the sea. Aranmore Island is the most populated and largest of a series of islands. It can be reached by ferry from Burtonport, an attractive, unspoilt fishing port. Gweedore, situated in spectacularly wild country, is a major holiday centre. From here there is a road of remarkable scenic beauty by loughs Nacung and Dunlewy into the Derryveagh Mountains.

Gortahork and Falcarragh are Irish-speaking and are good places from which to start a climb of Muckish Mountain. Dunfanaghy has a fine beach and is a good place to explore the granite promontory of Horn Head. Between Creeslough, attractively situated on Sheephaven Bay, and Carrigart is the romantic Doe Castle, almost surrounded by the sea. Rosapenna, a resort town with a good golf course, is on the way to the beautiful Rosguill Peninsula, with wonderful views of Melmore Head, Horn Head and Muckish Mountain. Milford is a pretty town from where the Fanad Peninsula with its sandy beaches can be explored. The tranquil village of Rathmullan is beautifully situated with a sandy beach and is famous for its historical associations. The road between here and Ramelton is one of the most beautiful in Ireland. Ramelton is also in a lovely location and is a planned Planter's town, begun in the early seventeenth century.

The Inishowen Peninsula, which lies between the waters of Lough Foyle and Lough Swilly, is quite different to the rest of Donegal. The centre is very hilly, Slieve Snaght at 615 metres being the highest point. From the Buncrana to Clonmany and Cardonagh road there are fine views of sea and mountains, and a road runs right to the tip of the peninsula at Malin Head. One of the best views to be had of this part of Donegal is from the Grianan of Aileach. It is 250 metres high and consists of a cashel, or stone fort, enclosed within three earthen banks. Cardonagh's chief glory is St Patrick's Cross, which dates from the seventh century, making it one of the very important Christian crosses.

Glenveagh lies in a deep gorge and is the setting for a fairytale castle, as well as wonderful gardens that were developed by Henry McIlhenny. The gardens and the estate are now a national park, and Mr McIlhenny has bequeathed the castle to the nation. Gartan, Kilmacrenan and Raphoe, which has a fine old cathedral, are all associated with St Columba.

ARDARA

Rose Wood House

Edergole, Killybegs Road, Ardara, Co Donegal

Tel: (075) 41168

Located on the edge of Ardara on the Killybegs road, Rose Wood House was originally a bungalow but had another storey added to it by Mr McConnell in 1990. Mrs McConnell is a most friendly lady who lived for 11 years in New York. There is a very large lounge/dining room with an open fire, and lovely views from the upper floor over the river. Freshly baked scones are served with breakfast. No smoking in the dining room. On the Killybegs road 1 km from Adara. Visa and Mastercard accepted.

OWNER Mrs Susan McConnell   OPEN All year except Christmas
ROOMS 3 double, 2 twin, 1 single (all en-suite)
TERMS B&B IR£14.50 p.p.; reductions for children; single supplement

Woodhill House

Ardara, Co Donegal

Tel: (075) 41112, Fax: (075) 41516

In a wonderful position up a valley from Ardara, Woodhill House stands on a site dating from the seventeenth century, overlooking the Donegal highlands. This historic country house formerly belonged to the Nesbitts, Ireland's last commercial whaling family. The present owners bought the property about 7 years ago and are continuing to make improvements; all the bedrooms are now en-suite. The 2 front rooms are large, simply furnished, with wonderful views. The house has a friendly and informal atmosphere and is surrounded by 4 acres of gardens, including a walled garden, which are open to guests. There is a high-quality restaurant and licenced bar. Handmade crafts are available for purchase. The area, famous for its Donegal tweeds and woollen goods, also offers salmon and trout fishing, shooting, pony trekking, golf, excellent bathing beaches and the Sheskinmore Wildlife Reserve. Kennels available for dogs. No smoking. A quarter of a mile from the village. All major credit cards accepted.

OWNER John and Nancy Yates   OPEN All year, except Christmas   ROOMS 4 double, 2 single (all en-suite)   TERMS B&B IR£22.00 p.p.; reductions for children; single supplement; evening meals from IR£17.00; lunch IR£8.00

BALLYSHANNON

Ardpatton Farmhouse

Cavangarden, Ballyshannon, Co Donegal
Tel: (072) 51546

A comfortable, informal seventeenth-century farmhouse set in its own grounds, with over 380 acres for beef cattle. The kitchen used to be the local school, and the house was the local post office. The present owners have modernised the house, with only 2 of the original bedrooms remaining. Six bedrooms have en-suite facilities, and all have TVs. The bedrooms are all spacious, fresh and clean, with views over the countryside. Mrs McCaffrey's delightful children ably assist during the school holidays. Fires are lit on most days in both the lounge and dining room. Breakfasts include freshly baked scones, cereals, juice and a full cooked breakfast. Evening meals are available, if prearranged; light meals including salads and sandwiches are also served. Just 3 miles (4¹/₂ km) to Ballyshannon and the restored mill. Pets welcome. No smoking in the bedrooms. There is a tearoom and craft centre on the premises. 3 miles (4¹/₂ km) from Ballyshannon and 11 miles (16¹/₂ km) from Donegal. Visa accepted.

OWNER Mrs Rose McCaffrey   OPEN 1 February–31 October   ROOMS 5 double, 1 triple (all en-suite)   TERMS B&B IR£13.50–£15.00 p.p.; reductions for children under 12; single supplement; evening meal IR£12.00

Cavangarden House

Ballyshannon, Co Donegal
Tel: (072) 51365

A square, stucco-covered house standing in its own grounds, approached up a long driveway through park and farmland in lovely countryside. A Georgian house dating from 1750, it has been considerably altered. The McCaffreys are only the second family to have lived in the house. Mr McCaffrey and his brother run the 380-acre arable farm. The interior is comfortable, with a long entrance hall. The dining room has one enormous table, seating 14 people, with an open peat fire, piano and old pictures; a warm and friendly room. The sitting room also has an open fire and is a comfortable room. The bedrooms are large with solid, old-fashioned furniture, and there is a view from all rooms. Three have TVs. Evening meals are served by arrangement at 7.30 pm, and there is a wine licence. Three miles (4¹/₂ km) from Ballyshannon on the main Donegal road. All major credit cards accepted.

OWNER Mrs Agnes McCaffrey OPEN March–October ROOMS 2 double/twin/family (all en-suite) TERMS B&B IR£15.00 p.p.; reduction for children; single supplement; evening meal IR£12.00

BRUCKLESS

Castlereagh House

Bruckless, Co Donegal
Tel: (073) 37202

This early-nineteenth-century house stands in well-kept gardens, with views of the Blue Stack Mountains and Donegal Bay. The house is impeccably maintained by the congenial owner, Elizabeth Henry – there are rich red carpets throughout and the house is well furnished. The bedrooms are tastefully decorated in soft pastel wallpapers; two of them have en-suite shower rooms, and a separate bathroom is also available. There is a comfortable lounge with a TV, and a lovely antique sideboard. Substantial breakfasts are served in the bright dining room, which also has a sitting area. Elizabeth Henry is a most attentive host who is always happy to give advice on what to see and do in the area and to recommend local establishments for evening meals. Pets outside only. Non-smokers preferred.

OWNER The Henry Family OPEN Easter through October ROOMS 1 double, 1 twin, 1 single (2 en-suite) TERMS IR£16.00 p.p.; reductions for children

BUNCRANA

Kinvyra

14 St Orans Road, Buncrana, Co Donegal
Tel: (077) 61461

A 1930s large whitewashed detached house close to town.
All the bedrooms are upstairs and are spotlessly clean,
freshly decorated, with solid old-fashioned furniture and
washbasins. There is a small TV lounge with open fire. A
cup of tea or coffee is available at any time at no extra
charge. Molly McConigly has been welcoming guests into
her home for over 20 years, offering true old-fashioned
hospitality. The rear of the house overlooks Snagh and
Farhn hill. No pets.

OWNER Mrs Molly McConigly OPEN All year, except Christmas
ROOMS 1 double, 2 twin, 1 family TERMS B&B IR£14.50 p.p.;
reductions for children

BUNDORAN

Conway House

4 Bayview Terrace, Bundoran, Co Donegal
Tel: (072) 41220

A newly decorated Georgian-style house overlooking
Donegal Bay, on the south side of the main Bundoran Road.
Conway House is situated close to all the amenities of this
popular seaside town, including Water World. Two of the
bedrooms have sea views, as does the dining room and
lounge; both have the original fireplaces, which are lit on
chilly days. This house certainly has an easy-going
atmosphere. Mrs McGureen does all the cooking, ably
assisted by her daughter Mairead, while Mr McGureen
keeps busy decorating, maintaining the house and restoring
antiques. There is a lot to see and do in the area and this is
definitely an ideal base from which to explore the region.
Horse-riding and golf are offered within a mile. No pets.

OWNER Dorothy McGureen OPEN Easter–31 September
ROOMS 3 double, 1 family (2 en-suite) TERMS B&B IR£12.50–
£15.00 p.p.; reductions for children under 12; single supplement

Strand View

East End, Bundoran, Co Donegal
Tel: (072) 41519

Strand View is an older, refurbished townhouse, right in the centre of Bundoran on the main road, with safe off-street parking. It is a functional guest house, with good-sized bedrooms and a pleasant dining room and TV lounge. There are views of the beach from the front bedrooms. No smoking is permitted in the dining room. The house is well maintained, and all the bedrooms are en-suite. Some have TVs . Evening meals are not available, but there are plenty of restaurants and pubs close by. No pets.

OWNER Mrs Mary Delaney and family   OPEN All year, except Christmas   ROOMS 1 double, 3 twin, 1 family (all en-suite)   TERMS B&B IR£14.00 p.p.; reduction for children; single supplement

Thalassa House

West End, Bundoran, Co Donegal
Tel: (072) 41685, Fax: (072) 41002

Thalassa, which is Greek for 'sea', is an impressive terracotta house on the main road in Bundoran. The house has been modernised over the years and has a mixture of pine and antique furniture. The rooms to the back of the house have sea views and there are also rooms in an adjacent annexe. One of the rooms has its own entrance, ideal for those who value privacy. Both continental and traditional cooked breakfasts are served. Evening meals are served, and vary from the traditional to monk fish, Indian or Chinese food. Terry Fergus-Browne and her son Aidan Browne also run the Stracomer Riding School, which has lovely views of the Atlantic Ocean. There are programmes for beginners, as well as advanced horse-riding and there are several horse-riding trails close by. In the evening guests, full of tales of their day, enjoy congregating in the large lounge.

OWNER Aidan Browne   OPEN April–30 September   ROOMS double/twin/family (all en-suite)   TERMS B&B IR£16.00 p.p.; reductions for children; single supplement; evening meal IR£15.00

CARRICK

Rockville House

Roxborough, Carrick, Co Donegal
Tel: (073) 39107

Midway between Killybegs and Glencolumbkille, this small, modern house stands in a slightly elevated position, with marvellous views of the sea at Slieve League. The cliffs at Bunglas, the highest marine cliffs in Europe, are 3 miles (4^1/$_2$ km) away. This is a popular destination with tourists from many parts of the world. Maureen Hughes has lots of energy, and she is responsible for organising walking tours in the Kilcar area. Teelin, an Irish-speaking area, lies close by and attracts people wishing to learn Irish. The house is about a mile (1^1/$_2$ km) from the nearest beach and from Carrick village. The family room has wonderful views, as does the lounge, which has a dining table at one end and sliding doors opening onto the patio. The bedrooms are small, but very bright, and prettily and simply decorated. All have TVS, tea- and coffee-makers, hairdryers, radio alarm-clocks and electric blankets and are located on the ground floor. Four-course meals are served on request between 7 and 9 pm, and breakfasts are served on plates specially made at a pottery in Sligo. There is no licence, but guests are welcome to bring their own wine. No pets. Take the Carrick road from Killybegs, then the coast road outside Killcar to Carrick.

OWNER Maureen Hughes   OPEN All year   ROOMS 1 double, 1 twin, 1 family (2 en-suite)   TERMS B&B IR£13.50–£14.50 p.p.; reductions for children; single supplement; evening meal IR£12.00

CASTLEFINN

Gortfad

Castlefinn, Co Donegal
Tel: (074) 46135

Gortfad has been the home of the Taylor family for 7 generations. The house has been built onto and adapted over the years, though the front is mainly Victorian and Edwardian. Gortfad is furnished with old-fashioned possessions and stained glass windows, and is set in peaceful grounds. The rooms are large, and there is a comfortable sitting room with a log fire. Mrs Taylor is a hospitable, kind lady who has been offering her special welcome for over 27 years – little

wonder that she has guests returning year after year. Home-baking, delicious scones and fruit cake are often offered with tea on arrival, at no extra charge. Evening meals are available only if prearranged, and there are several good eating establishments in the area. Guests can visit the tweed weaving area of Glenties and the 10,000 hectares of the National Park at Glenveagh Castle, as well as Derek Hill's remarkable art collection at Church Hill. There are 2 golf courses within 6 miles (9 km) and salmon, trout and coarse fishing are available in the River Finn. Lifford is 5 miles (7^1/$_2$ km) away and Donegal town only 25 miles (37^1/$_2$ km). Dogs by arrangement. Located on the north side of Castlefinn, signposted off the N15.

OWNER Mrs J Taylor   OPEN Easter–mid-September
ROOMS 2 double, 2 twin, 1 family (2 en-suite)
TERMS B&B IR£15.00 p.p.; reductions for children under 12; single supplement; evening meal IR£11.00

CLAR

Cranard

Birch Hill, Clar, Co Donegal

Tel: (073) 22584

A modern and immaculate bungalow in an elevated position with spectacular views of the Sligo Mountains and Lough Eske. The bedrooms are average in size and individually decorated in blue and pink. The one bedroom that is not en-suite has its own bathroom, and all have a radio. There is a separate dining room and lounge, which overlooks the view, and although there is a TV, guests seem to prefer to sit and chat and enjoy the beautiful scenery. This is an ideal spot for people who are looking for peace and serenity: there are some lovely walks close by, including a 12-mile (18-km) walk around the lake. Home-cooked evening meals are served at reasonable prices; fresh fish is a speciality of the house and is provided by Mr Ward, who is a fish merchant. Guests may choose what they would like for breakfast. There are few rules here – Deborah Ward is a very congenial host who wants guests to feel relaxed and at home in her warm and friendly house. Pets by arrangement. Signposted off the Letterkenny Road, 3 miles (4½ km) from Donegal.

OWNER Deborah Ward   OPEN 1 March–1 October
ROOMS 1 double/twin (2 en-suite)   TERMS B&B IR£14.00 p.p.; reductions for children; single supplement; evening meal IR£12.50

CULDAFF

Culdaff House

Culdaff, Inishowen, Co Donegal
Tel: (077) 79103

This large, slightly forbidding, grey stucco building is approached by a long driveway. Set on the edge of the attractive village of Culdaff, in the extremities of County Donegal, there are lovely views of hills and sea. The sombre exterior in no way reflects the fresh and bright interior. This is very much a family home, with large rooms and high ceilings. There is a large comfortable drawing room, with a fireplace and TV, a smaller dining room, and the beds have old Irish linen bedspreads. The property has been in Mr Mills' family for the last 300 years. Since taking over the house 7 years ago, the Mills have done a tremendous amount of remodelling and redecorating, gradually taking in bed-and-breakfast guests. There are no private bathrooms, but there are 3 bathrooms exclusively for guests' use. The motto of this informal, happy house is: "We share our home with our guests." Culdaff House was the recipient of the BHS Farmhouse of the Year award. Evening meals by prior arrangement. No smoking in dining room and no pets. On route via Carndonagh; take Beach Road in Culdaff.

OWNER Mrs Frances Mills   OPEN 1 March–30 November
ROOMS 4 double, 2 twin   TERMS B&B IR£15.00 p.p.; reductions for children; single supplement; evening meal IR£12.00

Ard Dallan

Stranacorkra, Derrybeg, Co Donegal

Tel: (075) 31209

The house is in an elevated position just off the main road, and has lovely views. Derrybeg is in an Irish-speaking area and many people come here to study the language. The TV lounge, dining room and one of the bedrooms have front-facing views. All the bedrooms are on the ground floor, and are small, bright and clean. No pets.

OWNER Mrs Anne Shovlin   OPEN 1 April–30 September
ROOMS 2 double, 1 twin (1 en-suite)   TERMS B&B IR£12.00 p.p.; reductions for children; single supplement

DONEGAL

Arranmore House

Killybegs Road, Donegal, Co Donegal

Tel: (073) 21242

The Keeneys built this house in 1968. It stands in its own grounds, and is located up a steep hill in a quiet, peaceful area, with lovely views, yet is only 3 minutes from town. Mrs Keeney, who comes from England, is a most friendly lady and runs a comfortable house with a pleasant atmosphere. The guest lounge has a TV and open fire. Substantial breakfasts are served in the bright dining room. The bedrooms are quite good-sized, with shower rooms, and all of them are on the ground floor. Smoking is not permitted in the dining room and pets are not allowed. Take the Killybegs road from Donegal, cross over the bridge; Arranmore is the sixth house on the left, past the library.

OWNER Mrs Doreen Keeney   OPEN April–October
ROOMS 3 double, 2 twin, 1 family (all en-suite)   TERMS B&B IR£14.00–£15.00 p.p.; reductions for children; single supplement

Belle View

Lurganboy, Donegal, Co Donegal

Tel: (073) 22167

Belle View is a modern bungalow set in an elevated position overlooking Donegal Bay. It stands in an acre of landscaped gardens one mile from Donegal town, on the Ballyshannon/ Sligo Road. Mary Lawne is an attentive host who welcomes her guests with home-baked scones and a hot drink. The bedrooms are average in size, with good bathrooms and comfortable beds. Breakfast only is served, but there is a wide choice of eating establishments in Donegal town. The guest lounge, which overlooks the mountains and bay, has an open fire and TV. There are some lovely walks close by, and boating and water sports are available at nearby Lough Eske. The house is easily located and is adjacent to a pitch and putt course. The nearby Donegal Craft Village is of special interest. Pets outside. Smoking in lounge only.

OWNER Mrs Mary Lawne   OPEN Easter–November
ROOMS 4 double/twin/family (2 en-suite)   TERMS B&B IR£14.00–£15.00 p.p.; reductions for children; single supplement

Shanveen House

Donegal Town, Co Donegal
Tel: (073) 21127

Shanveen House is an attractive house in an elevated position, overlooking the Blue Stack Mountains. Three minutes' walk from town, it stands opposite the eighteenth-century Presbyterian church. The bedrooms are spotlessly clean, and all have chairs and individual wardrobes. Although there are only two en-suite bedrooms, another does have its own shower. There is a comfortable lounge with Victorian furnishings and a piano, which guests are welcome to play. A lovely grandfather clock stands in the hallway and there is an interesting doll collection displayed in a cabinet on the landing. There is a pleasant homely atmosphere, and Mrs McGarrigle does everything possible to ensure her guests feel welcome and comfortable. No pets.

OWNER Mrs Anna McGarrigle   OPEN Easter–October
ROOMS 2 double, 1 twin, 1 family (2 en-suite)
TERMS B&B IR£15.50 p.p.; reductions for children; single supplement

St Ernan's House Hotel

St Ernan's Island, Donegal, Co Donegal
Tel: (073) 21065, Fax: (073) 22098

Just 2 miles (3 km) south of Donegal, St Ernan's was built

in 1826 by John Hamilton, a nephew of the Duke of Wellington. Situated on what was an island, the house is now linked to the mainland by a short causeway and covers some 8 acres. It is a most elegant, lovely country house in a beautiful position, offering peace and tranquillity in wonderful surroundings. It was turned into a hotel in 1983 and has been in the O'Dowds' hands since 1987. The rooms are beautifully proportioned and very spacious, each bedroom with marvellous views of sea and countryside and equipped with telephones and TVs. Dinner is served in the large dining room. Non-residents are encouraged to make reservations. The elegantly furnished drawing room is a good place to relax in at the end of the day. There is a bar that is used by residents. There are several golf courses close by, and horse-riding and fishing are available locally. Smoking is not permitted in the dining room and pets are not allowed, nor are children under six. The house is signposted from the main road between Donegal and Sligo. Visa and Access cards accepted.

OWNER Brian and Carmel O'Dowd OPEN Easter–1 November
ROOMS 12 double/twin/single (all en-suite)
TERMS B&B IR£52.00–£69.00 p.p.; reductions for children; single supplement; evening meal IR£25.50

DOWNINGS

Baymount Bed and Breakfast

Downings, Co Donegal
Tel: (074) 55395

Mrs McBride was born in the small house at the bottom of the driveway. Twenty-two years ago, she and her husband built their present house. At the time, Mr McBride was a builder; now he is a driving-test examiner. The house stands above the narrow country road, with spectacular views over the water to the mountains. At the time the house was built the family was very large; the couple had 12 children. Some have now left home, which has provided space for Mrs McBride's bed-and-breakfast business. The TV/VCR lounge is a large, bright room, enjoying the same magnificent views as the dining room, which has separate tables as well as a TV and sitting area, and sliding doors onto the terrace: a lovely place to sit on a fine day. A hairdryer and iron are available upon request. Smoking allowed in the lounge only. No pets. The house can be found half a mile from Downings village on Atlantic Drive.

128

OWNER Mrs Mary McBride   OPEN Easter–31 August
ROOMS 4 double, 2 twin (1 en-suite)   TERMS B&B IR£14.00–
£15.00 p.p.; reductions for children under 10; single supplement

DUNFANAGHY

Rosman House

Figart, Dunfanaghy, Co Donegal

Tel: (074) 36273

Standing on the edge of Dunfanaghy, Rosman House is in a
wonderful position: an elevated spot with marvellous views
all round. Mrs McHugh is a friendly lady who formerly was a
teacher in Falcarragh. Her husband looks after the 100-acre
dairy and sheep farm. There have been several improve-
ments to the property, and the spacious TV lounge, which
opens onto a well-kept patio and gardens, is an ideal spot to
relax in after a busy day. The bedrooms are of a high stand-
ard, all individually decorated in coordinated colour
schemes and fitted with tea-makers, TVs and electric blan-
kets. There are 5 ground-floor bedrooms. Breakfast is served
in the elegant dining room on separate tables, where guests
have views of Horn Head. Smoking permitted in the lounge
only. Rosman House has lovely scenic walks close by and an
18-hole golf course. The house is located by turning right
after the art gallery on the main Falcarragh road.

OWNER Mrs Roisin McHugh   OPEN All year   ROOMS 3 double,
2 family, 1 treble (all en-suite)   TERMS B&B IR£15.00 p.p.;
reductions for children; single supplement

DUNGLOE

Barr a' Ghaoith

Quay Road, Dungloe, Co Donegal

Tel: (075) 21389

Barr a' Ghaoith means "Top of the Wind" – an apt descrip-
tion, as this house is in an elevated position with panoramic
views. This is very much a family-run establishment with all
the family joining in to help with the work. There is a
separate dining room and a very comfortable lounge with
TV, VCR and games. The house is situated in a picturesque
seaside area, only 200 metres from the sea and within
walking distance of the town. The bedrooms are fresh and
clean, and all have tea-makers. Breakfasts include home-
baked breads and preserves. Close by, the visitor will enjoy

angling, golf, hill walking and scenic drives; tennis courts and a leisure centre are also available. Pitch and putt and deep-sea fishing can be organised if desired. Children are welcome. Pets welcome by arrangement.

OWNER Mrs Susan Gallagher   OPEN All year, except Christmas
ROOMS 2 double, 1 twin, 1 family (2 en-suite)   TERMS B&B
IR£12.50 p.p.; reductions for children under 12, children under 3 free; single supplement

DUNKINEELY

Bruckless House

Bruckless, Dunkineely, Co Donegal

Tel: (073) 37071, Fax: (073) 37070, E-mail: bruc@iol.ie

This attractive, creeper-covered Georgian house, with its traditional cobbled courtyard, was built around 1750. Standing in 18 acres in a lovely position right on the coast, it is surrounded by an attractive, award-winning garden, and a meadow with mature trees. Irish draught horses and Connemara ponies are bred here, and can often be seen grazing down by the shoreline. The house has recently been completely redecorated and is comfortably furnished in an oriental flavour, as the Evans family spent many years in Hong Kong. The 2 reception rooms have log fires and views of the bay. Dinner is not served, but arrangements can be made with one of the good restaurants in the area. There are 2 golf courses within easy reach, and a driving range in the village. No smoking. No pets. Twelve miles (18 km) from Donegal town, on the left-hand side.

OWNER Joan and Clive Evans   OPEN 1 April–1 October   ROOMS 1
double, 1 twin, 2 single (1 en-suite)   TERMS B&B IR£20.00–
£25.00 p.p.

FALCARRAGH

Sea View House

Upper Ray, Falcarragh, Co Donegal

Tel: (074) 35552

An attractive bungalow set in 3 acres of land in an elevated position, surrounded by open countryside and sweeping views of the mountains and sea – on clear days Tory Island can be seen. Guests are greeted upon arrival with a cup of tea or coffee, and substantial breakfasts, including homemade bread and preserves, are served in the new dining room. The lounge is bright, cheerful and comfortably furnished, and there is a TV. Evening meals are not served, but advice on good local restaurants is given, as well as information on what to see and do in the area. Mrs McFadden is a very helpful lady and guests are well taken care of here. Cots are available. This is a wonderful spot to relax in and there are lovely walks close by. Situated 2¹/₂ miles (4 km) from Falcarragh. Pets outside only.

OWNER Mrs Jean McFadden   OPEN Easter–30 September
ROOMS 2 double, 1 twin, 1 single   TERMS B&B IR£13.00 p.p.;
reductions for children; single supplement

GLENCOLUMBKILLE

Corner House

Cashel, Glencolumbkille, Co Donegal
Tel: (073) 30021

The Corner House is right in the centre of the village and, as its name implies, it is on a corner. Mrs Byrne, a very pleasant lady, runs the bed and breakfast as well as the adjoining small shop, and her son runs the pub. From the outside, the house looks quite modest, but it is surprisingly big inside, with an enormous dining room and small upstairs TV lounge. The house is well maintained; the bedrooms are small, but very clean. The one bedroom that is not en-suite has its own bathroom. The surroundings are beautiful, and it is a great place for walking and hill climbing. Sandy beaches are close by, and there is good fishing. No pets. There is a public phone.

OWNER Mrs John P. Byrne   OPEN 1 April–30 September
ROOMS 2 double, 1 family, 1 twin (3 en-suite)   TERMS B&B
IR£15.00 p.p.; reductions for children; single supplement

INVER

Cloverhill House

Cranny, Inver, Co Donegal
Tel: (073) 36165

Approached by a driveway lined on each side with high yew hedges, this attractive, long, low, whitewashed, modern building stands in an elevated position, with lovely views over the river. The house was constructed with some imagination. There is an enormous and very pleasant open sitting/dining room with a real fire, and the bedrooms are spacious and well furnished. Three of the bedrooms are on the ground floor, and en-suite facilities have recently been added to one of the bedrooms. An evening meal is available on request at 7 pm, and there is a wine licence. Pets are not permitted. Seven miles (10½ km) from Donegal town on the Killybegs road. Fishing, golfing and mountain climbing nearby.

OWNER June and Terry Coyle OPEN All year, except Christmas
ROOMS 2 double, 3 twin, 1 single (1 en-suite)
TERMS B&B IR£13.50–£16.00 p.p.; reductions for children; evening meal IR£12.00; high tea from IR£10.00

Hollyhaven

Kerrykeel, Co Donegal

Tel: (074) 50064

Hollyhaven has wonderful views over sea and mountains, and, although out in the country, it is only a 4-minute walk from the village. The small, whitewashed bungalow stands in an attractive front garden on a quiet country road. Mrs Dougherty is a most friendly lady who greets her guests with a cup of tea or coffee whenever possible, at no extra charge. Evening meals are served at 7 pm, if ordered in advance. There is no licence, but guests are welcome to bring their own wine. All the bedrooms are on the ground floor and all are very small, spotlessly clean and simply furnished. The dining room has lovely views, and there is a TV lounge. No pets.

OWNER Mrs Rose Dougherty OPEN Easter–31 October
ROOMS 2 double, 1 twin, 1 single (3 en-suite)
TERMS B&B IR£14.00–£16.00 p.p.; reductions for children; single supplement; evening meal IR£11.00; high tea IR£7.00

KILLYBEGS

Bannagh House

Fintra Road, Killybegs, Co Donegal

Tel: (073) 31108

Bannagh House may be recognised by the ambulance that stands occasionally in the driveway when Mr Melly, an ambulance driver, is off duty. Mrs Melly takes care of the bed-and-breakfast business and her 5 children. This modern house stands in an elevated position in a small front garden on the edge of Killybegs, with wonderful views over the harbour, town and hills both near and distant. Killybegs is a big fishing port, and the harbour always seems to be full of enormous fishing boats; consequently, it is an excellent place for fresh fish. Melly's Café does excellent fish and chips in vast portions. There is a TV lounge and dining room overlooking the bay. All the bedrooms are on the ground floor. No pets. An ideal location for touring the Donegal area. Located by driving through Killybegs; Bannagh House is the first bungalow on the left on Glencolmcille Road.

OWNER Mrs Phyllis Melly   OPEN 1 April–31 October
ROOMS 4 double, 1 twin, 1 family (all en-suite)
TERMS B&B IR£15.00 p.p.; reductions for children under 10; single supplement

Holly Crest Lodge

Donegal Road, Killybegs, Co Donegal
Tel: (073) 31470

This attractive, Georgian-style house is set just off the road, in a large, well-maintained garden. The owner, Anne Keeney, is a very personable lady who enjoys meeting people, and nothing is too much trouble to ensure her guests are comfortable. The house is very well decorated and is furnished to a high standard. The colour-coordinated bedrooms are on the ground floor, and one has a brass bed. There is a guest lounge with TV, and guests are welcome to sit in the garden on pleasant days. An excellent breakfast is served in the separate dining room and, though evening meals are not served in the house, there are plenty of eating establishments close by.

OWNER Anne Keeney   OPEN 1 April–1 September   ROOMS 3 double (2 en-suite)   TERMS IR£15.00; reductions for children; single supplement

LAGHY

Hillcrest

Ballyshannon Road, Laghy, Co Donegal
Tel: (073) 21837, Fax: (073) 21674

Three and a half miles (5 km) from Donegal, just off the Ballyshannon Road, Hillcrest offers a warm, friendly welcome. All the bedrooms, which are on the small side, have pretty, front-facing views and are located on the ground floor. Each bedroom has tea-making facilities. The small TV lounge has a piano and comfortable chairs, and the dining room has a pleasant view. The modern bungalow stands on the side of a hill and is set in an attractive front garden. No smoking is permitted in the dining room and pets are not allowed.

OWNER Mrs Sheila Gatins   OPEN 1 April–31 October
ROOMS 1 double, 3 family (2 en-suite)   TERMS B&B IR£13.00 p.p.; reductions for children; single supplement

LETTERKENNY

Hillcrest House

Lurgybrack, Letterkenny, Co Donegal
Tel: (074) 22300, Fax: (074) 25137

Spotlessly clean and offering a warm welcome, Hillcrest House is on the main Sligo road, just a mile from Letterkenny, so it is potentially noisy. However, there is a great view of the water, town and mountains. The Maguires are a friendly couple, with 5 children, and they serve guests with cakes and tea when they arrive. The rooms, although a little small, are comfortable, and there are 4 ground-floor bedrooms. No smoking is permitted in the dining room, a pleasant room with separate tables. There is a small TV lounge. Hillcrest House is RAC acclaimed and AA listed. Pets outside only. This is an ideal location for touring. One mile (1¹/₂ km) from the roundabout on Derry Road. All major credit cards accepted.

OWNER Larry and Margaret Maguire   OPEN All year, except Christmas   ROOMS 1 double, 2 twin, 3 family (5 en-suite)
TERMS B&B IR£15.00 p.p.; reductions for children; single supplement

White Gables

Dromore, Derry Road, Letterkenny, Co Donegal
Tel: (074) 22583

White Gables is a spacious house in an elevated position overlooking the river and town; the house is sandwiched between a new dual carriageway and the former main road. Double-glazed windows in the house keeps traffic noise to a minimum. There is a lovely view from the breakfast room/ lounge, which has a small sitting area and one table for breakfast facing the windows. The small bedrooms are clean and simply furnished; 2 are on the ground floor. There is quite an attractive rear garden. There are two ground-floor rooms. The house is on the Derry road about 2 miles (3 km) outside Letterkenny. No pets.

OWNER Mr and Mrs J. McConnellogue OPEN All year, except Christmas ROOMS 5 double/twin/family (4 en-suite)
TERMS B&B IR£13.50 p.p.; reductions for children; single supplement

LIFFORD

The Hall Greene

Porthall, Lifford, Co Donegal
Tel: (074) 41318

A neatly kept, whitewashed farmhouse dating from 1611 and standing back from the road, looking into Co Tyrone and the Sperrin Mountains. Salmon fishing is available on the river at the bottom of the garden. Licences can be obtained in Lifford. This is a wonderful place for children – it is off the road and has large rooms, and on the farm there are lambs, goats and a donkey. Mrs McKean, a very friendly lady, has 4 children of her own, so children are especially welcome. The house is a comfortable family home with a large TV lounge and open fire in an old fireplace. The bedrooms have tea-making facilities and hairdryers. The large dining room has 2 tables, and there is one family room,

which is very spacious, with massive pieces of old furniture. Evening meals are served at any convenient time if arranged in advance. There is no licence, but guests are welcome to bring their own wine or beer. The 150-acre farm has sheep, cattle, pigs and cereals. Non-smokers preferred. No smoking in the dining room. The house is signposted 1½ miles (2½ km) from Lifford.

OWNER Mervyn and Jean McKean OPEN All year, Christmas by arrangement ROOMS 1 double, 3 family (2 en-suite)
TERMS B&B IR£15.00 p.p.; reduction for children under 12 (sharing parents' room); evening meal IR£12.00, high tea IR£7.00

The Haw Lodge

The Haw, Lifford, Co Donegal
Tel: (074) 41397

A traditional farmhouse on the main road, about a mile (1½ km) from Lifford in the direction of Sligo. The rooms are decorated in pretty wallpaper and matching fabrics. The dining room at the back of the house was the original farmhouse kitchen, dating from over 100 years ago. There is a small front garden. Haw Lodge has one ground-floor bedroom, with a toilet and washbasin close by, and an ideal family suite, consisting of 2 self-contained, en-suite bedrooms. All the beds are orthopaedic and have electric blankets. A cot is available. The cosy lounge has a TV and fireplace. Evening meals or high teas can be served by arrangement. Salmon and trout fishing are available in the River Finn, which flows through the farm. Golf, walking, birdwatching and a fully equipped leisure centre are close by. A visit to the Lifford Old Courthouse, Visitor and Clans Centre is well worthwhile. This is a friendly house, with a home-away-from-home atmosphere. No smoking. Pets outside. Off the main Lifford to Sligo road. Visa and Access cards accepted.

OWNER Eileen Patterson OPEN 1 March–1 November
ROOMS 3 double, 3 twin, 1 family (3 en-suite)
TERMS B&B IR£13.00–£16.00 p.p.; reductions for children; single supplement; evening meal IR£12.00; high tea IR£8.00

Barraicin

Malin Head, Inishowen Peninsula, Co Donegal

Tel: (077) 70184

Barraicin takes its name from the field on which it was built by the Doyles in 1971, and means "the square toecap". Just 3½ miles (5 km) from Malin Head Point, Ireland's most northerly point, it is in a superb position – about half a mile from the sea and with lovely sea views. The small, cosy dining room, where guests share 2 tables, overlooks the pretty garden, which has an old pump. The large, bright lounge has an open fire and sea views. The Doyles are a very pleasant couple who started doing bed and breakfast in 1980. The bedrooms are clean and bright; all are equipped with washbasins, and one is en-suite. Tea- and coffee-making facilities and a hairdryer are available upon request. Home cooking a speciality. Pets are not permitted. There is no licence, but guests are welcome to bring their own beer or wine. Six miles (9 km) from Malin village, opposite public telephone in Malin Head.

OWNER Mrs M. Doyle   OPEN Easter–31 October
ROOMS 1 double/twin/family   TERMS B&B IR£13.00–£14.00 p.p.; reductions for children; single supplement

PORTNOO

Carnaween Guest House

Narin, Portnoo, Co Donegal

Tel: (075) 45122

Carnaween is named after one of the mountains in the Blue Stack Mountain range and is situated in an idylic setting overlooking Gweebary Bay. There are lovely sandy beaches close by, and during a full or new moon a fifteen-minute walk can be taken to Inniskeel Island. Be sure to check the tides or you could end up waving a red sweater for rescue. Owner, Nora Shovlin, formerly a teacher, was born in the house, is very knowledgeable about the area and is happy to give advice on what to see and do. The house was built in 1930 as a guest house and it has been extended and modernised over the years. The bedrooms are average in size and are clean and functional. This is a lovely spot for families, with the beautiful beaches close by. Narin and

Portnoo golf courses are within walking distance.

OWNER Nora Shovlin OPEN 17 March–30 September
ROOMS 10 double/twin/family/single (all en-suite)
TERMS B&B IR£14.00 p.p.; reductions for children; single
supplement

RAMELTON

Ardeen

Ramelton, Co Donegal
Tel: (074) 51243

An attractive, small country house on the edge of Ramelton,
standing in a most pleasant lawned front garden with views
of the River Leannon. The rooms are good-sized and
prettily decorated, and the front ones have lovely views.
Two bedrooms have TVs. There is a TV lounge and dining
room with one big table, and outside a hard tennis court at
the back of the house. The house at one time belonged to a
private nurse of King George V and, more recently, to 2
doctors. The Campbells bought the house about 17 years
ago. Mr Campbell is now retired from running a local shop
and Mrs Campbell, who has 3 grown-up children, concen-
trates on the bed-and-breakfast business. Smoking is not
permitted in the dining room. American Express accepted.

OWNER Mrs Anne Campbell OPEN Easter–31 October
ROOMS 2 double, 1 twin, 1 family (2 en-suite)
TERMS B&B IR£16.00–£17.50 p.p.; reductions for children; single
supplement

Gleann Oir

Ards, Ramelton, Co Donegal
Tel: (074) 51187

A modest, modern house located in a hilly area, with specta-
cular views all around of farmland and hills, situated about 3
miles (4¹/₂ km) from Ramelton and signposted off the
Letterkenny road. It is a quiet, peaceful, comfortable family
home, simply furnished. Mrs Crawford has 7 children, and
so children are especially welcome here. The 35-acre farm is
quite an attraction, with sheep, 2 milking cows and arable
land. There is a comfortable sitting room with TV and open
fire, a small rear dining room, and an additional family room
is now available. Evening meals are served to suit guests, if
arranged in advance. There is no licence, but guests are

welcome to bring their own wine. There are 2 ground-floor rooms, and all rooms have hairdryers.

OWNER Mrs Rosemary Crawford   OPEN Easter–31 October
ROOMS 2 double/family (3 en-suite)   TERMS B&B IR£14.00 p.p.; reductions for children; single supplement; evening meal IR£12.00

The Manse

Ramelton, Co Donegal
(074) 51047

The original house dates from 1690 and was a planter's cottage. It was built on to in later years and is now 3 storeys high. Mrs Scott, who is quite a character, moved into The Manse 36 years ago. It's somewhat faded and old-fashioned, but this lends to its charm. Visitors find the bathroom, with its original fittings, quite intriguing. The bathtub has the old shower, with an enormous head and vast brass taps that allow the water to come from three different directions, from above, the sides and below. Mrs Scott encourages her guests to have the run of the house, and most visitors forsake the more formal rooms for what is known as the 'warm' kitchen. The functional kitchen is known as the 'cold' kitchen and is in the room behind. Mrs Scott really enjoys her guests and

takes in 4 guests only so she has a chance of talking to them and filling them in on the area and old anecdotes. A downstairs cloakroom and WC were installed recently. Smoking is permitted in the study/library only. No pets. Seven miles (10¹/₂ km) north of Letterkenny on the shore of Lough Swilly, direct road from Dublin.

OWNER Mrs Florence Scott   OPEN Easter–mid-September
ROOMS 1 double, 2 twin   TERMS B&B IR£20.00 p.p.

County Galway

Galway contains the widely renowned area of Connemara, which stretches northwards from Galway city up to Killary Harbour and is bordered on the east by beautiful Lough Corrib, which boasts an island for every day of the year.

Galway, the 'city of the tribes', and the nearby popular resort of Salthill, which overlooks the famous Galway Bay, have lovely beaches, a promenade for walking, lots of restaurants: an ideal holiday spot.

Wild Connemara has inspired song and poetry. Today, Galway, Connemara and the west of Ireland are a haven for ancient customs and culture. You will hear lilting and evocative Irish music in the pubs and probably the Irish language being spoken as well. Travel offshore and you beome immersed even deeper into Ireland's traditional way of life, with trips to Inishbofin, County Clare, Achill and the Aran Islands.

There's plenty to see and do in the west of Ireland: pony trekking, dramatically located golf courses, angling (which is well catered for, with abundant salmon and trout in clean waters).

If you are interested in sixteenth-century castles, visit the ruins of Ardamullivan Castle, 5 miles (7¹/₂ km) south of Gort, an O'Shaughnessy stronghold. Fiddaun Castle, 5 miles (7¹/₂ km) south-southwest of Gort, is another of their strongholds.

Clarinbridge is a popular place in September when it hosts the Oyster Festival. While Portumna, a market town, is at the head of Lough Derg.

For the more adventurous, a climb up the Slieve Auchty Mountains is well worth the view.

Two castles worth seeing are Derryhivenny Castle, 3 miles (4¹/₂ km) northeast of Portumna. Built in 1653, it is well preserved, as is Pallas Castle, 6 miles (9 km) from

Portumna on the Loughrea Road.

Ballinasloe is well known for the October Horse Fair, which lasts for 8 days, and includes carnival events and show-jumping exhibitions.

ANNAGHDOWN

Corrib View Farm

Annaghdown, Co Galway

Tel: (091) 91114

A charming old farmhouse near Lough Corrib, approximately 2 miles (3 km) off the Galway-Headford-Castlebar road. Good old-fashioned hospitality is offered here, with the emphasis on a warm welcome and good food, featuring home-baking and local fresh produce. The rooms are clean and comfortable and all the bedrooms have tea- and coffee-making facilities. The family bedroom has en-suite facilities, and there are 2 additional bathrooms exclusively for guests. Corrib View has a separate dining room and TV lounge – smoking is permitted only in the lounge. Evening meals must be prearranged, and guests are welcome to bring their own wine. Pets outside only. Corrib View was a regional winner of the Agri-Tourism award, and is a convenient base for touring Connemara and the West. Trips to the Aran Islands can be arranged. Galway city is 8 miles (12 km) away, and Annaghdown Pier is a short drive away. Corrib View is signposted at Cloonboo Cross near Regan's Bar.

OWNER The Scott-Furey family   OPEN Easter–October
ROOMS 2 double, 1 twin, 1 family, 1 single (1 en-suite)
TERMS B&B IR£15.00–£17.00 p.p.; reductions for children; single supplement; evening meal IR£16.00

CASHEL

Cashel House

Cashel, Co Galway

Tel: (095) 31001, Fax: (095) 31077

Cashel House, formerly one of Connemara's most gracious private homes, stands at the head of Cashel Bay in a tranquil and secluded setting, a 40-acre estate of flowering shrubs and woodland walks. It has quickly gained an international reputation for good food and comfort in a quiet, relaxing atmosphere; carefully cooked, fresh garden and sea produce are its specialities, and there are open turf fires. In 1969, the

late General and Madame De Gaulle spent 2 weeks of their Irish holiday here. The house is furnished with fine antiques and other treasures. The charming, recently upgraded bedrooms are beautifully appointed and all have TVs, direct-dial telephones and hairdryers. The bathrooms have recently been redone. Beaches, golf, and sea fishing are available in the vicinity. There is a hard tennis court, tiny private beach and horse-riding facilities. No pets. Situated on the main Galway/Clifden road; turn left at Recess. All major credit cards accepted.

OWNER Dermot and Kay McEvilly   OPEN All year except 10 January–31 January   ROOMS 32 rooms: double/twin/family (all en-suite)   TERMS IR£49.00–£66.00 p.p.; reductions for children; evening meal from IR£27.00–£29.00

CLARINBRIDGE

Spring Lawn

Stradballey, Clarinbridge, Co Galway
Tel: (091) 96045

An attractive house set in 2¹/₂ acres in the heart of oyster country. There is a wooded area behind the house, and the sea is within walking distance. The bedrooms are good-sized, clean and freshly decorated, with modern, comfortable furnishings. All are en-suite. There is a sitting room for guests and a separate dining room. Maura McNamara has been in business for over 9 years and takes a personal interest in her guests. Breakfast only is served, but there are 3 restaurants close by. No smoking. No pets. Vouchers accepted.

142

OWNER Mrs Maura McNamara   OPEN 1 March–30 November
ROOMS 1 double, 1 treble, 1 family (all en-suite)   TERMS B&B
IR£13.50 p.p.; reductions for children; single supplement; evening
meal IR£11.50

CLIFDEN

Ardmore House

Sky Road, Clifden, Co Galway

Tel: (095) 21221, Fax: (095) 21100

Ardmore House is a luxury farmhouse set in beautiful scenic
countryside overlooking the sea. It is warm and inviting;
Kathy Mullen is a delightful and pleasant host, and guests
are assured of true Irish hospitality. The bedrooms are
immaculate and individually decorated, with comfortable
beds. There's a well-furnished TV lounge with open fires.
Evening meals with home-style cooking are served, if
prearranged, and seafood is a speciality. Lake and deep-sea
angling, pony trekking and beautiful walks, sandy beaches
and golf are all available in the area. No smoking. Situated 4
miles (6 km) west of Clifden (50 miles/75 km west of
Galway). Visa, Access and Eurocard accepted.

OWNER Kathy Mullen   OPEN 1 April–15 October   ROOMS 6
double/twin/family (all en-suite)   TERMS B&B IR£15.50 p.p.;
reductions for children; single supplement; evening meals
IR£14.00

Cregg House

Goulane, Clifden, Co Galway

Tel: (095) 21326

An immaculate Dormer bungalow standing in an elevated
position in its own grounds of 1 acre. The house has a
spectacular view of Roundstone Bog and the mountains
beyond. The bedrooms are prettily and individually deco-
rated in pink, blue, green or peach, with tasteful matching
fabrics; all are en-suite but one, which has its own bath-
room. The O'Donnells have been offering their special
brand of hospitality for over 11 years, and guests feel very
much at home here. There is a TV lounge with turf fires.
Breakfasts are excellent and include fresh fruits, homemade
yoghurt and soda bread. An ideal base from which to tour
Connemara, there is a fishing river less than 5 minutes away;
golf and horse-riding are also available. The O'Donnells

have 3 charming daughters, Lisa, Tracy and Lorraine. Pets by arrangement. Ideally situated 2 miles (3 km) from Clifden on the main Galway road.

OWNER Mary and Hugh O'Donnell   OPEN Easter–31 October
ROOMS 2 double/family/twin (5 en-suite)   TERMS B&B IR£15.00
p.p.; reductions for children, single supplement

Mallmore House

Off Ballyconneely Road, Clifden, Co Galway
Tel: (095) 21460

A lovely Georgian house with a friendly and warm atmosphere, set in 35 acres, within walking distance of the sea. The house overlooks the bay, and most of the bedrooms have lovely views. Mr and Mrs Hardman have been in business for 14 years, and during that time have been renovating the house, cleverly combining the old-world charm with modern conveniences. All of the bedrooms are on the ground floor and are spacious and comfortable. There is a comfortable, well-furnished lounge with TV and open peat fireplace. Guests are assured of personal service: Kathleen Hardman is a considerate and helpful host. Excellent breakfasts are served in the separate dining room, and there are several places to eat in the area. No smoking in the dining room. Situated approximately 1¹/₃ miles (2 km) from Clifden.

OWNER Mrs Kathleen Hardman   OPEN 1 March–1 November
ROOMS 2 double, 3 twin, 1 family (all en-suite)   TERMS B&B
IR£15.50 p.p.; reductions for sharing; single supplement

Sunnybank House

Clifden, Co Galway
Tel (095) 21437

A charming period house set in an elevated position in its own landscaped grounds overlooking Clifden town. The immaculate bedrooms are tastefully decorated and have their own en-suite bathrooms. There are two ground-floor rooms with private sitting rooms. There is a heated swimming pool, a sauna, tennis courts and mature gardens for guests' use. There is also a spacious lounge and drawing room. Evening meals are not served at Sunnybank House, but the charming owners, Jackie and Marion O'Grady, have an award-winning seafood restaurant with a bistro bar, which is open for lunch and dinner daily. Sunnybank would be an ideal base from which to explore this well-known and beautiful area of Ireland. Not suitable for young children.

OWNER Jackie and Marion O'Grady   OPEN 1 March–September ROOMS double/twin/family (all en-suite)   TERMS B&B from IR£20.00–£25.00 p.p.; single supplement

CLONBUR

Ballykine House

Clonbur, Co Galway

Tel: (092) 46150

Ballykine House is situated on the road between the picturesque villages of Cong and Clonbur, the gateways to Connemara. The house overlooks the famous fishing lake of Lough Mask with its own private grounds of gardens and lawns surrounded by beautiful woodlands. The oldest part of the house belonged to the Guinness family; the house and land were purchased by the family in 1940, and in 1992 an addition was added. Mr and Mrs Lambe have created a warm and inviting atmosphere – the rooms are bright and clean, and the bedrooms all have hairdryers. There is a cosy sitting room with open fire and a conservatory to relax in with tea- and coffee-makers provided, as well as an adjacent billiard room. There are wonderful forest walks (guides can be provided) as well as walks to the summit of magnificent Benlevi. The immediate area is a fisherman's paradise. Restaurants within walking distance of house. Pets outside only.

OWNER Ann Lambe   OPEN 1 April–1 November   ROOMS 1 double/twin/family (all en-suite)   TERMS B&B IR£15.00 p.p.; reductions for children; single supplement

CORRANDULLA

Cregg Castle

Corrandulla, Co Galway

Tel: (091) 91434

Cregg Castle, the last fortified castle to be built west of the Shannon, sits in a peaceful and secluded spot on 165 acres of wildlife reserve. This is a very lived-in and informal property and there are no strict rules here: guests may make tea or coffee at any hour of the day free of charge, or walk in the woods and spot the wildlife. Breakfast, which includes free-range eggs and homemade bread, is served in the Great Hall, with its huge log fire, until noon. The emphasis here is on relaxation, and guests are encouraged to get to know each other and enjoy conversation, which often goes on late into the night. Irish music is played here, and guests are able to enjoy an evening of music and fun. This is an ideal spot for those who want to be involved in Irish music. Owners Pat and Ann Marie are both experienced musicians, and are delighted to play for or with guests.

This is a unique property with many original features, such as the huge locks and security bars, the foot scraper with the rampant black cat of the Blake crest and the shutters on the big windows. The Blake crest is also on the fireplace with its black marble, which is believed to have come from the Menlo quarries. Outside in the courtyard is a Queen Ann bell tower, in the inner yard is the original forge and the remains of an oven for firing pottery. There is also a beautiful spring well that supplies Cregg Castle with natural spring water. Five rooms have private baths. Cregg Castle's welcome is aptly described on the front of their brochure: "Hail Guest, we ask not what thou art; if friend, we greet thee hand and heart; if stranger, such no longer be, our friendly faith shall conquer thee." Cregg Castle is a place to capture Ireland's history and culture. There is a wine licence. Stables outside for pets.

OWNER The Broderick family   OPEN 1 March–1 November
ROOMS 12 double   TERMS B&B IR£20.00–£25.00 p.p.; reductions for children; evening meal IR£12.00 p.p.

GALWAY

Eureka

Bushy Park, Galway, Co Galway
Tel: (091) 23229

Eureka is set back off the main road, five minutes from the city centre on the Clifden Road. The house is modern, clean, bright and well maintained. Bedrooms are of a high standard, tastefully decorated, with the front rooms having a view of the lake, river and golf course. There is a small sun lounge with a TV on the first floor, a good spot in which to relax after a busy day. Owners, Mary and John Connell, are an extremely friendly couple who go out of their way to assist their guests. A complimentary hot drink and biscuits are offered on arrival. Only breakfast is served, and guests not wanting the traditional Irish breakfast have a choice of yoghurts and fresh fruit. Mary and John are happy to recommend restaurants for evening meals. Their house is directly opposite the Glenlo Abbey golf course. Smoking restricted. No pets.

OWNER John and Mary Connell   OPEN 1 May–30 September
ROOMS 3 double/twin/family (all en-suite)   TERMS B&B IR£15.00 p.p.; reductions for children under 12; single supplement

Killeen House

Killeen, Bushy Park, Galway, Co Galway
Tel: (091) 524179, Fax: (091) 528065

This charming house, approached by a tree-lined driveway, is nestled in 25 acres of beautifully landscaped gardens that extend down to Lake Corrib. Catherine Doyle is a wonderful host with a flair for decor and a passion for antiques. The house has been totally refurbished, combining all modern comforts with the style of the original. The rooms are enormous and luxuriously appointed. One reflects the Victorian era, another the Edwardian. All have TVs, hairdryers, telephones and tea- and coffee-makers. The elegant drawing room has the original marble fireplace and an interesting teapot collection. A varied breakfast is served in the dining room. Evening meals are not available, but there is a wide choice of eating establishments close by. For those who enjoy gracious living in a tranquil atmosphere, Killeen House would be an excellent choice. Not suitable for children. No pets. Situated 4 km from the city centre on the Clifden Road.

OWNER Catherine Doyle   OPEN All year except Christmas
ROOMS 4 double/twin (all en-suite)   TERMS B&B from IR£25.00 p.p.; single supplement

LEENANE

Delphi Lodge

Leenane, Co Galway
Tel: (095) 42211, Fax: (095) 42296

Delphi Lodge is one of the finest sporting lodges in Ireland. Beautifully restored in 1988, this magnificent 1830s country house has a rich history. Set in 1,000 acres with 3 loughs, in a stunning lakeside location, and surrounded by ancient woodlands and towering mountains, the lodge is the ultimate Connemara retreat. The house has antique pine furniture and the bedrooms have lovely views. Originally the sporting estate of the Marquis of Sligo, Delphi is now the home of Jane and Peter Mantle; Jane is a Cordon Bleu cook who specialises in local seafood. The lodge has a strong emphasis on salmon and sea-trout fishing, and Delphi is one of the finest game fisheries in Ireland. The fishing season runs from spring to the middle of October. Outside the fishing season, the lodge is popular with shooting parties, ramblers and golfers. Horse-riding and hunting can also be arranged. Superb, safe and uncrowded beaches are within 20 minutes' drive, and the lodge is conveniently placed for visiting Westport and all the sites of Connemara. A huge snooker room and a magnificent library are open to guests. Evening meals are served at a superb old oak dining room table and the wine cellar is extensive. Not suitable for children. French spoken. No pets. There are 4 charming country cottages available for self-catering; ideal for families.

OWNER Jane and Peter Mantle   OPEN 1 February–31 October
ROOMS 11 double/twin (private baths)   TERMS B&B IR£30.00–£47.50 p.p.; evening meal £25.00

Glen Valley House and Stables

Leenaun, Co Galway

Tel: (095) 42269, Fax: (095) 42269

Glen Valley House is found down a rather bumpy private road in a remote location amidst lovely countryside. This large, modest farmhouse, nestled in the foothills of Lettershanbally Mountain, has spacious rooms, is clean and comfortable and is simply furnished. There is a small, cosy sitting room with TV and turf fires. This is an ideal base for those who enjoy hill walking; pony trekking is available on the farm, which is run by Mr O'Neill. Substantial breakfasts and evening meals, if prearranged, are served in the farmhouse dining room. Pets outside only. Situated $1^1/2$ miles ($2^1/2$ km) off the Clifden Road, down a private road, five miles ($7^1/2$ km) from Leenaun.

OWNER Joseph and Josephine O'Neill   OPEN Easter–31 October
ROOMS 1 double/twin/family   TERMS B&B IR£13.50 p.p.; reductions for children; single supplement; evening meal IR£13.00

Moycullen House

Moycullen, Co Galway

Tel: (091) 85566, Fax: (091) 85566

Moycullen House lies on a narrow, quiet road on one of the highest points in the area overlooking Lough Corrib. This large house was designed in the arts-and-crafts style and has great oak doors with the original iron locks and latches. It was built in the 1900s by Lord Campbell, a Scot who came to the West for sporting holidays. The house is set in 30 acres of rhododendrons and azaleas, and there is a pure spring that still provides the house with water. When Moycullen was first built it included a servants' wing and to this day bell pushes still exist in the sitting room, dining room and 4 of the bedrooms. The bedrooms are large, tastefully decorated and well furnished; most have period fireplaces. All have their own bathrooms. There is a lovely sitting room with an old stone fireplace, and a conservatory has been recently added. Philip and Marie are charming hosts who can organise coarse, trout and salmon fishing as well as boats on Lough Corrib. For golfers there are four 18-hole golf courses within a 30-minute drive. Excellent freshly prepared evening meals are served, if prearranged. This is a delightful, tranquil and peaceful spot from which to explore this scenic area. Smoking is not permitted in the bedrooms. No pets. Take the Clifden Road from Galway to Moycullen village. Turn left in the village centre onto Spiddal Road. Moycullen House is 1 mile (1½ km) on the left. American Express, Visa, Access and Mastercard accepted.

OWNER Philip and Marie Casburn   OPEN 1 March–30 November
ROOMS 5 double/twin (all private bathrooms)   TERMS B&B IR£27.50 p.p.; reductions for children; single supplement; evening meal IR£18.00

OUGHTERARD

Corrib Wave House

Oughterard, Connemara, Co Galway

Tel: (091) 82147, Fax: (091) 82736

Corrib Wave House is a three-star guesthouse in picturesque surroundings overlooking Lough Corrib. The bedrooms are modest and clean, most of them with views of the lake. There is a separate lounge with an open fire, and a licenced dining room where breakfasts and evening meals are served, if prearranged, which include fresh home-baking. This is an ideal spot for people who like the outdoors, with lovely walks close by, and salmon, trout and coarse fishing. Boats and engines for hire, gillies arranged. Swimming, canoeing and sailing on the lake. There is an 18-hole golf course within a mile (1½ km), and the house is conveniently located near Galway and Connemara. Smoking is not permitted in the dining room. No pets. Located off the Clifden Road, one mile (1½ km) east of Oughterard. Visa, Mastercard and Access accepted.

OWNER Maria and Michael Healy   OPEN 1 April–15 October
ROOMS 10 double/twin/family (all en-suite)   TERMS B&B
IR£18.00 p.p.; reductions for children; single supplement; evening meal IR£13.50

SALT HILL

Carraig Beag

1 Burren View Heights, Knocknacarra Road, Salt Hill,
Galway, Co Galway
Tel: (091) 521696

Carraig Beag is a luxurious red-brick house just off the promenade, with views of the bay. The bedrooms are a good size, furnished with every comfort in mind, and all have their own bathrooms and hairdryers. There are attractive rich wood doors and a handsome staircase. Breakfasts are served on separate tables in the elegant dining room, which has a beautiful crystal chandelier and marble fireplace. There is a lounge with TV where guests can relax after a busy day. An added bonus are the owners, Mr and Mrs Lydon, who are a most accommodating and helpful couple. Catherine and her husband often take walks along the promenade in the evening; guests may join them, but beware: you may find them hard to keep up with! Located close to the beach and all amenities. Pets outside only. Situated in Salt Hill, past the golf course, second road on the right.

OWNER Catherine Lydon   OPEN All year, except Christmas
ROOMS 2 double, 2 twin, 1 family (all en-suite)
TERMS B&B IR£15.00 p.p.; reductions for children; single supplement

The Connaught

Barna Road, Salt Hill, Galway, Co Galway

Tel: (091) 25865

An attractive residence set back off the road in a quiet position. The house has recently been redecorated and is impeccably maintained. The bedrooms are pleasantly furnished, with TVs, hairdryers and comfortable beds, which have electric blankets. There is a pleasant dining room and well-furnished lounge, which has rich carpeting throughout. An extremely cordial and helpful couple, the Keaveneys do everything they can to ensure their guests are comfortable and well taken care of: there is a warm and friendly atmosphere here, and the Connaught would be an ideal base from which to explore this lovely region. Public phone available. No smoking. No pets. To locate the Connaught, drive past the promenade along the seafront, continue approximately for 1 mile (1¹/₂ km), turn left at the T-junction – the house is on the right-hand side, the last house in the lay-by.

OWNER Mrs Colette Keaveney   OPEN 17 March–31 October
ROOMS 2 double, 1 twin, 3 family (5 en-suite)   TERMS B&B
IR£16.00 p.p.; reductions for children; single supplement

Dun Roamin

30 Beach Court, Gratton Road, Salt Hill, Galway,

Co Galway

Tel: (091) 582570

The Bogan family named their attractive modern red-brick house after their decision to stay put and enjoy all that Galway has to offer. The house has a warm and welcoming atmosphere, the rooms are clean and all the beds have duvets. Each bedroom has a TV and tea- and coffee-making facilities, and hairdryers are available. There's a cosy guest lounge and a separate dining room where freshly prepared breakfasts of cereals, fruit and savouries are served. Located less than 2 minutes from the beach, restaurants and other amenities. Jo Bogan is a helpful and considerate host. Guests are welcomed with a hot drink upon arrival. No pets.

OWNER Mrs Jo Bogan   OPEN 1 March–1 November
ROOMS 1 double, 3 twin (all en-suite)   TERMS B&B IR£14.00 p.p.;
reductions for children; single supplement

Mandalay

10 Gentian Hill, Salt Hill, Galway, Co Galway
Tel: (091) 524177

This beautiful, new Georgian-style house is in a superb
location overlooking the bay and the Aran Islands. Mr and
Mrs Darby, who built the house, are from Rhode Island in
the U.S. Mandalay is furnished and decorated to extremely
high standards: there are rich wood furnishings and
antiques. The rooms are spacious, 2 have balconies, all have
views and their own bathrooms. The entry hall and the
kitchen have Liscannor stone floors from the Burren. The
elegant lounge has a TV and piano and there are lots of
plants and exquisite dried-flower arrangements throughout
the house. Excellent breakfasts are served in the bright
dining room. For nature lovers, there are some nice walks
close by, and a bird sanctuary can be seen in front of the
house. For guests wanting luxury at modest prices, Manda-
lay is certainly an excellent choice. The house is open all
year, including the Christmas holiday period. No pets.
Smoking not permitted in the dining room or bedrooms.
Situated in upper Salt Hill – past the Spinnaker Pub,
signposted on the road. Visa, Access and Mastercard
accepted.

OWNER Georgianna Darby   OPEN All year   ROOMS 1 double, 2
twin, 2 family (all en-suite)   TERMS B&B IR£16.00 p.p.; reduc-
tions for children; single supplement

Seaview

Beach Court, Grattan Road, Salt Hill, Galway, Co Galway
Tel: (091) 582109, Fax: (091) 582109

A detached, attractive white house across from the bay. The
front bedrooms overlook the sea; they are all colour-
coordinated and have en-suite bathrooms; 2 have
orthopaedic beds, satellite TVs, hairdryers and tea- and
coffee-making facilities. There is a balcony for guests' use
and a small TV lounge. The house is a 5-minute walk from
the town centre and is directly across the road from the
beach. Private parking is available. No smoking in the dining
room. Pets by arrangement. Situated between Salt Hill and
Galway, just off Gratton Road overlooking Galway Bay. All
major credit cards accepted.

OWNER Mrs Bready Tracey   OPEN All year, except Christmas
ROOMS 3 double, 1 twin, 1 family (all en-suite)   TERMS B&B
IR£13.00–£18.00 p.p.; reductions for children; single supplement

SPIDDAL

Cala 'n Uisce

Green Hill, Spiddal, Co Galway
Tel: (091) 83324

Cala 'n Uisce's name means "little harbour" and this inn is
in a picturesque setting facing the bay. The house was
designed by owner Padraic Feeney and has leaded windows,
a red-brick exterior and is exceptionally well maintained.
There are 3 ground-floor bedrooms, attractively decorated
with colour-coordinated fabrics. Many interesting paintings
of local scenes by Mrs Feeney and other family members are
hung throughout the house. There is a comfortable lounge,
with a TV and turf fire, which leads out onto a patio. The
dining room, where a tasty breakfast is served on linen
tablecloths and pretty china, overlooks the bay. Padraic
Feeney's father was a cousin of John Ford, who directed
The Quiet Man. This is an Irish-speaking area and the
Feeney family speaks Irish. Cala 'n Uisce is a most comfort-
able and peaceful place; the house stands in an acre of
landscaped gardens, and there are beautiful bog areas and
sea walks close by. No smoking in the bedrooms. No pets.
Situated 1/2 mile (1 km) west of Spiddal village.

OWNER Mrs Moya Feeney   OPEN All year   ROOMS 3 double, 1
twin, 2 family (all en-suite)   TERMS B&B IR£15.00 p.p.; reduc-
tions for children; single supplement during high-season only

County Limerick

Bordered on the north by the expanses of the Shannon,
Limerick is a peaceful farming county with its fair share of
relics from the past.
   The origins of the city of Limerick go back to the days of
the Vikings. Always a principal fording point for the Shannon
River, it has played an important part in Irish history, parti-
cularly during the 1690s. Old English Town and the old
Irish part of the city across the river are the most interesting
parts of the city to explore, particularly around St John's
Square with its Georgian architecture. The most noteworthy
sights to visit are the Granary, a restored eighteenth-century

warehouse, which houses the tourist office as well as restaurants, shops and an exhibition gallery. King John's Castle, with its massive rounded tower, St Mary's Cathedral, dating from 1172, and the Hunt Collection at the National Institute for Higher Education can also be visited.

Adare has some splendid ruins to see, the finest one being the Franciscan Friary. Others include the Trinitarian Abbey, the Augustinian Abbey and St Nicholas Church. It is a most attractive town, with pretty thatched cottages and lovely views of Desmond Castle and Adare Manor on the river.

It is thought the 'limerick' may well have come from Croom, which was the meeting place of eighteenth-century Gaelic poets, who wrote extremely witty verse.

ADARE

Adare Lodge

Kildimo Road, Adare, Co Limerick

Tel: (061) 396629

Adare Lodge is a luxurious mock-tudor house on a quiet side street, surrounded by an award-winning garden. The picturesque centre of Adare village, with its thatched cottages, is just a two minute walk away. The house is tastefully appointed and the bedrooms are exquisitely decorated. Agnes Fitzpatrick is a charming and dedicated host who has a wonderful flair for decor and thoroughly enjoys her bed and breakfast. Guests are well looked after here and can enjoy high standards, with a taste of luxury at affordable prices. Excellent breakfasts are served in the bright attractive dining room and there is a conservatory/lounge where guests are allowed to smoke. Evening meals are not available at Adare Lodge, but there is a wide selection of pubs and restaurants in the village. All the bedrooms are on the ground floor, have en-suite facilities and have Ballygowan water for drinking. On pleasant days, guests can enjoy a cup of tea on the patio.

OWNER Agnes Fitzpatrick   OPEN All year   ROOMS 6 double/twin/family (all en-suite)   TERMS B&B IR£17.00 p.p.; reductions for children; single supplement

LIMERICK

Cloneen House

Ennis Road, Limerick, Co Limerick
Tel: (061) 454461

Mary Cusack took over this turn-of-the-century house in
April, 1993. There have been extensive improvements to the
property; both the interior and exterior have been redecorated
in keeping with the style of the house. The bedrooms have
been refurbished, have new orthopaedic beds, are spotlessly
clean, and have multi-channel TVs, hairdryers and tea-making
facilities. Guests are served tea on their arrival in the comfort-
able drawing room with its original fireplace. The breakfast
menu has been upgraded and includes freshly squeezed orange
juice, fresh fruit and cereals, as well as a traditional Irish
breakfast. Smoking is not allowed in the dining room. Car
parking is available. The bus to Shannon Airport stops close
to the house and the town centre is just 10 minutes walk.
Incoming phone calls are accepted for guests. This is a new
venture for Mary Cusack who came to Limerick from Dublin
and who offers her guests a warm and friendly welcome.

OWNER Mary Cusack OPEN All year, except Christmas ROOMS 3
double, 1 twin, 1 family, 1 single (all en-suite) TERMS B&B
IR£22.00–£25.00 p.p.; reductions for children; single supplement

Trebor

Ennis Road, Limerick, Co Limerick
Tel: (061) 454632

Trebor, which is the name of the owner's son, Robert, spelt
backwards, is a comfortable turn-of-the-century townhouse.
The bedrooms are spotless and tastefully decorated with
colour- coordinated wallpapers and fabrics. Three rooms
have en-suite facilities, and there are 2 additional bathrooms
exclusively for guests. Breakfasts include freshly squeezed
orange juice, muesli or porridge and homemade breads,
followed by a cooked breakfast. Trebor is popular with
cyclists: a small group from America returns every year.
Drying facilities are available. There is a lounge with TV.
Evening meals are available (vegetarian and special diets are
catered for) if prearranged. Smoking is not permitted in the
dining room. Pets by arrangement. Located on the main
Ennis road past Jurys' Hotel.

155

OWNER Mrs Joan McSweeney OPEN All year, except Christmas week ROOMS 1 double, 2 twin, 2 family (3 en-suite) TERMS B&B IR£14.00–£15.50 p.p.; reductions for children; single supplement; evening meal IR£11.00; high tea IR£9.00

LISNAGRY

Willowbank

Lisnagry, Co Limerick
Tel: (061) 336553

Willowbank is a spacious dormer bungalow, standing in a quiet position on 46 acres of land, which include a private lake inhabited by swans. The bedrooms are of a good size and are elegantly decorated. The furnishings are of a high standard, with fitted wardrobes and cheval mirrors. Excellent breakfasts are served in the tasteful dining room which overlooks the well-kept garden. Sean and Gerty Leonard have exacting standards and offer a touch of luxury in their bright and friendly home. Guests can enjoy walking on the property and there is fishing, golfing, boating and horse-riding close by. Willowbank is set back off the N7, five miles north of Limerick.

OWNER Sean and Gerty Leonard OPEN March–October ROOMS 4 double/twin (2 en-suite) TERMS B&B IR£15.00–£18.00 p.p.; single supplement; reductions for children

NEWCASTLE WEST

Limetree Lodge

Killarney Road, Newcastle West, Co Limerick
Tel: (069) 62850, Fax: (069) 62662

Limetree Lodge is a modernised Georgian house standing in its own beautifully landscaped garden. The house is spacious, well maintained and immaculate. Tastefully and individually decorated with matching fabrics, the bedrooms are also comfortably furnished, with lots of wardrobe space. All the bedrooms have TVs and hairdryers. There are heated towel racks in the bathroom. Guests are served breakfast in the conservatory, with linen napkins and pretty flower arrangements. Tea and delicious home-baked cakes or scones and jam are offered upon arrival and in the evening. If you are looking for a little luxury, with a host offering lots of personal service at reasonable prices, Limetree Lodge is the answer. However, many others have already discovered it, so reserve early. No pets. 1½ miles (2½ km) from Newcastle West, halfway between Shannon airport and Killarney.

OWNER Mrs Peggy Geary   OPEN All year, except Christmas
ROOMS 1 double, 1 twin, 1 family (all en-suite)   TERMS B&B
IR£14.00 p.p.; reductions for children; single supplement; evening
meal IR£12.00

County Mayo

County Mayo is a maritime county, with the Atlantic Ocean making deep inroads into its coastline on the west and on the north. The sea influences the shape of its beauty, from the long, narrow fjord of Killary Harbour to the island-studded Clew Bay. Castlebar is the county town of Mayo and a good centre for touring. The most interesting building in the town is that occupied by the art centre and the education centre. It was formerly a chapel, the cornerstone of which was laid by John Wesley in 1785.

Westport is a gem of a town. The architect is not known, although some locals believe it to be a French architect left behind from Humbert's expedition in 1798. The main feature is the Octagon, a fine piece of planning. In the centre stands a Doric pillar, mounted on an octagonal granite base, on which the statue of George Glendenning once stood.

Innisturk Island can be visited from Roonah Point. It is an exceptionally attractive island with a lovely harbour; there is a glorious beach on the south side.

Killary Harbour is a striking example of a fjord. Its 5½-mile (8-km) length cuts deep into the surrounding mountains.

At Knock there is the Knock Folk Museum, which pays tribute to the area's forefathers. The collections and exhibitions on show help us to understand what life was like for our ancestors.

ACHILL ISLAND

Aquila

Sraheens, Achill Sound, Achill Island, Co Mayo
Tel: (098) 45163

This cosy, clean modern bungalow is situated in an elevated position, with magnificent views of Achill Sound and the Corraun Mountains. The bedrooms are well appointed, prettily decorated with comfortable beds. One very popular room is the converted attic room. It is most attractive, with its sloping ceilings, but it is not suitable for everyone, as the approach is by a very narrow staircase. There are 4 rooms on the ground floor. There is a comfortable sitting room and lounge with TV/VCR and an open turf fire. A self-catering unit is also available. All types of outdoor activities are available: fishing, swimming, mountain-climbing, surfing, sailing and scuba diving. Cots are available. Pets in outside garage only. The house is located near three "Blue Flag" beaches. Well signposted off the Achill Sound road.

OWNER Mrs Kay Sweeney   OPEN Easter–31 October   ROOMS 3 double, 1 twin, 1 family (4 en-suite)   TERMS B&B IR£16.00 p.p.; reductions for children; single supplement

BALLINA

Ashley House

Ardoughan, Crossmolina Road, Ballina, Co Mayo
Tel: (096) 22799

An attractive Georgian-style dormer bungalow situated off the main road and set in a beautifully landscaped garden, three quarters of a mile from Ballina, Ashley House was established as a bed and breakfast over 9 years ago. The well-appointed bedrooms all have tea-makers and are on the ground floor. Carmel Murray is a friendly lady with a good sense of humour. The dormer was converted several years ago into private quarters for the family. Mr Murray is very handy and works hard to maintain the high standards. The owner's son is an enthusiastic fisherman and can advise guests on the best local fishing spots. Carmel is into set-dancing and, if guests are interested, could easily be per-suaded to give guests a lesson and/or a demonstration. No smoking in the dining room. Self-catering unit available. No pets. All major credit cards accepted.

OWNER Mrs Carmel Murray   OPEN 1 March–1 November ROOMS 3 double, 1 twin, 1 family (3 en-suite)   TERMS B&B IR£14.00 p.p.; reductions for children; single supplement

Belvedere House

Foxford Road, Ballina, Co Mayo
Tel: (096) 22004

A spacious, modern, two-storey house standing in its own grounds, a 10-minute walk from the town centre. The bedrooms are of a good size, attractively decorated and clean, and all have TVs, hair dryers and orthopaedic beds. There is a very large dining room and lounge, with TV and fireplaces. The owners are attentive and work hard to maintain the high standards. Breakfast only is served, but there are many fine eating establishments in the area. A popular place with fishing enthusiasts, Ballina is situated on the lower reaches of the River Moy and directly between Lough Conn/Cullen and Killala Bay. Bicycles for hire locally. For guests who would like a day trip to Dublin, there is a good local bus service. Pets by arrangement. Situated off the Dublin/Foxford road.

OWNER Mary Reilly   OPEN All year, except Christmas
ROOMS 2 double/twin/family (all en-suite)   TERMS B&B IR£14.50 p.p.; reductions for children; single supplement

Coolabah House

Culleens, Killala Road, Ballina, Co Mayo
Tel: (096) 70343

A "coolabah" is an Australian tree, and it's also the name of the town in New South Wales where the McGeever family lived for three years. The name and the design of the house are pleasant reminders of the time they spent there. The house is set in its own grounds, and there are some lovely walks nearby. Tea or coffee is offered on arrival. Mrs McGeever is an extremely artistic lady, as evidenced by the high standards of style and design of the interior. The large bedrooms are very comfortable, individually decorated, with quality furnishings, and some with satin bed covers. Irons and hairdryers are available on request. Coolabah is immaculate throughout and there is a peaceful and restful atmosphere. Smoking is not permitted in the dining room or bedrooms. Situated $1^1/_2$ miles ($2^1/_2$ km) to town centre, signposted off the Killala road.

OWNER Mrs Margaret McGeever   OPEN 1 May–30 September
ROOMS 2 double/twin/family (3 en-suite)   TERMS B&B IR£12.50–£13.50 p.p.; reductions for children; single supplement; high tea IR£8.00

Hillcrest House

Main Street, Bangor Erris, Ballina, Co Mayo
Tel: (097) 83494

A modern, cosy bungalow located in the centre of the village, very close to the Owenmore River. Mr and Mrs Cosgrove are a very congenial couple, and Mr Cosgrove was born in the village. The restaurant, which is part of the house, is very popular with the locals. Mrs Cosgrove, who does all the cooking, has built up an excellent reputation for providing good food. The bedrooms are comfortable; hot water bottles and hairdryers are provided. There's a TV lounge with VCR. This is a popular spot with fishermen, with river and lake fishing close by. No pets. No smoking in the bedrooms. Bangor Erris is 25 miles ($37^1/_2$ km) from Ballina.

OWNER Evelyn Cosgrove OPEN All year, except Christmas
ROOMS 3 twin, 1 family (1 en-suite) TERMS B&B IR£13.00 p.p.; reductions for children; single supplement

The Yellow Rose

Belderigg, Ballina, Co Mayo
Tel: (096) 43125

This bright, modest bungalow is in a remote spot with such spectacular views of the surrounding countryside that it is hard not to imagine you are sitting on top of the world! There is a prehistoric farm site within walking distance. The rooms are clean and comfortable; there are plans to make them all en-suite for 1996. The owners are a most congenial and welcoming couple. Excellent evening meals are served here and include home-baked breads, spring lamb and fresh wild salmon, courtesy of Stephen McHale, who is a fisherman. Two of the bedrooms have views of the sea and of an impressive ruin in the distance. An outside shed is provided for guests' dogs. Situated 5 miles from the Ceidi Fields interpretive centre and 25 miles from Ballina.

OWNER Mrs Eileen McHale OPEN All year except Christmas
ROOMS 5 twin/double/single/family TERMS B&B IR£11.00 p.p.; reductions for children under 12 (under 3 free); evening meals from IR£7.00

BALLYCASTLE

Keadyville

Carrowcubbic, Ballycastle, Co Mayo
Tel: (096) 43288

Keadyville is situated on a beautiful site overlooking Downpatrick Head. Mrs Kelly went into the bed-and-breakfast business as more tourists came to the area to visit the interpretative centre of the fascinating Ceidi Fields, which are older than the Pyramids. The top floor, all in pine, was added to the property in the summer of 1992. The bedrooms are average in size, clean and comfortable, and all offer lovely scenic views. The one bedroom that is not en-suite has a very large adjacent bathroom. One ground-floor room has its own shower. The owners are local people and greet guests with a cup of tea. They are happy to provide information on the area. There is a cosy guest lounge/dining room where a fire is lit on chilly days There are self-catering units available. Evening meals are available if prebooked and there is also a local pub close by that serves food.

OWNER Mrs Barbara Kelly   OPEN All year except Christmas
ROOMS 4 twin/double (3 en-suite)   TERMS B&B IR£13.00 p.p.; reductions for children under 12; single supplement; evening meals IR£10.00

Hilltop House

Ballycastle, Co Mayo
Tel: (096) 43089

A modest bungalow on a dry-stock farm, with panoramic views of the countryside, the sea and Downpatrick Head. A cup of tea and some delicious homemade cake are offered on arrival. The lounge is comfortable and overlooks a glorious view. There are a VCR and TV where guests can watch the Ceidi Field project video and learn about the oldest en-closed farmland in the world. Older than the pyramids, the enclosure and neolithic tombs are preserved by a blanket of bog. The project is 5 miles (7¹/₂ km) west of Ballycastle, and an interpretative centre is open. Home-cooked evening meals are available, if prearranged. Pets outside only. No smoking in the dining room. Take the Ballycastle road from Ballina; the farm is well signposted.

OWNER Séan and Annette O'Donnell   OPEN 1 May–30 September
ROOMS 2 double, 1 twin, 1 family (2 en-suite)   TERMS B&B IR£14.00 p.p.; reductions for children; single supplement; evening meal IR£12.00

CASTLEBAR

Fort Villa House

Moneen, Castlebar, Co Mayo

Tel: (094) 21002

This handsome Georgian house stands in one and a half
acres of beautiful gardens full of flowers, mature shrubs and
trees. The bedrooms are individually decorated, have solid,
old-fashioned furniture (the high back walnut bed is of
particular interest) and all have TVs and teamakers. The
house was built by the present owners' great-grandfather
and has always been in the family. There is a cosy guest
lounge with a gas fire and lots of interesting china displayed
on ceiling racks. There is a good choice for breakfast, which
is served in the lovely dining room which has a beautifully
carved, antique sideboard. This is a most comfortable and
friendly house and the owners, Patrick and Breeda
Flannelly, enjoy chatting with their guests and are happy to
provide information on what to see and do in the area. No
smoking in the dining room. Fort Villa is easily found on the
Dublin Road, beside the roundabout.

OWNER Patrick and Breeda Flannelly   OPEN All year, except
Christmas   ROOMS 5 double/twin/family (all en-suite)
TERMS B&B IR£15.00 p.p.; reductions for children; single supplement

Ashfort

Airport/Knock Road, Charlestown, Co Mayo

Tel: (094) 54706

A large, modern mock-tudor style house set off the road in
spacious grounds. The bedrooms are well appointed, all
have en-suite facilities and rich wood furnishings. The
house is decorated to a high standard throughout; there are
plush carpets, and a luxurious lounge for guests to relax in.
Charlestown is perhaps a little off the tourist track but there
are lot of things to see and do in the area. Owners Carol
and Philip O'Gorman are a delightful couple who are
always happy to assist guests with itinerary planning.
Evening meals are not available, but there are several good
eating establishments close by. Philip O'Gorman is a
teacher, but helps out around the inn during the summer.
Ashfort is a most comfortable property for touring the lovely
area of County Mayo.

OWNER Carol and Philip O'Gorman   OPEN March–31 October
ROOMS 5 double/twin/single (all en-suite)   TERMS IR£15.00 p.p.;
reductions for children; single supplement

CROSSMOLINA

Kilmurray House

Castlehill, Crossmolina, Co Mayo
Tel: (096) 31227

Kilmurray House is a large, attractive, two-storey farmhouse
on 55 acres of dry-stock farmland, beautifully situated under
Nephin Mountain. It is hard to believe that the house was a
ruin before Joe and Madge Moffatt lovingly restored the
interior, cleverly combining modern conveniences and a
traditional setting. The original oak staircase and wooden
doors have been retained, as has the fireplace, made by a
local craftsman, in the lounge. Recipient of two awards:
"Farmhouse of the Year" and "BHS and Bord Fáilte Farm-
house Award". The bedrooms are large, tastefully decorated
with matching fabrics and comfortably furnished. A turf fire
burns brightly in the TV lounge on chilly days. It's an ideal
base from which to explore this scenic area and a fisher-
man's delight – the farm has its own boats for guests' use
on Lough Conn. Excellent farmhouse dinners are served if
prearranged, and guests are welcome to bring their own
wine. Very enjoyable Irish musical evenings a quarter of a
mile away, as well as Irish dancing by the family. Historic
Heritage Museum for tracing ancestry 1½ miles (2½ km)
away. Babysitting available. No smoking in the dining room.
Pets outside by arrangement. Three miles (4½ km) from
Crossmolina on Castlebar road.

OWNER Joe and Madge Moffatt   OPEN April–mid-October
ROOMS 1 double, 2 twin, 2 family, 1 single (4 en-suite)
TERMS B&B IR£13.50–£15.00 p.p.; reductions for children; single
supplement; evening meal IR£12.00

KILLALA

Gardenhill Farmhouse

Crossmolina Road, Killala, Co Mayo
Tel: (096) 32331

A large, modern farmhouse set in 50 acres of mixed farm-
land, situated one mile south of Killala, on the Crossmolina
Road. The bedrooms are spacious, colour-coordinated and

163

have en-suite shower rooms. There is one ground-floor room. Owner Mary Munnelly is a registered nurse and an alternative medicine practitioner skilled in reflexology. There is a small, cosy lounge with an open fire, and the hearty farm breakfasts are served in the dining room, which overlooks the surrounding hills. Evening meals can be served, if pre-arranged, and local salmon often features on the menu. Tea-making facilities are available in the hallway. The interpretative centre for the Ceidi Fields is within easy driving distance and there is golf, deep-sea and shore fishing and miles of sandy dunes and beaches at Killala harbour.

OWNER Mary and Kevin Munnelly   OPEN All year except Christmas   ROOMS 6 double/twin/family (all en-suite)   TERMS B&B IR£15.00 p.p.; reductions for children under 12; single supplement; evening meals from IR£11.00

KNOCK

Ballyhowley House

Knock, Co Mayo
Tel: (094) 88339

Ballyhowley House is a spacious, beautifully kept Georgian residence approached by a sweeping drive through open fields. Thoughtfully and tastefully restored, it is furnished in keeping with the character of the house. This is a comfortable place to stay: all the bedrooms are en-suite, there is a guest lounge with a TV and a piano which guests can play. Evening meals are available, if prearranged. There are also plenty of eating establishments in Knock, which is a five-minute drive away. Owner, Mary Merrick, is a personable lady, who takes good care of her guests, offering tea or coffee on arrival. Guests can take a walk along the river that runs through the property and view the ruins of a Norman castle. Golf, fishing, pony-trekking and scenic walks are available close by.

OWNER Mrs Mary Merrick   OPEN 1 April–1 November   ROOMS 5 double/twin/family (all en-suite)   TERMS B&B IR£14.50 p.p.; reductions for children under 10; single supplement; evening meals IR£11.50

LOUISBURGH

Rivervilla

Shraugh, Louisburgh, Co Mayo
Tel: (098) 66246

Rivervilla is a bungalow situated in a peaceful and secluded setting along the banks of the Runrowen River, on a 25-acre sheep farm. Salmon and trout fishing are available, as well as lovely riverside walks. A real home-away-from-home atmosphere pervades here; all meals are freshly prepared, and home-baked breads and desserts are a feature. The bedrooms are tastefully decorated, some have glorious views of Shreffy Mountain and of Croagh Patrick. Of special interest is the Great Famine and Granvaile interpretive centre. There is a TV lounge. All the bedrooms have tea-makers, and for the 2 bedrooms that are not en-suite there are 2 guest bathrooms. Guests may bring their own wine. Dogs are welcome – outside sheds available. Located 1 mile (1½ km) from the village off the Westport/Louisburgh road. Ideal touring centre for Connemara, Mayo and Galway.

OWNER Mary O'Malley   OPEN 1 April–31 October   ROOMS 1 double, 1 twin, 2 single, 1 family (2 en-suite)   TERMS B&B IR£13.50–£14.50 p.p.; reductions for children under 12

NEWPORT

Loch Morchan Farm

Kilbride, Newport, Co Mayo
Tel: (098) 41221

This is a working sheep and cattle farm situated in a quiet location with good views all round, just 10 minutes from Clew Bay. The house is fresh and bright, the bedrooms average in size with comfortable beds. One of the nicest things about Loch Morchan Farm is Mrs Chambers herself, a delightful lady who is a most caring and attentive host; the bed and breakfast was established over 17 years ago, with many guests returning for the special hospitality found here. Evening meals are available by prior arrangement, and there are several good eating establishments close by. Loch Morchan has a TV lounge and separate dining room. The area is excellent for sea, river and lake fishing, with special group rates for fishing groups. An 18-hole golf course is close by. Smoking is not permitted in the dining room. No pets.

OWNER Mrs Chambers   OPEN 1 May–30 September   ROOMS 1 double, 2 twin, 1 family (1 en-suite)   TERMS B&B IR£13.00–£14.00 p.p.; reductions for children; single supplement

Altamont House

Ballinrobe Road, Westport, Co Mayo
Tel: (098) 25226

Altamont House is a pre-Famine, wisteria-covered farm-house situated within a 5-minute walk of the town centre. This is a most pleasant and welcoming house. Established as the first guest house in the area, it has built up an excellent reputation for offering good service at reasonable prices. The spotless bedrooms are prettily decorated, and the rooms to the rear of the house overlook the lovely gardens, as does the lounge, which has an open fire. The prize-winning gardens are a popular spot with guests. Breakfasts are served in the attractive dining room; silver service is employed, and, when possible, there are fresh flowers on the table. A new addition to the property is a sun lounge and patio. Evening meals can be had at several good pubs and restaurants close by. No pets.

OWNER Mrs Rita Sheridan   OPEN 1 February–30 November
ROOMS 2 double, 3 twin, 3 family (5 en-suite)   TERMS B&B
IR£13.50–£15.50 p.p.; reductions for children; single supplement

Cedar Lodge

Kings Hill, Newport Road, Westport, Co Mayo
Tel: (098) 25417

This is a pleasant family home in a quiet residential area, a five-minute walk from the town. The bedrooms are most attractive, and there is a comfortable family suite all in pine. The TV lounge has polished wood-block flooring and very comfortable chairs to relax in. Breakfast only is served, but there are several eating establishments in town. Pets are not permitted. Easily located on the Newport road, first turn to the left after passing the tennis court in the town centre.

OWNER Maureen Flynn   OPEN All year, except Christmas
ROOMS 1 double, 1 twin, 2 family (3 en-suite)
TERMS B&B IR£13.50–£15.50 p.p.; reductions for children; single supplement

Coral Reef

Lecanvey, Westport, Co Mayo

Tel: (098) 64814

Coral Reef is an attractive house standing in its own grounds. Located across the road from the beach, it has magnificent views of Clew Bay and is in the shadow of Croagh Patrick, where a pilgrimage climb takes place in July. This is a superb location with lovely walks close by. An added bonus is the wonderful, welcoming atmosphere created by the friendly owners. The house is well furnished; three of the bedrooms are on the ground floor, while a further two are reached by a spiral staircase. Anne Colgan is a good cook and evening meals are available if prearranged. All breads, cakes and desserts are homemade. There is an extensive breakfast menu, and a specialty of the house is the homemade health bread, the recipe of which has been taken to many parts of the world by satisfied guests. There is a cosy guest lounge with TV. Located 8 miles (12 km) west of Westport, on the Westport-Louisburgh Road.

OWNER Anne Colgan   OPEN Easter–31 October   ROOMS 2 double, 2 twin, 1 family (2 en-suite)   TERMS B&B IR£13.50–£15.00 p.p.; reductions for children under 12; single supplement

Moher House

Liscarney, Westport, Co Mayo

Tel: (098) 21360

Marion O'Malley is a delightful lady who knows just how to make her guests feel at home, offering a cup of tea and some of her delicious homemade scones upon arrival. The bedrooms are clean, with pretty duvets; there are electric blankets and hot-water bottles, and hairdryers are provided upon request. Excellent breakfasts and evening meals are served, using the best cuts of meat provided by Mr O'Malley, a local butcher. Vegetarians are also catered for. There is a pleasant sitting room with TV. This is an ideal spot for walking; there are 4 designated walks in the area, and for the more adventurous, Croagh Patrick Mountain, with its magnificent view of 365 islands. Washing and drying facilities are available. Fishing is available in Moher Lake across the road from the house. No pets. Five miles (7^1/$_2$ km) from Westport, on the main Clifden-Westport road.

OWNER Marion O'Malley   OPEN 1 March–31 October   ROOMS 2
double, 1 twin, 1 family (2 en-suite)   TERMS B&B IR£14.00 p.p.;
reductions for children; single supplement; evening meals
IR£11.00

Riverbank House

Rosbeg, Westport Quay, Co Mayo
Tel: (098) 25719

An inviting, spacious country house with attractive black
shutters, flower baskets and window boxes, situated in a
peaceful spot adjacant to a river, one mile (1½ km) from
Westport. The rooms are a good size, with modern furnish-
ings, and are clean and comfortable. There's a relaxing guest
lounge with TV and open fires. Kay O'Malley is pleased to
help guests plan activities or day trips. Home-cooked
breakfasts are served in the sunny dining room, and vegetar-
ians can be catered for upon request. Local amenities
include shooting at the Tirawley Game Reserve, bathing,
boating, trout and salmon fishing and golf. Smoking
permitted in the lounge only. No pets.

OWNER Mrs Kay O'Malley   OPEN 1 April–30 November
ROOMS 4 double, 3 twin, 1 family (5 en-suite)   TERMS B&B
IR£13.50–£15.50 p.p.; reductions for children; single
supplement

Seapoint House

Kilmeena, Westport, Co Mayo
Tel: (098) 41254

Seapoint House is situated in a beautiful, unspoilt setting
overlooking an inlet of Clew Bay. Most of the rooms have
views of the sea and mountains. There is a very large lounge
with a fireplace and a tastefully decorated dining room,
which leads out onto a sun porch. Dinners are served, if
prearranged, featuring fresh farm food, home-baking, fresh
vegetables, homemade soups and local fish and meat. The
bedrooms are functional and spotlessly clean. Self-catering
is available and there is a pony for children to ride. Non-
smokers preferred. Fishing, sailing, walking and an 18-hole
golf course are available nearby. Baby-sitting can usually be
arranged. Situated midway between Newport and Westport,
approximately 5 miles (7½ km) from Westport.

OWNER The O'Malley family OPEN 1 March–15 October
ROOMS 6 double/ twin/family (all en-suite) TERMS B&B IR£16.00
p.p.; reductions for children; single supplement; evening meals
IR£13.00

County Sligo

County Sligo is located in one of the most beautiful and
least explored regions of Ireland, surrounded by rugged
mountains and rolling hills. The landscape is a patchwork of
picturesque lakes, lush forests and sparkling rivers, its
coastline dotted with peaceful coves.

Sligo's seaside resorts stretch along the coast from
Innishcrone to Mullaghmore, with sandy beaches, fishing,
golfing, beautiful walks and horse-riding – there is so much
to do in this uncrowded corner of Ireland.

Explore the Gleniff Horseshoe, the Ladies Brae, visit
Lissadell House and, for the more adventurous, climb to the
summit of Queen Maeve's Cairn.

Tour the loughs – Arrow, Gill, Easky, Gara, Glencar,
Templehouse and Talt – and feast your eyes on Sligo's
beauty.

W. B. Yeats, the poet, is buried at Drumcliffe. He called
Sligo "The Land of Hearts' Desire", and after you have
visited, you will too.

BALLINCARROW

Westleigh House

Ropefield, Ballincarrow, Co Sligo
Tel: (071) 84135

Guests are treated as family friends in this turn-of-the-
century house. It stands in a very large front garden, full of
mature shrubs and lawns. Owners Olive and Arthur
Thickett are a down-to-earth couple whose motto is
"welcome friends and stay awhile and enjoy our hospitality".
The rooms are modestly furnished and spotlessly clean. An
excellent, freshly cooked breakfast is served in the cosy
beamed dining room, with home-baked bread and home-
made marmalades. Light snacks are available on request,
Evening meals are available, if prearranged, and there is a
good pub, the Woodside Inn, only a quarter of a mile
away, which serves dinner. Smoking in the lounge only. No
pets.

OWNER Olive and Arthur Thickett   OPEN All year except
Christmas   ROOMS 3 double/twin/family   TERMS B&B IR£14.00
p.p. for two or more nights, IR£15.00 p.p. for one night; reduc-
tions for children under 12

BALLYMOTE

Temple House

Ballymote, Co Sligo
Tel: (071) 83329, Fax: (071) 83808

Approached through an impressive gateway bordered by
white iron railings, the drive meanders through parkland to
this massive Georgian mansion. Set in 1,000 acres of farm-
and woodland, the estate has been in the Perceval family
since 1665, the present house having been redesigned and
refurnished in 1864. The entrance to the house is through a
portico to a large square entrance hall with tiled floor and
shooting gear, which leads to a second larger hall, off which
is an enormous dining room and 3 sitting rooms, all with
open fires. The larger room has lovely views over the garden
to the lake and a ruined castle, built by the Knights Templar
in 1200. The bedrooms are enormous, furnished with
antiques and family portraits. Some have original bathroom
fittings, curtains, carpet, etc; consequently, some are faded
and worn, but this all lends charm and atmosphere to the
house. All are en-suite but one, which has its own bathroom.
   The Percevals are a very friendly couple. Mrs Perceval
does all the cooking and Mr Perceval runs the farm, which is
stocked with sheep, Kerry cattle, pigs and poultry, providing
the kitchen with meat, bacon, eggs, vegetables and fruit. The
vegetables and fruit are grown organically in a walled garden
and the surplus is sold locally. Almost everything is home-
grown and homemade, including yoghurt, jams and cream
cheese. Evening meals are served at 7.30 pm, if ordered in
advance. The house has a wine licence, and guests may also
bring their own spirits. Temple House is within easy reach
of beautiful beaches, mountains, trout lakes and golf
courses. The house is signposted from the main Galway-to-
Sligo road, 9 miles (13¹/₂ km) south of Sligo. No smoking.
No pets. Visa, Access, American Express and Mastercard
accepted. *Please note:* Mr Perceval is chemically sensitive, so
guests are asked to avoid all perfumed products.

OWNER Mrs D Perceval   OPEN 1 April–30 November   ROOMS 2
double, 2 twin, 1 single (4 en-suite)   TERMS B&B IR£40.00 p.p.;
reductions for children; single supplement; evening meal IR£18.00

Villa Rosa

Bunduff, Cliffoney, Co Sligo
Tel: (071) 66173

This family home has wonderful views of the Donegal
Mountains and Bunduff Beach and it overlooks a bird
sanctuary and megalithic tombs. There have been several
improvements made to the property in the past year; there is
a new TV lounge downstairs and the house has been freshly
decorated. John McLoughlin is a qualified chef and the
meals are a special feature here, with seafood a speciality of
the house. Cookery classes can be provided, if arranged in
advance. Dinners are served between 6–8.30 pm and there
is a wine licence. Guests feel very much at home in this
warm and friendly house. There is one ground-floor, en-
suite room. Smoking in the bedrooms only. Guide dogs only
permitted. American Express and Visa accepted.

OWNER John and Beatrice McLoughlin   OPEN April–November
ROOMS 5 double/family/twin/single (3 en-suite)   TERMS B&B from
IR£13.00 p.p.; single supplement; dinner IR£15.00

COLLOONEY

Union Farm

Collooney, Co Sligo
Tel: (071) 67136

This 300-year-old house, painted pale blue, stands in a very
neat front garden in quiet, peaceful countryside, about a
mile (1½ km) off the main road, with lovely views. The
house is part of a 50-acre cattle farm and is well kept, with a
comfortable TV lounge and attractive dining room. Low
doorways and thick walls abound, and the bedrooms are
small and furnished simply. Evening meals or high tea are
served at 7 pm if arranged in advance, and there is a wine
licence. No smoking permitted in the dining room. Pets by
arrangement.

OWNER Des and Tess Lang   OPEN 1 March–15 October
ROOMS 1 double, 2 twin, 1 family, 1 single (2 en-suite)
TERMS B&B IR£14.00 p.p.; reductions for children; single supple-
ment; evening meal IR£12.00, high tea from IR£5.00

Benbulben Farm

Drumcliff, Co Sligo
Tel: (071) 63211, Fax: (071) 63211

A large, modern farmhouse set amidst lovely mature gardens on 90 acres of sheep farming land with unparalleled views of Ben Bulben Mountain and 100 square miles of beautiful Yeats country. This is very much a family home, and Mr and Mrs Hennigan are very congenial people, offering a welcome tray of tea or coffee upon arrival. The rooms are spotlessly clean and furnished simply with fitted wardrobes and firm beds. Evening meals are available by arrangement, featuring fresh farm produce and home-style cooking. A lovely area for walking (there is a nature walk on the farm), fishing and hang gliding. Sligo also has some fine examples of early megalithic tombs. There is no licence, but guests may bring their own wine. There is also a TV lounge. Visa accepted. Located approximately 3 miles (4½ km) north of Drumcliff.

OWNER Ann Hennigan   OPEN 1 April–31 September   ROOMS 2 twin, 3 family, 1 single (5 en-suite)   TERMS B&B IR£13.50–£15.00 p.p.; reductions for children; single supplement; light evening meal from IR£7.50

Urlar House

Drumcliff, Co Sligo
Tel: (071) 63110

Urlar House is a Georgian house in a quiet location off a private drive, 1 mile (1½ km) north of Drumcliff. This spacious house has a comfortable lounge with the original marble fireplace and 2 archways with the original Wedgewood figure design. The bedrooms vary in size; there is a family suite, consisting of a twin and double room with en-suite facilities, ideal for friends or a family travelling together. Excellent breakfasts are served family-style on a large antique table, and consist of a choice of yoghurts, stuffed pancakes, fish cakes, omelettes, full Irish breakfast, and home-baked breads. Mrs Healy is a proud recipient of the northwest region Agri-Tourism award and the 1992 Galtee Breakfast award. Excellent home-cooked dinners are also available if prearranged. There is an enclosed sun porch for the children to play in, and this leads out to the garden. Pets by arrangement. Six miles (9 km) north of Sligo.

OWNER Mrs Healy   OPEN 1 March–1 November   ROOMS 2 double, 2 twin, 1 family, (2 en-suite)   TERMS B&B IR£15.00–£16.00 p.p.; reductions for children; single supplement; evening meal IR£13.00

ENNISCRONE

Ceol na Mara

Main Street, Enniscrone, Co Sligo
Tel: (096) 36351

Ceol na Mara, whose name means "Music of the Sea", is a 120-year-old house, though because of its renovations it looks quite new; with its modern windows, and stucco façade. The house was recently redecorated in a tasteful, homely style and 4 new bedrooms added. All the rooms are en-suite and have TVs and telephones. The O'Regans are both teachers and the house was owned by Mr O'Regan's parents. They took over the house when they married and have carried out a lot of renovations. The house stands in the middle of Enniscrone, one side on the main street, the other with sea views. There is a large lounge with an open fire, which is lit on chilly evenings, and the large dining room has sea views at one end. All twin-bedded rooms have double beds, so they can also be used as family rooms. The rooms are quite good-sized and simply furnished. The championship golf course at Enniscrone draws many visitors. Evening meals are served on request. Two bedrooms are on the ground floor. Pets are not allowed. The 3-mile-long beach at Enniscrone has been awarded the Blue Flag and is one of the finest in Ireland. Located 8 miles (12 km) west of Ballina. Visa and Mastercard accepted.

OWNER Mairéad O'Regan   OPEN 1 February–30 November   ROOMS 1 double, 4 twin, 4 family (all en-suite)   TERMS B&B IR£16.50 p.p.; reductions for children; single supplement; evening meal IR£14.00; light meals available

Gowan Brae

Pier Road, Enniscrone, Co Sligo
Tel: (096) 36396

An unusual find in the midst of the town centre, this pleasant Georgian house is set back off the road, in three-quarters of an acre of grounds with plenty of parking. Gowan Brae has been refurbished: there are new carpets, pretty wall-

173

paper, and stripped pine doors. The bedrooms, with en-suite shower rooms, are spotlessly clean and modestly furnished with comfortable beds. All but one have views of the bay and harbour. There is a cosy lounge with a slate fireplace, TV and piano. Owner Brenda Quinn attends catering classes to ensure that her guests receive the best meals. Light snacks are also available. Smoking permitted in the lounge. No pets.

OWNER Mrs Brenda Quinn   OPEN 1 April–31 October   ROOMS 1 double, 3 twin, 1 family (all en-suite)   TERMS B&B from IR£15.00 p.p.; reductions for children; single supplement; evening meals from IR£12.00

RIVERSTOWN

Coopershill

Riverstown, Co Sligo

Tel: (071) 65108

Approached through parks, woods and farmland, the long drive winds its way up to this wonderful Georgian mansion, which has splendid views over woods, hills and the River Arrow, which runs through the property. It was built in 1774 and seven generations of the O'Haras have lived in it since then. Peacocks strut on the front lawn and the building has recently been cleaned up to reveal the pristine stonework. The present O'Haras have lived in the house for the last nine years and have restored it to an extremely high standard of comfort, without in any way detracting from the ambience of the house's period. In fact, much of the furniture is original. Family portraits adorn the walls, the rooms are big enough to make massive pieces of furniture look insignificant, and the dining room has enormous sideboards covered with gleaming family silver. Mr O'Hara farms the 500-acre estate with his brother, and Mrs O'Hara takes care of the guests and does all the cooking. There is a large, comfortable drawing room with a log fire, and 5 of the bedrooms have four-poster or canopy beds. Boats and gillies, can be arranged for fishing on Lough Arrow and boating; trout and coarse fishing are also available on the River Arrow. There is also a tennis court and croquet lawn. Evening meals, if arranged in advance, are served at 8.30 pm, and a light lunch or a picnic can also be provided. There is a wine licence. Hairdryers and tea- and coffee-making facilities are in all bedrooms. Guests are asked to smoke in the drawing-room and lounge only. Pets outside only. Signposted from the Drumfin crossroads. 11 miles (16^1/$_2$ km) southwest of

Sligo on the Dublin road. All major credit cards accepted.

OWNER Brian and Linda O'Hara   OPEN 16 March–31 October
ROOMS 6 double, 1 twin (6 en-suite)   TERMS B&B IR£42.00–
£45.00 p.p.; single supplement

Ross House

Ross, Riverstown, Co Sligo
Tel: (071) 65140

A 100-year-old house in attractive farmland surroundings,
standing in a small, pretty front garden, with the farmyard
stretching to the back of the house. It is well signposted from
the main Dublin road into Sligo and is located 3 miles (4^1/$_2$
km) from Drumfin, and approached down narrow lanes. Mrs
Hill-Wilkinson is a very friendly lady who loves baking, and
she is very happy for guests to come into the kitchen and see
how it is done. Home-cooked evening meals are available on
request at 7 to 7.30 pm, and a cup of tea is provided later in
the evening. It is a simple family home, and guests have use
of a TV lounge with peat fire and a dining room. One bed-
room is small; the other 3 are of average size, all have tea-
making facilities and hairdryers. There are 2 more large, en-
suite bedrooms on the ground floor, suitable for disabled
guests. This is a wonderful place for children; there is a
donkey, hay-making and cows on a 120-acre mixed farm.
Many come for the fishing on Lough Arrow, and fishermen
are able to hire boats, tackle and engines from the Hill-
Wilkinsons. There is also a tennis court for guests' use.
Smoking is not allowed in the dining room. Sligo has many
ancient monuments at Carrowmore, Carrowkeel, Creevykeel
and Deerpark, some dating back 3,000 years. There are
many beautiful beaches close by. Pets by arrangement.

OWNER Oriel and Nicholas Hill-Wilkinson   OPEN 1 March–1
November   ROOMS 1 single, 3 double, 2 family (2 en-suite)
TERMS B&B IR£17.00 p.p.; reductions for children; single supple-
ment; light meals available, evening meals from IR£12.00

ROSCOMMON

Munsboro House

Sligo Road, Roscommon, Co Sligo
Tel: (903) 26375

Munsboro House is a lovely Georgian house situated 300
yards off the main road in a peaceful and tranquil setting.

The Dolan family run an intensive sheep-rearing, cattle and tillage farm on the 150 acres surrounding the house. Munsboro House is also known as the Munsboro Equestrian Centre, which specialises in horse-riding and activity holidays; qualified instruction is provided in all cases, though the emphasis is on fun and enjoyment. The rooms are spacious, and you will find a warm welcome in this comfortable house with open fires, whether you are there to relax or to partake in any of the activities. Excellent evening meals are available and are prepared from fresh local produce, served in the lovely dining room. The Dolans are justly proud of their BHS Farmhouse of the Year award. The house now has a recreation centre featuring an 18-hole golf course, crazy golf, squash court and sauna facilities. For those looking to escape the chaos of modern life, Munsboro House is an excellent choice. Lovely forest walks in Moate Park 1¹/₂ miles (2¹/₂ km) away. Wine licence. No pets.

OWNER Mrs Delia Dolan   OPEN 1 June–1 October   ROOMS 2 double/twin   TERMS B&B IR£15.00 p.p.; reductions for children; single supplement; evening meal from IR£15.00

SLIGO

Aisling

Cairns Hill, Sligo, Co Sligo
Tel: (071) 60704

176

Aisling, whose name means "Irish dream", is an immaculate bungalow standing in its own grounds in an elevated position on the south side of Sligo. The bedrooms are average in size and comfortably furnished; all are on the ground floor and have TVs and hair dryers. Des and Nan Faul are a down-to-earth, congenial couple who share the work. Nan cooks breakfast, which is flexible (there is a varied choice), and Des enjoys chatting to guests and helping them plan daily activities. Breakfast only is served, but there are plenty of good restaurants close by. Aisling has a comfortable lounge with a TV and coal fire. Not suitable for children. No pets. Smoking not permitted in the bedrooms. Situated 300 metres off Pearse Road (the Dublin/Galway road).

OWNER Des and Nan Faul   OPEN All year, except Christmas
ROOMS 6 double/twin/family (3 en-suite)   TERMS B&B IR£14.00–£15.50 p.p.; single supplement

Hillside

Kilsellagh, Enniskillen Road, Sligo, Co Sligo
Tel: (071) 42808

This attractive, small, cream-coloured farmhouse standing just off the main Sligo-to-Enniskillen road, has a pretty front garden and lovely views. The house is about 200 years old and was originally a one-storey building. It belonged to Mrs Stuart's grandfather, and she has been doing bed and breakfast there for over 27 years. The house is well kept and cosy, with small, freshly decorated bedrooms, a dining room and small TV lounge with open fire. Tea and coffee are available on request. Smoking is not encouraged in the dining room or bedrooms. There is one downstairs bedroom. Pets by arrangement. Convenient to sandy beaches, golf, horse-riding, fishing and mountain climbing. Off the main Enniskillen road, 3 miles (4¹/₂ km) from Sligo.

OWNER Mrs Elma Stuart   OPEN 1 April–31 October   ROOMS 2 family/twin (both en-suite)   TERMS B&B IR£14.00–£15.00 p.p.; reductions for children; single supplement

Lisadorn

Lisnalurg, Donegal Road, Sligo, Co Sligo
Tel: (071) 43417

A spacious, modern, two-storey house just off the main road

in the heart of Yeats' country. Lisadorn is set back off the main road in a large, beautifully maintained garden with colourful flowers, manicured lawn and lovely views. No expense has been spared in making this a top-class bed and breakfast. The rooms are spacious and the decor and furniture of a high standard. All the twin-bedded rooms have double beds, so they can also be used as family rooms. Each room has a TV and electric blankets. The dining room, where breakfast only is served, is attractively furnished with separate tables and good views; the TV lounge has an open fire. Tea and coffee are available when required, at no extra charge. Pets by arrangment. Lisadorn is an ideal base from which to explore the northwest region. On the Donegal road.

OWNER Mrs Lily Diamond   OPEN All year, except Christmas
ROOMS 2 twin, 1 triple, 3 family (all en-suite)   TERMS B&B
IR£15.00 p.p.; reductions for children; single supplement

Lissadell

Pearse Road, Sligo, Co Sligo
Tel: (071) 61937

An attractive, whitewashed, creeper-clad house with red front door, standing just back from the main road close to the centre of town. The Caddens moved here approximately 5 years ago. Mrs Cadden is a friendly lady, and it is a pleasant, spacious house. The bedrooms are quite good-sized, and all have TVs and tea- and coffee-making facilities. A warm and comfortable house in the heart of Yeats' country. There is a large rear garden. Smoking is not permitted in the dining room. No pets. Situated 4 minutes' walk from the town centre.

OWNER Mrs Mary Cadden   OPEN All year, except Christmas
ROOMS 2 double/twin (all en-suite)   TERMS B&B IR£15.00 p.p.;
reductions for children; single supplement

Sea Park House

Rosses Point Road, Sligo, Co Sligo
Tel: (071) 45556

The Fullertons built this modern bungalow about 14 years ago and later extended it. It is a low, one-storey white-washed building just off the main road in Rosses Point, and has pleasant views of sea and mountains. The bedrooms are small and spotlessly clean, and guests have use of a hairdryer, iron and telephone. Breakfast only is served in the bright dining room and there is a TV lounge. Tea or coffee and scones available at any time. Smoking is not permitted in the dining room, and pets are not allowed. Situated on the main Sligo-to-Rosses Point road on the left-hand side, 3 miles (4½ km) out of town and overlooking the sea.

OWNER Thomas and Ismay Fullerton OPEN All year ROOMS 3 double, 1 twin, 2 family (4 en-suite) TERMS B&B IR£13.50– £15.00 p.p.; reductions for children; single supplement

Tree Tops

Cleveragh Road, Sligo, Co Sligo

Tel: (071) 60160 or 62301,
E-mail: treetops@internet-eireann.ie

Tree Tops is a spacious, modern, attractive house in a secluded location, set in a pretty garden with a fishpond, an 8-minute walk from town. The immaculate bedrooms are large, prettily decorated, and all have TVs, hairdryers, telephones and tea- and coffee-making facilities. The house is well maintained and tastefully furnished; there is also a collection of prints and paintings. Substantial, wholesome breakfasts are served in the dining room/lounge, which has a TV and period furniture. No smoking. There are some lovely walks and views close by. No pets. Signposted as you enter Sligo. Access, Visa and Mastercard accepted.

OWNER Ronan and Doreen MacEvilly OPEN All year, except Christmas ROOMS 5 double/twin (4 en-suite) TERMS B&B IR£14.50–£16.00 p.p.; reductions for children; single supplement

TUBERCURRY

Cruckawn House

Ballymote Road, Tubercurry, Co Sligo

Tel: (071) 85188, Fax: (071) 85239

Mrs Walsh, who is director of the North West Regional Tourism Organisation and an expert on all local attractions, makes this a special place to stay. An extremely outgoing, friendly lady, she likes her guests to feel that they are at home. Cruckawn House is very much a family house. It stands back a little from the road on the edge of town and

179

overlooks the golf course; there are clubs and caddies for hire, and the green fees are moderate. The bedrooms are small and have en-suite facilities, with hairdryers and TVs on request. There is a comfortable TV lounge that leads into the dining room. Excellent home-cooked meals are served, if arranged in advance. Separating the dining room from a small sun lounge are sliding glass doors with the family crests of the owners' families engraved in the middle of each door. There is a wine licence, so guests may enjoy a drink with dinner. Dog kennels are provided. Laundry facilities available. Local amenities include salmon and trout fishing, game shooting, mountain climbing, horse-riding and pony trekking. Tubercurry is quite a lively place, with traditional Irish music every Thursday, June through to September. Located 300 metres off the Galway-to-Sligo road, signposted in centre of town. Visa accepted.

OWNER Jo and Maeve Walsh   OPEN All year   ROOMS 1 double, 2 twin, 2 family (all en-suite)   TERMS B&B IR£16.00 p.p.; reductions for children; single supplement; evening meal IR£13.00

Pine Grove

Ballina Road, Tubercurry, Co Sligo
Tel: (071) 85235

A square, whitewashed house standing in a pretty front garden, just on the edge of town on the Ballina Road. Mrs Kelly caters for non-residents for lunch as well as evening meals, which are served in a large dining room at the back of the house, overlooking the back patio. The breakfasts are excellent. The house is furnished very simply, with rather old-fashioned furniture. The lounge with open fire and TV is comfortable. There is no licence, but guests are welcome to bring their own wine and beer. All the beds have electric blankets, and there are an iron and hairdryer available. Pets by arrangment. Located on the Ballina Road.

OWNER Mrs Teresa Kelly   OPEN All year, except Christmas   ROOMS 1 double, 3 twin, 1 family (all en-suite)   TERMS B&B IR£15.00–£16.00 p.p.; reductions for children; evening meal IR£14.00

The Midlands

County Carlow

One of the smallest counties in Ireland, Carlow lies just below Wicklow and is in an area of rich farmland.

The county town, Carlow, has had an eventful history, including being captured by Cromwell in 1650. Now it manufactures beet sugar and has quite a few sights worth looking at, including the ruins of a Norman castle, a Gothic Revival Catholic Church, the Carlow Museum and the fine courthouse with a Doric portico fashioned after the Parthenon.

There is a ruined twelfth-century church at Killeshin, with a fine Romanesque doorway, and fourteenth-century Ballymoon Castle, which has apparently never been occupied.

BAGENALSTOWN

Lorum Old Rectory

Kilgreaney, Bagenalstown, Co Carlow

Tel: (0503) 75282, Fax: (0503) 75455

Dating from the eighteenth century, Lorum Old Rectory is set in 18 acres, nestling beneath the Blackstairs Mountains. It is surrounded by open countryside, with views as far as Tipperary. There are plenty of animals about, including goats, horses, dogs, a peacock and Jacob sheep. The bedrooms are spacious, furnished with antiques, and all have their original fireplaces. There is a comfortable, informal atmosphere, and Don and Bobbie Smith are a friendly couple. Five-course, imaginative dinners are available, with homegrown organic vegetables. There is a wine licence and a tiny snug with a fireplace and chaise-longue. Smoking in public rooms only. Visa and Access cards accepted.

OWNER Bobbie Smith   OPEN All year, except Christmas
ROOMS 3 double, 1 family (all en-suite)   TERMS B&B IR£25.00 p.p.; reductions for children; single supplement; evening meal IR£18.00.

CARLOW

Barrowville Town House

Kilkenny Road, Carlow, Co Carlow

Tel: (0503) 43324, Fax: (0503) 41953

This eighteenth-century house stands in its own gardens on the main road to Kilkenny on the edge of town. The

Dempseys, who come from hotel ownership, did the whole house up four years ago. It has been attractively decorated and furnished and offers very comfortable, spacious bedrooms all with bathrooms, TVs, telephones, hair dryers, and tea- and coffee-making facilities. Breakfast is served buffet-style in the small, cosy basement dining room. Access to the lovely, private backyard and conservatory is through the tiny sitting room, which also has a TV. Access, Visa and Mastercard accepted.

OWNER Randal and Marie Dempsey   OPEN All year   ROOMS 6 double/twin (all en-suite)   TERMS B&B IR£17.00–£19.50; reductions for children; single supplement

RATHVILLY

Lisnavagh

Rathvilly, Co Carlow
Tel: (0503) 61104

Approached up a great wide driveway, past farm buildings and bordered by rhododendrons, Lisnavagh is a splendid Victorian Gothic country house built in 1848 for the Rathdonnells, who have owned the property for 300 years. It was then redesigned in 1952, mostly by demolishing about half the building. It is hard to imagine that what now is the most attractive library was formerly the kitchen: beautifully carved bookshelves encase the room, interspersed with family portraits, a stone fireplace and comfortable chairs and sofas. There is one enormous four-poster bedroom with an old-fashioned en-suite bathroom. The other bedrooms are smaller, but still of a good size, with private bathrooms. The house is set in 1,000 acres of farm and woodlands and is surrounded by expansive lawns, beyond which are lovely views. The heated outdoor swimming pool is set in its own beautiful walled garden; there is a grass tennis court, and clay pigeon shooting can be arranged. Golf, riding, squash, hunting, shooting and fishing are all available with notice. No pets. Not suitable for children.

OWNER Lord Rathdonnell   OPEN 1 March–31 October   ROOMS: 1 double, 2 twin, 1 single (1 en-suite, others private bathroom)   TERMS B&B IR£45.00–£55.00 p.p.; evening meal IR£18.00

County Kildare

County Kildare is famous for horse breeding and training, which takes place on the Curragh, a great plain leading into a boggy area, the Bog of Allen. Many horse-race meetings are held here, including the Irish Sweep Derby, the Irish 2,000 Guineas, the Irish Oaks and the Irish St Leger. The town of Kildare is the centre for horse breeding and has a well-preserved Church of Ireland cathedral and round tower.

At Robertstown, the eighteenth-century buildings along the Grand Canal have been restored to look as they did when this was a great water thoroughfare. Here it is possible to visit Europe's largest falconry. Two of Ireland's greatest Georgian country houses, Carton and Castletown, are located at Celbridge. A music festival takes place in June at Castletown, as does one of the hunt balls held during the Dublin Horse Show week.

The very pretty village of Leixlip has many associations with the Guinness family; the twelfth-century Norman castle belongs to Desmond Guinness.

Remains of a Franciscan Abbey can be seen at Castledermot, and Athy has many historic sights worth exploring, including the sixteenth-century Woodstock Castle, just out of town. Moone High Cross, one of Ireland's most beautiful high crosses, is at Moone Abbey, 8 miles (12 km) from Athy.

BALLITORE

Griesemount

Ballitore, Co Kildare

Tel: (0507) 23158

This small Georgian house lies just off the N9 and has lovely views to the ruined mill on the river Griese, which is a well-known trout stream. Griesemount is a comfortable, informal house full of pictures, books and flowers. The rooms are large, and the double has a half tester bed. The attractive white-washed building at the back of the house is the workshop where owner Carolyn decorates pots and watering cans, etc. – a great idea for presents. An ideal centre for golf or racing.

OWNER Carolyn Ashe   OPEN 1 February–30 November   ROOMS 1 double, 1 twin   TERMS B&B IR£18.50–£25.00 p.p.; reductions for children

Windgate Lodge

Barberstown, Co Kildare

Tel: (01) 6273415

An attractive, red-brick two-storey house set back off the road in an acre of landscaped gardens. The house is in good decorative order, and there are 2 bedrooms on the ground floor, one of which has its own bathroom. This is an ideal location to reach either the Dublin airport or Dublin city; there is a train station 2 miles (3 km) away at Maynooth where cars can be left, as well as a frequent bus service to Dublin. Pat Ryan is pleasant, always eager to offer assistance to guests, and she serves a good home-cooked, freshly prepared breakfast. There is a separate dining room and TV lounge. Easy access to Naas and the South. Dublin airport approximately 40 minutes' drive away. Pets by arrangement. There is a self-catering unit available. Situated on the Maynooth-to-Straffan road.

OWNER Mrs Pat Ryan   OPEN All year, except Christmas Day
ROOMS 2 twin, 2 family (1 en-suite)   TERMS B&B£15.00 p.p.;
reductions for children; single supplement IR£3.00

CASTLEDERMOT

Kilkea Lodge Farm

Castledermot, Co Kildare

Tel: (0503) 45112

A comfortable family house set in rolling parkland with a pleasant, rural aspect; it is approached down a long driveway off the Castledermot Road, about half a mile from Kilkea Castle. Kilkea Lodge, which has belonged to the Green family since 1740, has a relaxed, informal atmosphere and friendly owners. Marion Greene runs the riding centre, offering a variety of instructional and fun holidays, and Godfrey runs the 260-acre farm. There is an enormous studio, converted from an old barn, with its own entrance, 4 beds, a small loft and a sitting area in the middle: ideal for families or small groups. There is a comforable drawing room with fireplace and piano. Traditional home-cooked dinners are served in the dining room. No smoking in bedrooms. No pets.

OWNER Godfrey and Marion Greene   OPEN All year, except

Christmas and January   ROOMS 2 double, 1 twin, 1 single plus 1 family studio sleeping 6 (3 en-suite)   TERMS B&B IR£25.00 p.p.; reductions for children; evening meal IR£12.00–£20.00; single supplement

DUNLAVIN

Grangebeg

Dunlavin, Co Kildare
Tel: (045) 51367

Grangebeg house probably dates from the first half of the eighteenth century, and when acquired by Aine McGrane's father in the 1930s was twice as big as it is today. Although half the house was pulled down in the 1940s, today it has a neat, square and complete look to it, with a front porch and classical lines. Grangebeg stands in a park-like setting on a quiet country lane, about 1¹/₂ miles (2¹/₂ km) from Dunlavin. Aine McGrane was born here, and now that her 6 children have moved away or gone to school, she has plenty of room for guests. The eldest daughter runs the riding centre, with stables at the back of the house, and there is a cross-country course. The house is decorated in an individual style with flamboyant wallpapers and matching curtains and chair covers. There's a formal dining room, a smaller dining room off the kitchen, a pleasant drawing room with open fire and a smaller TV room. Guests are welcome to use the tennis court. This is a delightful, friendly place and very handy for the Punchestown Races. Grangebeg can be found off the Naas-to-Kilkenny road.

OWNER Aine McGrane   OPEN All year, except Christmas
ROOMS 3 double, 2 twin, 1 single (all en-suite)   TERMS B&B IR£25.00–£30.00 p.p.; evening meal IR£15.00–£18.00

KILDARE

Fremont

Tully Road, Kildare, Co Kildare
Tel: (045) 21604

Fremont is a modern bungalow in a private setting, 3 minutes' walk to the town centre and the twelfth-century cathedral. The bedrooms, all on the ground floor, are spotlessly clean, with modern furnishings and shower units. The bathrooms, hall and dining room have been completely refurbished. The comfortable TV lounge has a lovely Leitrim stone fireplace, and the bright dining room has a beautiful unit, displaying a fine collection of Waterford, Galway and Cavan crystal. Mrs O'Connell is a considerate host who enjoys meeting people, and she extends a warm welcome to everyone. Breakfasts only are served, but there are several restaurants and pubs within walking distance. A short drive or a 15-minute walk to the Irish Stud and the Japanese Gardens. No smoking in the bedrooms. Private parking. Signposted from the town centre.

OWNER Mrs Frieda O'Connell   OPEN 10 January–10 December
ROOMS 2 double, 1 twin (1 en-suite)   TERMS B&B IR£14.00 p.p.; reductions for children; single supplement

Mount Ruadhan

Old Road, Kildare, Co Kildare
Tel: (045) 21637

Mount Ruadhan is easily located, as it is signposted at the only traffic light in Kildare! The bungalow is situated 1 mile (1^1/$_2$ km) from town in an elevated position surrounded by landscaped gardens. All the bedrooms are on the ground floor. The owners are always on hand to answer questions or make a pot of tea. The Japanese Gardens, Irish National Stud and St Brigid Cathedral are close by. Other amenities include 2 golf courses, horse-riding and the Peatland World Interpretative Centre. Breakfasts only are served, but there are several venues for good food in town. Smoking in the TV room only.

OWNER Mrs Eileen Corcoran   OPEN 1 March–30 November
ROOMS 1 treble, 1 double, 1 twin (2 en-suite)   TERMS B&B IR£14.50–IR£17.00 p.p.; reductions for children; single supplement

STRAFFAN

Barberstown Castle

Straffan, Co Kildare
Tel: (01) 6288157, Fax: (01) 6277027

Dating from the early 13th century, this historic castle was one of the first great Irish country houses to open for guests, becoming a hotel in 1973. The castle keep, which was built in the thirteenth century, is the venue for banquets, and larger groups of up to 150 people are entertained in the 16th-century Banqueting Hall. The Elizabethan part dates from the second half of the 16th century, and the Victorian house was built in the 1830's. It is said that a man is interred between the top of the stairs and the roof of the tower. His family did this to prevent their eviction as tenants, as the lease stated that if he was put underground, it would expire. The bedrooms are spacious and comfortable, and the food creative and beautifully served. Barberstown is an interesting and relaxing place to stay within easy reach of Dublin. Major credit cards accepted.

OWNER Kenneth and Catherine Healy   OPEN All year except Christmas   ROOMS 10 double/twin (all en-suite)   TERMS B&B IR£55.00 p.p.s. (+10% service charge); single supplement; dinner from IR£25.00

County Kilkenny

Kilkenny, the county town, is one of the oldest and most interesting towns in Ireland. It comes alive at the end of August during the Kilkenny Festival, which is one of Ireland's foremost cultural festivals. Kilkenny Castle stands in the centre, dominating the town, and just opposite are the Kilkenny Design Centre workshops, which can be visited. The cathedral stands on the site of a monastery built by St Canice in the sixth century and from which the city took its name. The Kilkenny Archaeological Society houses its collection in a most interesting Tudor merchant's house, Rothe House, and the City Hall, built in 1761, was formerly the Tolsel, or Toll House. Some well-known writers, including Swift, Berkeley and Congreve, were educated at Kilkenny College, a fine Georgian building.

The Kilkenny countryside is pretty and compact, and places of interest to visit are the attractive town of Thomastown, near to which is Dysart Castle, former home of George Berkeley, after whom the city and university in California, Berkeley, is named. Near to Callan on the King's River is Kells, a fortified, turreted and walled collection of early ecclesiastical buildings, and near Urlingford are the ruins of 4 castles.

CASTLECOMER

Wandesforde House

Castlecomer, Co Kilkenny
Tel: (056) 42441

Wandesforde House was built in 1824 by Lady Ann
Ormonde as a school for the children of the Castlecomer
estate. When the Flemings bought it in 1989, it was almost a
ruin. They have cleverly united the whole building by
enclosing the front porch behind glass and putting in a new
front door; at the back of the house is a lovely conservatory,
which leads onto a sunny patio. The 2 enormous school
rooms with high ceilings to each side of the house have been
converted into a sitting room/restaurant for guests and into
the family living quarters. The central area, where the
teacher lived, has been altered to accommodate the bed-
rooms, which are comfortable and attractively decorated.
David is a trained chef, and interesting meals are available,
if booked in advance. The Flemings have horses, and guests
are welcome to bring their own. Packed lunches are avail-
able. There is a wine licence, and pets are accepted by
arrangement only. Located 10 miles (15 km) from Kilkenny
on the main Dublin road. All major credit cards accepted.

OWNER David and Phil Fleming   OPEN All year, except Christmas
ROOMS 3 double, 3 twin (all en-suite)   TERMS B&B IR£20.00 p.p.;
single supplement; evening meals IR£15.00

FRESHFORD

Kilrush House

Freshford, Co Kilkenny
Tel: (056) 32236

An interesting family house built in 1820, with large rooms
containing many of the original furnishings. Kilrush House
stands in lawns, gardens and parkland, surrounded by its
250–acre farm, which supports sheep and a few thorough-
bred National Hunt mares. The St George family have lived
at Kilrush for 3 centuries, and until the present house was
built they inhabited the old Tower House, which in spite of
its age still stands. One of the features of the house is the
graceful cupola that is set high above the hall, the circular
landing on the first floor accentuating its lines. Home-
cooked meals including vegetables, lamb and free-range
pork from the farm are served in the enormous dining room,

which has the furniture originally made for the house and the old, somewhat faded wallpaper dating from around

1820. There is a hard tennis court; hunting holidays can be arranged during the winter. Pets by arrangement. Kilrush can be found on the road to Cashel, 2 miles (3 km) from Freshford.

OWNER Richard and Sally St George OPEN mid-April–mid-October ROOMS 3 double (all en-suite) TERMS B&B IR£39.00–£45.00 p.p.; reductions for children; single supplement; evening meal IR£20.00

GRAIGUENAMANAGH

Stablecroft

Moneen, Graiguenamanagh, Co Kilkenny

Tel: (0503) 24714

The Forrests came to Ireland for the first time in 1990 and liked it so much they bought Stablecroft, which was an old stone barn. They have built their stone home from scratch, using stones from the barn. Stablecroft exudes a relaxed atmosphere; the house is comfortable and simply furnished, mostly with pine furniture. Delicious evening meals are available, if arranged in advance. The house has wonderful views to Mount Leinster and the Blackstairs Mountains, and there are plenty of opportunities for golf, walking and fishing.

OWNER Sheila and Alan Forrest OPEN All year ROOMS 1 single, 3 double/twin, 1 single (3 en-suite) TERMS B&B IR£17.00; reductions for children; single supplement; dinner IR£14.00

Berryhill

Inistioge, Co Kilkenny
Tel: (056) 58434, Fax: (056) 58434

A most attractive country house, built by the family in 1780 and standing in 200 acres of farmland with wonderful views to the Nore Valley and to the hills on the other side. It is a favourite retreat of the actress Mia Farrow, who has stayed here with her 6 children. There is a pleasant garden, croquet lawn, private fishing and lovely walks. Accommodation is in the three exceptional suites, one of which has an outside terrace from where one can enjoy the view. Dinner, if arranged in advance, is served in the dining room, which has a fireplace and bay window, and guests can relax in the long drawing room in front of a log fire. Belinda Dyer is a charming and attentive hostess.

OWNER George and Belinda Dyer   OPEN All year, except Christmas and March   ROOMS 3 doubles (all en-suite)   TERMS B&B IR£30.00–£35.00; single supplement; dinner IR£25.00

Cullintra House

The Rower, Inistioge, Co Kilkenny
Tel: (051) 23614, Fax: (051) 23614

This attractive, ivy-covered, 200-year-old house is approached by a long driveway through a park of grazing cattle. The rooms, including a garden conservatory and a converted barn, reflect Miss Cantlon's artistic talents. There are a great many friendly cats and a local fox who comes to eat dinner in the garden every evening. Miss Cantlon specialises in good food, served by candlelight in an unhurried fashion and breakfast can be taken as late as you wish. There are 230 acres of farmland, and a private path leads to beautiful Mount Brandon. The studio/conservatory with a small kitchen for making drinks is available for guests and can also be used as a small conference room.

OWNER Patricia Cantlon   OPEN All year   ROOMS 6 double/family (3 en-suite)   TERMS B&B IR£23.00; reductions for children; single supplement; dinner IR£16.00

Blanchville House

Dunbell, Maddoxtown, Kilkenny, Co Kilkenny
Tel: (056) 27197, Fax: (056) 27636

Blanchville House is an elegant Georgian residence standing in its own grounds, approached by a tree- and shrub-lined private drive. It is beautifully furnished with antiques and has large comfortable bedrooms, all of which are now en-suite and have tea- and coffee-making facilities. The spacious drawing room, with the original wallpaper and service bells,

has a TV, grand piano and open fireplace. All the rooms overlook the lovely green countryside. Evening meals, if booked in advance, are served in the atmospheric dining room and are tastefully prepared with homegrown produce; vegetarian and special diets catered for. A wonderful retreat to return to after a day's sightseeing. Local amenities include golf, tennis, horse-riding, hunting and fishing, as well as flying at the Kilkenny Air Club. A 10-minute drive from Kilkenny: turn right off the Dublin road at Barlow Ford (approx 3 miles (4¹/₂ km) from this point). If in doubt, call for directions. All major credit cards accepted.

OWNER Tim and Monica Phelan   OPEN 1 March–1 October
ROOMS 3 double, 2 twin, 1 family (all en-suite)   TERMS B&B
IR£25.00–£27.00 p.p.; reductions for children; single supplement; evening meals IR£17.00

Burwood Bed and Breakfast

Waterford Road, Kilkenny, Co Kilkenny

Tel: (056) 62266

A modern bungalow with old-fashioned hospitality, set back off the main road, with a small, pretty front garden. The bedrooms, all on the ground floor, are immaculate and individually decorated with pastel-flowered wallpaper. There's a comfortable TV lounge for guests. Joan Flanagan is a most accommodating host, and a cup of tea or coffee is offered upon arrival and in the evening. She is proud of the personal attention she gives to her guests, making them feel relaxed and welcome. The house is close to all amenities and local restaurants. No smoking. Dogs welcome. Located on the Waterford road, 1 mile (1¹/₂ km) from the medieval city of Kilkenny.

OWNER Joan Flanagan OPEN 1 June–1 October ROOMS 2 double, 1 twin (2 en-suite) TERMS B&B IR£13.00 p.p.; reductions for children

Dunromin

Dublin Road, Kilkenny, Co Kilkenny

Tel: (056) 61387

The standard of maintenance is exceptionally high throughout the public rooms and bedrooms of this house, situated on the edge of town. There are views of the countryside at the back of the house, and a golf course lies to the front. The bedrooms are spacious, with a mixture of traditional mahogany and wicker furnishings, and are immaculately clean. Guests enjoy the secluded, landscaped garden, with furniture for guests' use, and there is a wonderful friendly atmosphere. Mr Rothwell plays the accordian and he enjoys entertaining guests; Dunromin is well known for its informality and great musical evenings. Tea or coffee is offered on arrival, and breakfasts include home-baked breads and homemade preserves. No smoking in the dining room.

OWNER Mrs Valerie Rothwell OPEN All year ROOMS 4 double, 5 twin (4 en-suite) TERMS B&B IR£14.00 p.p.; reductions for children; single supplement

Hillgrove

Bennettsbridge Road, Kilkenny, Co Kilkenny
Tel: (056) 22890 or 51453

This delightful family home is set back off the New Ross Road, 3 km from Kilkenny. Margaret Drennan used to work for the Irish Tourist Board and knows everything there is to know about Kilkenny. She is happy to suggest itineraries and help with planning your stay. She is a National Galtee Breakfast Award winner and has a varied breakfast menu. The house is furnished in a mixture of old and reproduction furniture, and guests are offered coffee or tea on arrival.

OWNER Margaret and Tony Drennan   OPEN 1 February–30 November   ROOMS 3 double, 2 twin (all en-suite)   TERMS B&B IR£16.00; reductions for children; single supplement

Shillogher House

Callan Road, Kilkenny, Co Kilkenny
Tel: (056) 63249

A large modern brick house built by the owners, which stands in its own grounds on the outskirts of Kilkenny, on the Callan road; only a few minutes' walk to the town centre. The Morgans are very welcoming people, and the house has a friendly atmosphere. The rooms are immaculately clean and decorated with pretty wallpaper and curtains, and all have TV, phones and hairdryers. Tea and coffee are available in the conservatory and there is a lounge off the breakfast room. The menu gives guests an excellent choice for breakfast. No smoking in the bedrooms and no pets allowed. Visa and Access cards accepted.

OWNER Bill and Margaret Morgan   OPEN All year, except Christmas   ROOMS 5 double/twin/family (all en-suite)   TERMS B&B IR£15.00–£17.50 p.p.; reductions for children

PILTOWN

Fanningstown House

Piltown, Co Kilkenny
Tel: (051) 43535

This attractive country house was built in 1710 by the Walsh family, and lies at the foot of the mountains named

194

after them. It is a pure coincidence, though, that the present owners, John and Judith Walsh, have the same surname. They bought the house eight years ago, when it was in virtual ruins – there were two feet of water in the basement kitchen and a tree growing through the drawing room! Major renovation has made this a comfortable home, tastefully decorated and furnished. Two of the double rooms are on the first floor, while on the second floor there are a further three pretty attic-type rooms. Facilities include a sauna and hard tennis court. Hunting and shooting holidays are arranged in the winter and pony trekking is also available. Judith trained in hotel and catering management, so you can be assured of excellent meals. Visa and Access accepted.

OWNER Judith Walsh   OPEN All year except October   ROOMS 3 double, 2 twin (all en-suite)   TERMS B&B IR£25.00; reductions for children; single supplement; dinner IR£16.50

THOMASTOWN

Abbey House

Jerpoint Abbey, Thomastown, Co Kilkenny

Tel: (056) 24166 or 24192, Fax: (056) 26275

Abbey House is an attractive building located opposite Jerpoint Abbey. The house may have been built as early as 1540, and a mill here dates from the twelfth century. Ruins of the old mill, which Helen Blanchfield would love to restore, lie behind the house. The house itself was in a very bad condition when the Blanchfields bought it in 1988, and only one original wall is left after doing the restoration work. Helen is an amusing, chatty lady with a lot of energy. She runs not only the bed and breakfast but also provides lunches, teas, dinners and snacks for non-residents. The house is spacious, with a drawing room, and simply furnished bedrooms all equipped with hairdryers, telephones and trouser presses; the pleasant dining room has small tables. Abbey House is located on the Dublin-to-Waterford road. Visa, Access and Eurocard accepted.

OWNER Mrs Helen Blanchfield   OPEN All year   ROOMS 5 double, 1 single (all en-suite)   TERMS B&B IR£16.50 p.p.; reductions for children; single supplement; evening meal IR£15.00, also à la carte

County Leitrim

Leitrim is a county of charming beauty, with distinctive hill formations and lovely lakes. This long, narrow county is divided in two by Lough Allen, one of the many lakes of the Shannon River. The county is a very popular place for anglers, and the main topic of conversation everywhere seems to be fishing.

Dromahair is a pretty village, located about 8 miles (12 km) from Manorhamilton. The road from here is scenically superb, with views of Lough Gill and beautiful wooded countryside.

Fenagh, which is located in the hills, has the ruins of a Gothic church, all that remains of the monastery St Columba founded as a school of divinity. You can fish to your heart's content in this area, which is full of lakes, beautiful scenery and wildlife.

Carrick-on-Shannon is the centre of river cruising on the Shannon. There is a large marina, several cruising companies, and lots of restaurants and pubs, which during the season have traditional Irish music.

BALLINAMORE

Glenview

Aughoo, Ballinamore, Co Leitrim
Tel: (078) 44157, Fax: (078) 44814

Glenview is a most attractive farmhouse situated on the outskirts of Ballinamore, beside the Woodford River, part of the Ballinamore-Ballyconnel Canal and the Shannon-Erne Link – a delightful rural setting. There are extensive gardens here, as well as a pony, donkey and cart for children's enjoyment; a games room and pool table are available for guests' use. The house is efficiently run; bedrooms are tastefully furnished and there is a very large lounge with a marble fireplace and an antique chaise longue. There are many lakes close by and guests are advised on the best places to fish. A tackle shed, cold room and bait service are provided. Owner Theresa Kennedy has been very successful with her bed and breakfast during the past 11 years and is the proud recipient of the BHS Agri-Tourism award. Glenview has its own gourmet, licenced restaurant; guests should reserve in advance for evening meals. No pets. Self-catering available. Visa accepted.

OWNER Brian and Theresa Kennedy   OPEN All year, except Christmas   ROOMS 1 double, 5 twin (4 en-suite)

CARRICK-ON-SHANNON

Ard-na-Greine House

St Mary's Close, Carrick-on-Shannon, Co Leitrim
Tel: (078) 20311

A modern, three-storey house within easy walking distance of the River Shannon and town centre. Helen Dee is a friendly, outgoing lady who thoroughly enjoys her guests and is happy to offer advice with local sightseeing. The well-furnished lounge rooms are bright and spotlessly clean, and freshly prepared breakfasts are served in the cosy dining room overlooking the woods. Traditional home-cooked evening meals are available if prearranged; vegetarians catered for. There are 2 comfortable lounges where a cup of tea or coffee is served in the evening. Helen Dee is proud to have American Senator McGovern as a regular guest. Located off the main road in a cul-de-sac, opposite the Bush Hotel. Visa accepted.

OWNER Helen Dee OPEN All year ROOMS 4 double, 4 twin, 2 family (4 en-suite) TERMS B&B IR£13.50–£14.50 p.p.; reductions for children; single supplement; evening meal IR£11.00

Caldra House

Carrick-on-Shannon, Co Leitrim
Tel: (07) 21606

Caldra House is set in a secluded spot, in 72 acres of farmland through which the River Shannon flows, and is a perfect choice for a peaceful and relaxing holiday. This recently restored Georgian residence combines the ambience and charm of its era with modern comforts. The owner's daughter, Miriam O'Connell, runs the business and is adept at making guests feel welcome. Tea or coffee is offered upon arrival. There are two comfortable sitting rooms and a conservatory, which is delightful in good weather, while there are fires in both the dining room and the lounge for chilly days. There are boats and a bait-and-tackle room for guests' use. There are 41 coarse fishing lakes within a 5-mile radius. Evening meals, all home-cooked, with tasty desserts, can be prearranged. Traditional music can be enjoyed in local pubs. No pets.

OWNER Joseph and Maura O'Connell   OPEN March–October
ROOMS 6 double/twin/family (4 en-suite)   TERMS B&B IR£16.00;
reductions for children; single supplement; evening meals
IR£12.00

Corbally Lodge

Dublin Road, near Carrick-on-Shannon, Co Leitrim

Tel: (078) 20228

A country-style house in an attractive garden with an infor-
mal, friendly atmosphere approx. 1½ miles (2½ km) from
Carrick-on-Shannon. The bedrooms are fresh and clean,
and 2 are on the ground floor. There are antique furnish-
ings, and an attractive guest lounge with TV and turf fires.
Mrs Rowley is a very friendly lady who takes excellent care
of her guests. Breakfasts and dinners, with wholesome foods
and fresh-baked breads, are served in the bright dining
room. The River Shannon is close by; there are numerous
lakes in the area, plus golf, swimming and local boat hire
available. From Dublin, take the road to Mullingar; the
house is 1½ miles (2½ km) away on the left-hand side .

OWNER Mrs Valerie Rowley   OPEN All year   ROOMS 1 double, 3
twin (3 en-suite)   TERMS B&B IR£13.50–£14.50 p.p.; reductions
for children; single supplement; evening meal IR£11.00.

Lake View House

Drumcong, Carrick-on-Shannon, Co Leitrim

Tel: (078) 42034

This old-style country house overlooks Carrickport Lake to
the front and Lough Scur to the rear. It has a warm and
homely atmosphere and the owners, Tom and Nancy
McKeown, are hospitable and friendly. Originally owned by
the parish priest, the house and its five acres were purchased
by Tom and Nancy in 1972 and they have been welcoming
guests for the past five years. The house has a lived-in feel;
the bedrooms are large, modestly furnished and most have
views of the lough. There is only one en-suite bedroom, but
there are plans to add an additonal en-suite facility soon.
There are seven lakes close by, and guests can fish for perch,
pike, bream and rudd, while Lough Carrickport and Scur
are within a five-minute walk. Guests have use of a spacious
tackle room and fridge. The cosy lounge has a turf fire, and
breakfasts and dinners are served in a separate dining room.

There is a pub featuring traditonal music and entertainment within a two-minute walk. Pets outside only.

OWNER Tom and Nancy McKeown   OPEN March–October
ROOMS 4 double/twin/family (1 en-suite)   TERMS B&B IR£15.00
p.p.; reductions for children

County Longford

The most central county of Ireland, Longford lies in the basin of the Shannon, and the landscape is consequently low and flat, interspersed with small streams and lakes dotted with islands. Longford has strong associations with writers, particularly Oliver Goldsmith, Padriac Colum, Maria Edgeworth and Leo Casey, and is a popular place for coarse fishing.

The town of Longford is spaciously laid out with wide streets, a Renaissance-style court house and a nineteenth-century cathedral, which is built of grey limestone and has impressive towers.

Close to Newtonforbes is beautiful Castle Forbes, a fine seventeenth-century castellated mansion. St Patrick is said to have founded a church at the old village of Ardagh in a pretty wooded setting, the ruins of which can still be seen.

LONGFORD

Sancian House

Dublin Road, Longford, Co Longford

Tel: (043) 46187

A warm and informal atmosphere pervades Sancian, and there is a welcoming pot of tea and plate of scones on arrival. The rooms are simply furnished, spotlessly clean, fitted with colour TVs and clock radios. The house is set back off the road, the front garden is full of roses and there are colourful window boxes. Martha O'Kane is an outgoing, friendly lady who is very knowledgeable regarding family heritage and is willing to assist guests wishing to trace their ancestry. An 18-hole golf course is located across the street, and it is a 5-mile drive to the lovely village of Ardagh. Pets permitted by arrangement. Located on the edge of town on the east side of the Dublin road.

OWNER Martha O'Kane   OPEN All year, except Christmas
ROOMS 2 double, 1 twin, 2 single (3 en-suite)   TERMS B&B
IR£15.50 p.p.; reductions for children

Counties Offaly and Laois

These 2 counties lie in the central part of Ireland, with the River Shannon forming their western border.

Clonmacnois is an important name in Irish history. St Ciaran founded a monastery here in AD 548, which became one of Ireland's best-known religious centres. A pilgrimage is held here each September on the feast of St Ciaran.

There is an attractive castle at Clononey, and Anthony Trollope first started writing novels whilst living at Banagher, a pretty little village on the canal. At Birr, the gardens of the castle are open to the public, and in Portarlington, built on the canal, the gardens of the old town houses run down to the river instead of to the street.

BIRR

Minnocks Farm Guesthouse

Clonkelly, Birr, Co Offaly

Tel: (0509) 20591

This attractive Georgian-style house with colonnades, Georgian doors and windows, and ceiling rose and cornices was cleverly converted from a farmhouse in 1991. There are 2 bedrooms on the ground floor – all have TVs and new firm beds, are individually decorated in soft pastel shades and have matching fabrics and curtains. This comfortable and peaceful house is set on a 100-acre dairy farm. Breakfasts are sumptuous and include freshly made scones, potato bread, eggs, bacon, and fresh milk and cream from the farm. Five-course dinners are available, if prearranged. Veronica Minnock is a most gracious host and has been awarded the Golden Thoughts Tourist award, an accolade for "service above and beyond the call of duty". A cup of tea is offered upon arrival; in fact, at Minnocks Farm the kettle is rarely

off the boil. There is a separate sitting room for guests' use. Located on the Birr-to-Roscrae Road, 3 miles (4¹/₂ km) from Birr, convenient to Birr Castle and the Clonmacnois and West Offaly Railway.

OWNER Noel and Veronica Minnock   OPEN All year
ROOMS 2 double, 2 twin, 3 family (all en-suite) TERMS B&B IR£15.00 p.p.; reductions for children under 12; single supplement; evening meal IR£12.00

RAHAN

Canal View Country House

Killina, Rahan, Tullamore, Co Offaly
Tel: (0506) 55868

Canal View is an attractive, modern dormer bungalow in a peaceful positon backing onto the Grand Canal. One can fish from the back garden for bream, rudd, tench and perch, and angling maps are available. Guests can walk along the canal bank and watch the cruisers pass by or take a ten-minute stroll to the ancient Rahan Church. A patio and picnic and play area is available for guests. A sauna, steamroom, Jacuzzi and pedal and rowing boats are all available to guests at no extra cost. Breakfast and evening meals are served in the pretty dining room, which overlooks the canal. The bedrooms, all of which are en-suite, are spotlessly clean and tastefully decorated with matching fabrics and wallpapers. All have TVs, radios, tea-making facilities and hairdryers. Canal View offers extremely high standards and guests are assured of a warm welcome and attention to detail in this pleasant house. Complimentary snack tray on arrival. No pets.

OWNER Bernadette Keyes   OPEN All year   ROOMS 2 family, 2 double (all en-suite)   TERMS B&B IR£16.00 p.p.; reductions for children under 12; single supplement

TULLAMORE

Pine Lodge

Ross Road, Screggan, Tullamore, Co Offaly
Tel: (0506) 51927, Fax: (0506) 51927

Pine Lodge, set in 2 acres of lawned gardens, with outstanding views of the surrounding countryside, provides the ultimate in relaxation. This is an exceptionally well-maintained house with extremely high standards. All but one of the well-appointed bedrooms have pine furnishings. There is a sitting room with TV and a separate dining room, where excellent breakfasts are served on separate pine tables. Claudia Krygel is from Germany and prides herself on the wholesome food served. Breakfast consists of smoked salmon, eggs and pancakes, as well as the traditional fare. Little wonder that Claudia was a winner of the National Irish Breakfast Award. Imaginative evening meals are also served (advance notice required). Vegetarian and special diets are catered for. There are some lovely countryside walks, and golf and fishing are close by. A log-cabin building has been added, which houses a large, heated indoor pool, sauna, steam room and sun bed. Massage and reflexology also available. Not suitable for children under 12. No pets. Smoking in designated area only. Head to Birr, turn off 3 miles (4½ km) from Tullamore to the left, signposted after 1 mile (1½ km), on the left.

OWNER Claudia Krygel   OPEN 1 February–1 December   ROOMS 2 double, 2 twin (all en-suite)   TERMS B&B IR£20.00 p.p.; no reductions for children; single supplement; evening meal IR£12.00–£17.50

DONAGHMORE

Castletown House

Donaghmore, Co Laois
Tel: (0505) 46415, Fax: (0505) 46788

Castletown House is an early-nineteenth-century farmhouse set in scenic surroundings on a 200–acre beef and sheep farm, on which the ruins of a Norman castle remain (approached through open fields full of grazing sheep). The house was completely renovated in 1979, at which time the 30-inch-thick outer walls were raised by 18 inches. This must be one of the best-value accommodations in Ireland: the bedrooms are of a good size and there are several interesting pieces of antique furniture. Fresh farmhouse breakfasts and evening meals with home-baking are served in the dining room, which has a marble fireplace; there is a sitting room with TV. Guests enjoy gathering in the farm kitchen for a cup of tea and chatting to the friendly owners. Castletown House was the recipient of a regional Agri-Tourism award. A wonderful spot to stay a while and enjoy the many things to see and do in the area, including the Italian Heywood Gardens and the Agricultural Museum in the old

Donaghmore Workhouse. Guests interested in genealogy can be assisted by Moira Phelan. A path leads down to the River Erkina, where fishing is allowed. Pets outside. No smoking in the bedrooms. Visa and Access cards accepted.

OWNER Moira Phelan   OPEN 1 March–1 December, or by arrangement   ROOMS 2 double, 1 twin, 1 family (all en-suite)   TERMS B&B IR£14.00 p.p.; reductions for children under 12; evening meal IR£12.00

STRADBALLY

Tullamoy House

Stradbally, Co Laois
Tel: (0507) 27111

A lovely nineteenth-century stone house standing in its own grounds, with acres of parkland and a 150-acre mixed farm. The bedrooms are large and are furnished with some unusual antique furniture. There is a large lounge with a log fireplace and a pleasant dining room where guests can enjoy farm breakfasts and wholesome evening meals. There is a small museum on the premises, which houses various items found in the locality. There are also the ruins of an old castle on the property. The owner, Kathleen Farrell, is a down-to-earth friendly lady who has created a pleasant ambiance in her informal, comfortable house. Guests are encouraged to use the lounge, and Kathleen is always happy to advise guests on what to see and do. She has also compiled a most informative portfolio of local attractions for the benefit of her guests. There are also lots of interesting books available for guests to read. The National Stud and the Irish Horse

Museum in Tully, and the Japanese Gardens, considered to be Europe's finest, are all close at hand.

OWNER Mrs Kathleen Farrell OPEN May–October ROOMS 3 double/twin/family TERMS B&B IR£15.00 p.p.; reductions for children; single supplement

County Roscommon

County Roscommon is an inland county 40 miles (60 km) in length. Two-thirds of the county is bounded by water. In the north are the largest lakes: Lough Key, Lough Gara and Lough Boderg, with the great Lough Ree in the east. The limestone foundation of the whole county and the numerous lakes make it a fisherman's paradise.

Large areas of arable land are to be found in the centre of the county, and the principal occupation of the people is raising cattle and sheep.

Roscommon is a county of abbeys and castles. You can visit Clonalis House, Castlerea, once the home of two of Ireland's high kings in the twelfth century; Strokestown Park House, with its records of Famine-ridden Ireland; prehistoric Rathcroghan; St John's Interpretative Centre; medieval Boyle and picturesque Lough Key with its forest park.

For those interested in contemporary art, the Glebe House Gallery is situated midway between Boyle and Carrick-on-Shannon at Crossna, Knockvicar.

CARRICK-ON-SHANNON

Avondale

Roosky, Carrick-on-Shannon, Co Roscommon
Tel: (078) 38095

An attractive, modern two-storey house standing in its own grounds, 500 yards from the River Shannon. This is very much a family-run establishment, with a relaxing, homely atmosphere. Carmel Davis was initially in the hotel trade but missed the personal contact with guests and decided to run a B&B; she and her husband were successful from the beginnning and soon added on 2 additional bedrooms. The 5 bedrooms are clean and comfortable, with orthopaedic beds and all are en-suite. There is a TV lounge with turf fires. Excellent home-cooking for breakfasts and evening meals, if prearranged, is served. Avondale is an ideal base for anglers – there is a tackle room with fridges and drying facilities.

Bait is available locally, and boat hire can be arranged on request. Roosky is an excellent base for touring, midway beween Longford and Carrick-on-Shannon; Lough Rinn House and Gardens are just 6 miles (9 km) away. No pets. Signposted on the N4 at Rooskey, half a kilometre over the bridge. All major credit cards accepted.

OWNER Carmel and John Davis   OPEN All year, except Christmas   ROOMS 2 double, 1 twin, 2 family (5 en-suite)   TERMS B&B IR£15.00 p.p.; reductions for children; single supplement

Glencarne House

Carrick-on-Shannon, Co Roscommon

Tel: (079) 67013

This charming Georgian house is located in scenic country-side with lovely views of fields and grazing sheep. A very warm welcome awaits you at Glencarne House; Mrs Harrington has received several awards, including the Galtee Breakfast Award and the Agri-Tourism National Award. The house is warm and peaceful and the bedrooms have every comfort, including armchairs, hot-water bottles and electric blankets; some have antique brass beds. There is a comfortable guest lounge with a marble fireplace, which, along with the dining room, has a blazing fire on chilly days. Mrs Harrington is an excellent cook; evening meals are all prepared fresh daily and the desserts feature some of the best pastry in Ireland. Wine licence. There is a golf course within half a mile and boating, fishing and shooting are available locally. Pets outside by arrangement. Situated $4^{1}/_{2}$ miles ($6^{1}/_{2}$ km) from Carrick-on-Shannon, midway between Boyle and Carrick-on-Shannon.

OWNER The Harrington family   OPEN 1 March–1 October   ROOMS 2 double, 2 single, 2 family (4 en-suite)   TERMS B&B IR£17.00–£20.00 p.p.; reductions for children under 12; single supplement; evening meal IR£14.00

STROKESTOWN

Church View House

Strokestown, Co Roscommon

Tel: (078) 33047, Fax: (088) 602909

Church View House is a spacious, 200–year-old, rambling country house in a scenic setting. It has been in the Cox family for four generations and there is a 250-acre farm. The original structure of a famine fever hospital is in the grounds. The good-sized bedrooms are simply furnished; two are en-suite, and there are ample bathrooms. Guests have use of two lounges, one with a TV, and another quieter one with an original marble fireplace. Evening meals are served, if ordered in advance, and guests are welcome to bring wine. There are many coarse fishing lakes in the area, the most well-known being Grange and Kilglass, which are also trout fishing lakes. Guests can trace their ancestry at the Country Heritage Centre nearby. Church House is signposted from Strokestown, which is three and a half miles away. Pets outside. Smoking in the lounge only.

OWNER Harriet Cox   OPEN Mid-March–October   ROOMS 6 double/twin/family (2 en-suite)   TERMS IR£16.00–£18.00 p.p.; reductions for children

County Tipperary

Located right in the centre of the southern part of Ireland, Tipperary is a beautiful county of rich farmland. From the top of Slievenamon there is a splendid view. To the north you can see the Rock of Cashel, a steep outcrop of limestone topped by impressive ruins – a truly spectacular sight, particularly during the summer when it is floodlit at night. From early times the rock was a fortress and seat of chieftains, and later it became an important religious site. Today you can see the vast ruins of the gothic cathedral, which dates from the thirteenth century; the tower of the Castle; the cross of St Patrick, the massive base of which is said to be the coronation stone of the Munster kings; and Cormac's Chapel, a very interesting building dating back to 1130.

The Cashel Palace Hotel is a very fine Queen Anne-style house, formerly the residence of Church of Ireland archbishops, located in the busy town of Cashel. A fine collection of sixteenth- and seventeenth-century books can be found in the Diocesan Library in the precincts of the St John the Baptist Cathedral, and there's a good craft shop where one can buy Shanagarry tweed. Situated between Thurles and Cashel, Holycross Abbey was built in 1110, to house a part of the True Cross, and later became a popular place of pilgrimage.

Cahir, a most pleasant town on the River Suir, has a beautifully restored fifteenth-century castle on an island in the river, and now houses the tourist office. Tipperary, famous for the World War I marching song "It's a Long Way to Tipperary", is a great farming centre. The mountains between Nenagh and Toomvara were the home of Ned of the Hill, the local Robin Hood, and nearby is Nenagh Round, all that is left of an old castle built in 1200.

Kilcooly Abbey, the Abbey of the Holy Cross and the attractive old church at Fethard are all worth seeing. At Ahenny are two elaborately carved eighth-century stone crosses, and at Carrick-on-Suir is a very fine example of a Tudor mansion, which can be visited by request.

BALLINDERRY

Gurthalougha House

Ballinderry, Near Nenagh, Co Tipperary
Tel: (067) 22080, Fax: (067) 22154

Gurthalougha House is approached through a peaceful avenue that winds for a mile (1^1/$_2$ km) through 150 acres of mature forest. Built in the nineteenth century, the house is situated on the banks of the River Shannon; in the distance can be seen the mountains of Clare and Galway. This is an informal and relaxed house, with huge log fireplaces and antique furnishings. The bedrooms are large, with wooden floors and comfortable beds, and one has a balcony overlooking the lake. Breakfast goes on until noon and is available in bed or in front of the fire in the dining room. Michael Wilkinson, your host, enjoys cooking, and all foods are prepared with fresh, wholesome ingredients. There is a wine licence. There are lovely woodland walks with a great variety of wildlife: red squirrels, badgers, otters and kingfishers. Boats and windsurfboards are available at no extra charge, with swimming from the jetty and croquet on the lawn. There are 4 golf courses, pony trekking, 2 hard tennis courts and a sailing school close by. No pipes or cigars in the dining room. Pets by arrangement.

OWNER Bessie and Michael Wilkinson OPEN All year, except Christmas and February ROOMS 6 double, 2 twin, 2 family (all en-suite) TERMS B&B IR£36.00–£42.00 p.p.; reductions for children under 10; evening meal IR£22.50

Bansha Castle

Bansha, Co Tipperary
Tel: (062) 54187, Fax: (062) 54187

Built in the 1830s, Bansha Castle is a large country house
with a square tower at one end and a round tower at the
other. It stands at the edge of the village, with an attractive
walled garden to the rear of the house, and is surrounded
by 45 acres of land. Bansha Castle has been in the Russell
family for 40 years, and 13 years ago Teresa and John
moved in and started updating it. This is a pleasant house,
restfully decorated and featuring comfortable rooms. The
dining room is an attractive oval-shaped room, where
delicious, attractively served breakfasts are accompanied by
a welcoming open fire on chillier mornings. Evening meals,
which are prepared where possible with local, organically
grown produce, must be booked in advance. There is a wine
licence. The Russells specialise in walking holidays, but can
also arrange riding, golf and fishing. No pets.

OWNER Teresa and John Russell   OPEN All year   ROOMS 3
double, 2 twin, 1 family (4 en-suite)   TERMS B&B IR£18.00–
£21.00 p.p.; reductions for children; single supplement; evening
meal IR£15.00

Bansha House

Bansha, Co Tipperary
Tel: (062) 54194, Fax: (062) 52499

Bansha House is 200 yards from the village of Bansha on the
main road from Shannon to Waterford. It is a lovely Geor-
gian residence approached by an avenue of beech trees, set
in 100 acres of land. The house is tastefully decorated, with
some lovely antique furnishings dotted about. Two of the
bedrooms are on the ground floor. The delightful lounge has
a log fire and leads onto the gardens. A relaxed and comfort-
able atmosphere pervades, and guests can often be found in
the kitchen with Mary, chatting about what to see and do in
the area. John and Mary breed and train racehorses, and
riding is available on an hourly basis. Cooking is of a very
high standard, with homemade breads, tarts and pies.
Glorious scenic tours can be taken from here. This is a
superb house for guests wanting some peace and tranquil-

lity. Some smoking restrictions and no pets allowed. A self-catering cottage is also available.

OWNER John and Mary Marnane   OPEN All year, except Christmas   ROOMS 4 double, 2 twin, 1 single (4 en-suite)   TERMS B&B IR£15.00–£17.00 p.p.; reductions for children; single supplement; evening meals IR£12.50

Lismacue House

Bansha, Co Tipperary
Tel: (062) 54106, Fax: (062) 54126

Lismacue House has been in Kate Nicholson's family since it was built in 1813, a classic, beautifully proportioned Irish country house, set in its own extensive grounds at the foot of the magnificent Galtee Mountains. The approach to the house is via one of the most impressive lime tree avenues in Ireland. The spacious drawing room and library have the original wallpaper. Breakfasts and dinners are served in the imposing dining room. There is central heating throughout the house. All rooms have telephones, hairdryers and trouser presses. Traditional log fires burn in the warm and welcoming reception rooms. Special-interest holidays are available; pony trekking for adults and children, and, during November to February, hosted hunting holidays; also trout fishing on the estate's own river (tuition available). There are 3 golf courses and tennis close by, not to forget the Rock of Cashel and Cahir Castle. Lismacue has a wine licence. No pets. Situated on the Tipperary/Cahir Road.

OWNER Mrs Katherine Nicholson   OPEN All year, except Christmas   ROOMS 3 double, 2 twin (3 en-suite)   TERMS B&B IR£33.00–£40.00 p.p.; reductions for children; single supplement; evening meals from IR£21.00

CAHIR

Ashling Guest House

Dublin Road, Cahir, Co Tipperary
Tel: (052) 41601

Ashling guest house is a pink-washed, low building on the main Dublin road, about 1 mile (1$^{1}/_{2}$ km) outside Cahir, with lovely views from the front of the house. Breda Fitzgerald is a very friendly, chatty lady, who keeps an immaculately clean and tidy house. The rooms are on the small side, but comfortably furnished, and there is a large sitting room off the dining room. The house stands in beautifully kept gardens. No pets. No smoking.

OWNER Breda and Michael Fitzgerald   OPEN All year   ROOMS 4 rooms (3 en-suite)   TERMS B&B IR£15.00–£17.00 p.p.; reductions for children; single supplement

CASHEL

Ardmayle House

Cashel, Co Tipperary

Tel: (0504) 42399, Fax: (0504) 42420

A spacious, creeper-covered, unpretentious farmhouse surrounded by a 200–acre working farm. The bedrooms, furnished with old-fashioned and antique furniture, are large and comfortable. The open log fire in the sitting room is the ideal setting for making friends and enjoying a cup of tea and some delicious homemade scones. Guests are welcome to explore the dairy farm; sheep and horses are also kept. Annette is a warm, kindly host who is anxious for guests to experience the best of rural living. They are welcome to fish both banks on the 1-mile-long private stretch of the River Suir that runs through the property. Golf, forest walks and horse-riding can all be arranged locally. Approximately 4 miles (6 km) from Cashel. Evening meals by advance arrangement. There are also 2 four-star, self-catering cottages on the farm.

OWNER Annette Hunt   OPEN 1 April–30 September   ROOMS 1 double, 1 twin, 4 family (3 en-suite)   TERMS B&B IR£14.00–£16.00 p.p.; reductions for children; single supplement; evening meals IR£12.50

Knock-St-Lour House

Cashel, Co Tipperary

Tel: (062) 61172

A circular driveway leads to this large, square, modern whitewashed house with its stone-pillared porch. Knock-St-Lour lies just off the Cork-to-Cashel road, 1^1/$_2$ miles (2^1/$_2$ km) from Cashel, and is surrounded by 32 acres of beef and tillage farming. The drawing room is very formal, but the TV lounge has comfortable chairs, a piano and a fireplace. The rooms on the whole are large and comfortable, and the house enjoys views of the Rock of Cashel. Dinner is available by arrangement. No smoking in dining room and no pets.

OWNER Eileen O'Brien   OPEN 1 April–1 October   ROOMS 7 double/twin/family (7 en-suite)   TERMS B&B IR£16.00 p.p.; reductions for children; single supplement; evening meal IR£13.00

Maryville

Bank Place, Cashel, Co Tipperary

Tel: (062) 61098

This is a popular property, situated in the town centre. An extension was added 9 years ago to accommodate more guests, but early reservations are still necessary. The rooms are clean and functional, and there is a small TV lounge with tea- and coffee-making facilities. The back bedrooms have a lovely view of the Rock of Cashel, floodlit at night. There is a pretty, secluded garden with furniture for guests' use, and, adjoining the garden, the remains of a thirteenth-century Dominican Abbey. This is a photographers' delight. Mary and Pat Duane are helpful people, and in the lounge there is information on what to see and do. There is music, dance and song Tuesday to Saturday at Bru Boru, 2 minutes' walk away. No smoking in public areas and no pets. Visa, Access and Eurocard accepted.

OWNER Mary and Pat Duane   OPEN All year, except Christmas ROOMS 2 double, 2 twin, 4 family (4 en-suite)   TERMS B&B IR£14.50–£16.50 p.p.; reductions for children; single supplement

Rahard Lodge

Cashel, Co Tipperary

Tel: (062) 61052

Rahard Lodge is approached up a tree-lined drive and is set in glorious landscaped gardens. There are superb views of the Rock of Cashel, which is floodlit at night. Built by the owners 27 years ago, this long, low, whitewashed house is surrounded by its 130-acre beef and sheep farm. The bedrooms are large, comfortable and well appointed. Mr and Mrs Foley are a delightful couple who are interested in antiques, and there are some interesting pieces about. The house is impeccably maintained, there are rich carpets and a spacious lounge with an open fireplace. Freshly prepared breakfasts are served, and guests are greeted with a hot drink and homemade cake or scones. Evening meals are available, if prearranged, and there is a wide selection of good restaurants and pubs serving evening meals within a 10-minute walk. Guests are welcome to sit in the lovely gardens, which were awarded first prize in County Tipperary and third prize in the All-Ireland competition. No smoking. No pets. Visa accepted.

OWNER Moira Foley   OPEN March–December   ROOMS 1 twin, 4 family (all en-suite)   TERMS B&B IR£14.00–£16.00 p.p.; single supplement; reductions for children

Ros-Guill House

Dualla Road, Cashel, Co Tipperary

Tel: (062) 61507

This small, neat-looking house was built by the owners 26 years ago, and Mrs Moloney has been running a bed and breakfast here for 24 years. Ros-Guill House is well shielded from the road by evergreen trees and has a small enclosed front garden. The rooms are on the small side, but immaculately clean, and the dining room has views of the castle and the Galtee Mountains. There is also a TV lounge for guests' use. Mrs Moloney, who is a most friendly lady, has won 2 garden awards as well as the 1987 Galtee Regional Breakfast award. Ros-Guill House is on the Dualla Road, three-quarters of a mile from Cashel.

OWNER Evelyn Moloney   OPEN 1 April–1 October   ROOMS 2 double, 2 twin, 1 family (3 en-suite)   TERMS B&B IR£14.50–£17.50 p.p.; reductions for children; single supplement

CLONMEL

Clonanav Farm Guesthouse

Ballymacarbry, Clonmel, Co Waterford

Tel: (052) 36141, Fax: (052) 36141

The Ryans built this long, low house for themselves twenty years ago. With eight children, and now a guesthouse business, they added on to the original building as the need arose. Their house stands in lovely countryside, and is used primarily by fishermen. Andrew is an expert fisherman and an approved fishing instructor. Most of the bedrooms are in a purpose-built wing and are equipped with telephones and bathrooms. The sitting room has a fireplace and TV. Tea and coffee are available in the entrance area, and there are pleasant views from the dining room. Eileen is a very friendly, energetic lady and is very attentive to her guests. For guests not wanting to fish, there are excellent walks nearby. Visa and Access accepted.

OWNER Larry and Eileen Ryan   OPEN 1 February–15 November ROOMS 7 double/twin, 3 single (all en-suite)   TERMS B&B IR£20.00; reductions for children; single supplement; dinner IR£14.00

Woodrooffe House

Cahir Road, Clonmel, Co Tipperary

Tel: (052) 35243

Woodrooffe House is a spacious and elegant house surrounded by a lovely garden full of mature trees and flowers, set on 270 acres of mixed farming. This is a warm and inviting house, and even though it was only built in 1977 it has the ambience of a bygone era. The four spacious en-suite bedrooms are beautifully decorated with matching Sanderson wallpapers and fabrics. Guests enjoy the log fires on chilly evenings. Owner, Anne O'Donnell, is a most gracious host who offers complimentary refreshments on arrival. Evening meals are available, if prearranged. Anne is a good cook; a favourite dish with guests is her baked fish with its delicious sauce, and her mouthwatering desserts, such as pavlova with fresh fruit or orange-coffee cheesecake, are equally popular. There are walks through the farm, and Cahir, Cashel and Clonmel are within driving distance.

OWNER Anna O'Donnell   OPEN March–October   ROOMS 4 double/ twin/family (2 en-suite)   TERMS B&B IR£14.00 p.p.; reductions for children; single supplement; evening meal IR£12.00

NENAGH

Otway Lodge Guest House

Dromineer, Nenagh, Co Tipperary

Tel: (067) 24133 or 24273

Otway Lodge is in a lovely position overlooking Lough Derg. Parts of the house are over 100 years old, as it was formerly part of a barracks. It has been extended and tastefully modernised since then. The rooms are a good size, as are the bathrooms, and are modestly furnished. There is a spacious guest lounge with a peat fire, TV, harp and piano. Frank and Ann enjoy their business and work as a team – they always have a pot of tea on the hob! There is a small shop on the premises offering sweets, lemonade and other items. This is an ideal spot for families and water sports enthusiasts, as there is windsurfing, sailing, waterskiing and trout and coarse fishing available. There are boats for hire.

OWNER Ann and Frank Flannery   OPEN Easter–November
ROOMS 6 double/twin/family (4 en-suite)   TERMS B&B IR£15.00 p.p.; reductions for children; single supplement

Riverrun House

Terryglass, Nenagh, Co Tipperary
Tel: (067) 22125, Fax: (067) 22187

An attractive house standing in its own grounds of 1½ acres, situated in Terryglass – the recipient of the famous Tidy Village award. Tom and Lucy Sanders are an enthusiastic couple, fairly new to the B&B business, having opened in the autumn of 1991. Three of the bedrooms, all of which have telephones, hairdryers and tea-making facilities, are located on the ground floor, tastefully decorated in pretty pastel floral colours with matching fabrics and furnished in pine. Two have pretty lake views. This is a most comfortable house with lots of character, full of interesting antiques. A pleasant 5-minute stroll away is the busy harbour set on the northeast shore of Lough Derg, largest of the lakes on the Shannon system. Riverrun House has a hard tennis court, bicycles for guests' use, and fishing boats and engines for hire. There is an 18-hole golf course close by. Excellent breakfasts are served, including freshly squeezed orange juice, home-baked soda bread and yoghurts, as well as traditional fare. Vegetarian breakfasts available upon request. Evening meals also available. Visa, Access and Mastercard accepted.

OWNER Tom and Lucy Sanders   OPEN All year, except Christmas
ROOMS 2 double, 2 twin, 1 family (all en-suite)   TERMS B&B IR£22.50 p.p.; reductions for children; single supplement

THURLES

Willmount House

Ballingarry, Thurles, Co Tipperary
Tel: (052) 54108

Formerly Pittman's summer home (he of shorthand fame), this country house was built in 1814. Located in a rural setting at the foot of Slievenamon, Willmount House is surrounded by pleasant lawned gardens and entered under an arched bell tower and through a courtyard. The house extends around 3 sides of the courtyard; the comfortable drawing room with open fire and dining room with separate tables take up one side and overlook the garden. The bedrooms are spacious and plainly decorated and furnished. There is a games room with Ping-Pong, pool and darts, and a heated outdoor swimming pool. Courses are available in cooking, creative writing and stencilling. Riding and hunting can be arranged and dogs are welcome. The house has a wine licence. Laundry services available. It is advisable to get directions, but the house is signposted from the Dublin to Cork road.

OWNER Ellen Collinson OPEN All year, except Christmas ROOMS 5 double (1 en-suite) TERMS B&B IR£15.00 p.p.; reductions for children; evening meal IR£15.00; children's menu

TIPPERARY

Arra View

Emly Road, Tipperary, Co Tipperary
Tel: (062) 51879

Anne Cronin is a most accommodating host who is dedicated to ensuring her guests feel welcome. The bedrooms, although a little small, are spotlessly clean. There is an en-suite family room on the ground floor, and all but one of the other rooms have their own bathrooms. There is a pleasant lounge with a TV and a piano, which guests are welcome to play, and a sun lounge for guests' use. The house is located in a scenic area overlooking the Galtee Mountains and the town centre is only a 10-minute walk away, on the Killarney Road. No smoking in the dining room. Pets outside only. Large private car park for guests.

OWNER Anne Cronin OPEN April–31 October ROOMS 3 twin, 1 family (3 en-suite) TERMS B&B IR£14.00 p.p.; reductions for children; single supplement; evening meals IR£14.00

Barronstown House

Emly Road, Tipperary, Co Tipperary
Tel: (062) 55130

Easygoing Mr and Mrs O'Dwyer provide old-fashioned hospitality and comfort at Barronstown House, a lovely old house furnished with antiques, which belonged to Mr O'Dwyer's ancestors. The house is situated in the heart of the Golden Vale, overlooking the Galtee Mountains. Rooms are large and comfortable and there is a quiet spot on the landing, ideal for reading or playing cards. The TV lounge has the original fireplace. The motto of the house, "An Irish home – where every guest is a friend", certainly describes the welcome that guests receive here. A good base for exploring the Glen of Aherlow and Rock of Cashel, and for salmon and trout fishing on the River Suir. The house is located 3 miles (4¹/₂ km) from Tipperary, off the Tipperary/Killarney Road.

OWNER Mr and Mrs J. O'Dwyer   OPEN 1 May–1 September
ROOMS 1 double, 2 twin, 1 family   TERMS B&B IR£15.00 p.p.;
reductions for children; single supplement

Clonmore House

Galbally Road, Tipperary, Co Tipperary
Tel: (062) 51637

An immaculate, detached house set back from the main road on the edge of town. The bedrooms are tastefully decorated and colour-coordinated, with modern fitted wardrobes. Breakfasts are served in the attractive dining room with its pretty lace tablecloths. The spacious lounge/dining room overlooks the gardens, which are available for guests' use. A fire is lit in the lounge on chilly days, and guests may enjoy a hot drink in the evening; a pleasant spot to unwind in after a busy day of sightseeing. On fine days the sun lounge is a popular place to sit. Mary Quinn is a delightful hostess who prides herself on personal service. She is pleased to advise on good local restaurants. There is no need to worry about driving or parking in town, as Clonmore House is just five minutes' walk away. Smoking in the lounge only.

OWNER Mrs Mary Quinn   OPEN 1 April–1 October   ROOMS 2 double, 3 twin, 1 family, (all en-suite)   TERMS B&B IR£14.50 p.p.; reductions for children; single supplement

County Westmeath

Centrally located, this county offers a peaceful and beautiful landscape, excellent fishing and lots of history.

The main attractions are its lakes, the 4 larger ones being loughs Owel, Ennell, Derravaragh and Lene. Beautiful Lough Sheelin is farther north and there are a number of small lakes too, as well as Lough Ree, an expansion of the Shannon, which is now popular for sailing, cruising and coarse fishing. On many of the islands that dot the lakes are remains of early Christian churches.

Mullingar, the county town, is a thriving commercial centre and attractive market town. It is in one of the best cattle-raising districts of Ireland, and is also a great centre for hunting, shooting and fishing.

Athlone is the largest town in the county; originally a fording point of the Shannon, it is now a busy market town, major road and rail terminus, and harbour on the inland waterways system. Athlone Castle, now housing a museum dealing with local history, is a strongly fortified building with many interesting features. It has been a famous military post since its original construction in the thirteenth century.

Lough Derravaragh, one of the most beautiful in County Westmeath, is associated with the most tragic of Irish legendary romances, when the Children of Lir were changed into swans by a jealous stepmother and spent 300 years on its dark waters.

Near Castlepollard is Tullynally Castle, seat of the Earls of Longford, with a spectacular façade of turrets and towers, and at Fore is the most historic Christian site in Westmeath. There are several ruins to see, dating from the tenth century, among them St Fechin's Church, an unusual feature of which is the massive cross-inscribed lintel stone.

ATHLONE

Cluain-Inis

Summerhill, Galway Road, Athlone, Co Westmeath
Tel: (0902) 94202

A friendly, cosy bungalow located off the Galway road 2½ miles (4 km) from town. The lounge is tastefully decorated with matching pink and red fabrics, attractive lights and wall lamps. Tea- and coffee-making facilities are also provided. The bedrooms are all on the ground floor, and are prettily decorated and comfortable. Hairdryers are provided. One double room has an en-suite. An ideal location for touring Clonmacnois and Deer Park, with fishing and golf close by.

OWNER Kathleen Shaw   OPEN 1 April–31 October   ROOMS 1 double/twin/family (1 en-suite)   TERMS B&B IR£14.00 p.p.; reductions for children; single supplement

Riverdale House

Clonown Road, Athlone, Co Westmeath

Tel: (0902) 92480

A turn-of-the-century house pleasantly situated on the Connaught side of the River Shannon in its own grounds, just a few minutes' walk from the town centre. The bedrooms and lounge are large and comfortable, with traditional furnishings, and the house has a warm, old-fashioned atmosphere. All of the bedrooms have a TV, tea- and coffee-making facilities and hairdryers. The stones surrounding the marble fireplace in the lounge were specially made to preserve the character of the house. The front door has beautiful stained-glass depicting a peacock. Mr and Mrs Lyons have been established for over 27 years and were one of the first bed and breakfasts in the area. They have built up an excellent reputation; most of their guests are repeat visitors, and advance reservations are recommended. Riverdale House is just 200 yards from the River Shannon and specialises in coarse-fishing holidays; group rates and holiday packages are available upon request. South of the town lies the ancient monastic settlement of Clonmacnoise, and there is an 18-hole golf course, tennis and walking trails close by.

OWNER Mrs Anne Lyons   OPEN All year   ROOMS 1 double, 2 twin, 1 single, 3 family (2 en-suite)   TERMS B&B IR£15.00 p.p.; reductions for children; single supplement; evening meal IR£12.00.

Shelmalier House

Cartrontroy, Athlone, Co Westmeath

Tel: (0902) 72245, Fax: (0902) 73190

A modern, spacious house standing in its own grounds with an attractive front garden. The 7 bedrooms are beautifully appointed, with firm, comfortable beds, and 2 of them are on the ground floor. All have hairdryers, telephones and TVs. Very much a family-run establishment, with considerable hosts who do everything possible to ensure their guests' comfort. There is a spacious TV lounge. Guests may help themselves to tea and coffee in the sun porch. Jim and Nancy Denby specialise in coarse-fishing holidays, but a warm welcome is extended to all visitors. Excellent evening meals are served, with the emphasis on fresh food and home-baking. There is an 18-hole golf course on the shores of Lough Ree, trail walks, and a heated swimming pool within 10 minutes' walk. Shelmalier is a delightful house offering excellent value. No pets. Visa accepted.

OWNER Jim and Nancy Denby   OPEN All year except Christmas   ROOMS 3 double, 2 twin, 2 family (all en-suite)   TERMS B&B IR£15.00 p.p.; reductions for children; single supplement; evening meal IR£13.00

HORSELEAP

Temple House

Horseleap, Moate, Co Westmeath
Tel: (0506) 35118, Fax: (0506) 35118

Temple House has been in the same family for 3 generations, set among mature trees and gardens on a 140-acre cattle and sheep farm. It was built on the site of a sixth-century monastery, hence the name. This lovely 200–year-old country house with its old-world atmosphere has marble washstands and fireplaces, and brass beds. Bernadette is an excellent cook; dinners are served family-style in the large dining room, featuring farm-fresh meat and vegetables, with delicious homemade desserts. After dinner, guests gather

round the open fire in the lounge, often joined by
Bernadette and Declan. All the bedrooms are now en-suite,
and a new games room and library were added in 1991. All-
inclusive walking, cycling and relaxation holiday packages
are available; rates upon request. Fishing and golfing holidays
at championship courses can be arranged for small groups.
Reservations should be made as much ahead as possible.
Vegetarians catered for if prearranged. There is a wine licence.
An ideal location in which to relax, unwind and enjoy the
best of Ireland. Access, Visa and Mastercard accepted.
Situated 1 mile (1 1/2 km) west of Horseleap village.

OWNER Declan and Bernadette Fagan   OPEN 1 March–30
November   ROOMS 2 double, 1 twin, 1 family (all en-suite)
TERMS B&B IR£22.50 p.p.; reductions for children; single supple-
ment; evening meals IR£15.00

MOATE

Cooleen Country Home

Ballymore Road, Moate, Co Westmeath
Tel: (0902) 81044

This is a well-maintained and very attractive modern bunga-
low in a country setting of 1 1/2 acres. The rooms are good-
sized, tastefully furnished, and decorated with comfortable
beds. A warm welcome is received; guests are treated as one
of the family, and tea or coffee is offered upon arrival at no
charge. Breakfasts, which include fresh home-baked scones,
are served in the lush conservatory on warm days. There is a
guest lounge with a TV where peat fires burn in the evening.
Bicycles are available and there are some lovely walks
winding past the bog. For guests looking for a home-away-
from-home atmosphere, Cooleen is an excellent choice.

OWNER Ethna Kelly   OPEN All year except Christmas   ROOMS 4
double/twin (all en-suite)   TERMS B&B IR£13.50 p.p.; reductions
for children; single supplement

MULLINGAR

Grove House

Blackhall, Mullingar, Co Westmeath
Tel: (044) 41974

Grove House is very centrally located and is found on a
quiet cul-de-sac. Mrs Buckley is a delightful lady who runs

an immaculate and friendly house. There is a comfortable lounge with a TV and fireplace, which is lit at the first sign of a chill in the air. A guest lounge and a tastefully furnished dining room overlook the garden, full of mature shrubs, flowers and a fishpond. All bedrooms have satellite TV and hair dryers. Gladys Buckley has created a real home-away-from-home atmosphere; guests often book in for a night or two and end up staying a week. Gladys enjoys cooking and serves fresh home-baked bread. Seamus Buckley helps out when needed and takes care of the lovely gardens. Light snacks are available upon request at reasonable prices, as well as a cup of tea or coffee just about any time at no charge. Smoking is not permitted in the dining room. No pets in the house.

OWNER Gladys Buckley   OPEN All year, except Christmas
ROOMS 1 double/twin/family (1 en-suite)   TERMS B&B IR£14.00 p.p.; reductions for children

Hilltop

Delvin Road, Rathconnell, Mullingar, Co Westmeath
Tel: (044) 48958, Fax: (044) 48013

An exceptionally well-maintained, spacious, split-level house. Approached by a private gravel drive, the house sits in an elevated position with views of the Sheever Lough in the distance, and of the city at night. The house was specifically designed for bed and breakfast; the bedrooms are all large, with a high standard of decor and with comfortable, firm beds. Breakfasts are served in the bright dining room overlooking pretty countryside. One of the en-suite bedrooms is on the ground floor and has its own entrance. Dympna and Sean are extremely hospitable and helpful, and are happy to assist with itinerary planning. Hilltop has facilities for the angler, including a tackleroom with fridges and drying facilities. Boat hire can also be arranged. No smoking in the dining room. Dinners must be ordered in advance. Situated 2 miles (3 km) from Mullingar.

OWNER Dympna and Sean Casey   OPEN 1 March–1 November
ROOMS 2 double, 2 twin, 1 family (all en-suite)   TERMS B&B from IR£16.00 p.p.; single supplement; evening meal IR£12.50

Keadeen

Irishtown, Longford Road, Mullingar, Co Westmeath
Tel: (044) 48440

There is a comfortable, easygoing atmosphere at Keadeen, a well-maintained bungalow in a quiet location on the edge of town. To quote Madge Nolan, "I have never had a guest I didn't like", which could have something to do with her helpful attitude. The bedrooms are clean and fresh, individually decorated in bright colours, with warm duvets and purple carpets. Breakfast is served from 7.00 to 10.30 am and consists of homemade marmalades, preserves and fresh-baked bread. Dinners available by prior arrangement; vegetarians catered for. Local amenities include golf, fishing, swimming and boating. No smoking in the dining room. No pets. Located 100 yards off the N4 past the county hospital.

OWNER Mrs Madge Nolan   OPEN All year   ROOMS 1 double/twin/family (2 en-suite)   TERMS B&B IR£14.00 p.p.; reductions for children; evening meal IR£11.00

Lough Owel Lodge

Cullion, near Mullingar, Co Westmeath
Tel: (044) 48714, Fax: (044) 48714

Lough Owel Lodge is a most attractive country house approached by a long private drive, standing in 50 acres of farmland. The property extends down to the lake where there are gillie and boats available, as well as windsurfing, and several golf courses are located nearby. The house is well appointed and the spacious, well-furnished TV lounge overlooks the beautiful gardens and hard tennis court, which is available for guests' use. The bedrooms are individually furnished and comfortable; one has a four-poster bed. There are several interesting pieces of antique furniture about. This delightful property in a beautiful setting is an ideal haven of peaceful seclusion and tranquillity. No smoking in the dining room or bedrooms. No pets. Approximately 2¹/₂ miles (4 km) north of Mullingar, signposted at the lake.

OWNER Martin and Aideen Ginnell   OPEN 1 March–1 December   ROOMS 2 double, 1 twin, 1 single, 2 family (all en-suite)   TERMS B&B IR£15.00–£16.00 p.p.; reductions for children; single supplement; evening meal IR£12.00; high tea IR£7.50

Pettiswood House

Mullingar, Co Westmeath
Tel: (044) 48397

An attractive 1940s country house, set in 3 acres of beautiful landscaped grounds, approached by a tree-lined drive. The garden furnishings are for guests' use. The bedrooms are fresh and clean, and all have electric blankets. The elegant dining room, furnished with antiques, is exceptionally pleasant. Sumptuous breakfasts are served, with a wide choice of cereals, unlimited fruit juice, home-baked bread and a full cooked breakfast. Dinners are available, but advance notice is required. Evening snacks are served in the TV lounge. There are several pieces of antique furniture about, including a very nice chaise-longue. Lovely walks, fishing, golf and boating are available close by. Located 1 mile (1½ km) from Mullingar.

OWNER Marie Cox   OPEN All year   ROOMS 2 double, 1 twin, 1 single (2 en-suite)   TERMS B&B IR£15.00 p.p.; reductions for small children; single supplement

Woodlands Farm

Streamstown, Mullingar, Co Westmeath
Tel: (044) 26414

A charming 200–year-old farmhouse surrounded by ornamental trees, on a 120-acre dry cattle farm. Woodlands Farm is a marvellous spot for families; Mrs Maxwell has created a wonderful, informal, welcoming atmosphere. Guests are encouraged to explore the farm and there are free riding ponies for the children. The bedrooms are spacious and there are lots of antique furnishings, including a chaise-longue and a lovely dresser. Guests enjoy sitting around the log fires in the spacious lounge, which has a grand piano, and musical evenings are encouraged. Four of the bedrooms are on the ground floor, 2 are en-suite. There are 2 bathrooms, 2 shower rooms and 4 toilets. Excellent evening meals are served, if prearranged, using fresh homegrown and local produce. Wine licence. Golf and fishing holidays can be organised.

OWNER Mrs M. Maxwell   OPEN 1 March–1 November   ROOMS 2 double, 2 twin, 1 single, 1 family (2 en-suite)   TERMS B&B IR£13.00–£15.00 p.p.; reductions for children

Mornington House

Multyfarnham, Co Westmeath
Tel: (044)72191, Fax: (044) 72338

Mornington House has been the home of the O'Hara family
since 1856: 5 generations of the family have lived here.
Tucked away on a slope above Lough Derravagh, it is
surrounded by mature trees and parkland and ringed by the
hills of north Westmeath. Mornington is an oasis of peace
and tranquillity and an ideal location from which to explore
the midlands; it is within 1¹/₂ hours' drive from Dublin. The
original Manor, built on the site of an ancient castle, was
extended in the late nineteenth century. Today, Mornington
is a gracious family home still furnished with its original
furniture and portraits. Succeeding generations of the family
have added to the collection of family memorabilia. The
house is centrally heated and the reception rooms have open
fires. Anne and Warwick are charming hosts; Anne is an
excellent cook, and superb dinners are served in the candle-
lit dining room, featuring fresh fruit, vegetables and herbs
from the walled garden, with the best of local produce. The
house has a wine licence, enabling guests to enjoy a glass
with their meal. The bedrooms are large, 2 have brass beds,
all have their own bathrooms. Children by arrangement.
Take Castlepollard exit from N4. After 5 miles, turn left in
Crookedwood.

OWNER Warwick and Anne O'Hara   OPEN 16 March–31 October
ROOMS 5 rooms (all en-suite)   TERMS B&B from IR£25.00 p.p.;
single supplement; evening meal IR£18.00

Northern Ireland

County Antrim

County Antrim's attractions are many. The county town of Belfast lies on the shores of Belfast Lough, in a most attractive setting, surrounded by hills that can be seen from most parts of the town. It became a thriving commercial centre and port in the nineteenth century and now has a population of some 300,000, nearly a third of the population of all Northern Ireland. Among the many sights to see in Belfast is the Ulster Museum, which contains the treasures from the wreck of the Spanish Armada vessel, the *Girona*.

The town of Antrim is set back from Lough Neagh, the largest expanse of inland water in the British Isles and famous for its eels. The main fishery is at Toomebridge. One of the best ways to see the lough is from the Shane's Castle Railway at Randalstown, Ireland's only working narrow-gauge railway.

Country Antrim's stretch of coastline is among the most spectacular and scenic in Europe. Carrickfergus to the south, the oldest town in Northern Ireland, is dominated by its castle, while further north lies Larne, an important port, just a two-and-a-half-hour ferry ride from Scotland. Beyond Larne the coast road, built in the 1830s, affords breathtaking views of the coast and cliffs; along this stretch it is possible to see the formation of the earth's outer crust.

The coast road connects each of the 9 famous Glens of Antrim: green valleys running down to the sea, with rivers, waterfalls, wild flowers and birds. From south to north they are: Glenarm, Glencloy, Glenariff, Glenballyeamon, Glenaan, Glencorp, Glendun, Glenshesk and Glentaisie, which are said to mean: glen of the army, glen of the hedges, ploughman's glen, Edwardstown glen, glen of the rush lights, glen of the slaughter, brown glen, sedgy glen, and Taisie's glen (referring to the legendary princess of Rathlin Island). The resort town of Ballycastle is famous for its "Oul' Lammas Fair", which once lasted a week and now takes place over 2 hectic days at the end of August. Ballintoy, a picturesque, Mediterranean-looking fishing village, is one of the prettiest towns on the coast and beyond it is one of the world's most amazing natural wonders, the Giant's Causeway. This is made up of a mass of basalt columns, altogether some 40,000, which are tightly packed together, reaching heights of 40 feet, and which disappear into the sea. They reappear at Staffa Island on the Scottish coast, and all kinds of legends are attached to this natural phenomenon.

Colliers Hall

50 Cushendall Road, Ballycastle, BT54 6QR, Co Antrim
Tel: (012657) 62531

An interesting eighteenth-century pebble-dashed farmhouse offering comfort, excellent value and a homely atmosphere. The bedrooms are spacious, with the washbasins cleverly incorporated into marble washstands, and all have tea- and coffee-making facilities. The house is furnished with a mixture of traditional and antique furniture, and one twin room has handmade beds while another has a four-poster bed. The large TV lounge has an original marble fireplace and is furnished with antiques. Of particular interest is the china cabinet and beautiful marble clock, which was a wedding present given to Mr McCarry's grandmother. There are lovely walks through the woods, with views of the Knocklayde Mountains and Glenshesk Valley. An 18-hole golf course is situated close by. Located 2 miles (3 km) from Ballycastle. No pets. Smoking in lounge only.

OWNER Mrs Maureen McCarry   OPEN 1 April–1 October
ROOMS 3 family, 1 twin, 2 double (2 en-suite)   TERMS B&B
£15.00–£17.00 p.p; reductions for children and pensioners; single supplement; evening meal from £12.00, high tea from £6.00

Drumawillan House

1 Whitepark Road, Ballycastle, BT54 6HH, Co Antrim
Tel: (012657) 62539

An attractive old whitewashed house standing in mature gardens, right on top of the hill above Ballycastle; here one has wonderful views over the town to the sea and to Scotland beyond. The building was once a church school and has been in Mrs Todd's family for some years. It is a comfortable family home, attractively decorated. No smoking. Pets by arrangement.

OWNER Jeanette and Jackson Todd   OPEN All year   ROOMS 1 double, 1 twin, 1 family   TERMS B&B £16.00 p.p.; reductions for children; single supplement; evening meal from £11.00

Fair Head View

26 North Street, Ballycastle, BT54 6BW, Co Antrim
Tel: (012657) 62822

A small, family-run bed and breakfast, situated 2 minutes from the beach and tennis court, with the Ballycastle golf course a little farther away. The bedrooms are clean and simply furnished, and there is a cosy TV lounge with a peat fire, lit at the first sign of a chill in the air. With just 3 bedrooms, Mrs Delargy is able to offer her guests personal service, proferring cups of tea or coffee upon arrival. Fair Head View offers good basic accommodation at reasonable prices. There is a public car park close by. No pets.

OWNER Mrs K. Delargy   OPEN All year   ROOMS 2 double, 1 twin   TERMS B&B £12.50 p.p.; reductions for children

BALLYMONEY

Moore Lodge

Ballymoney, BT53 7NT, Co Antrim
Tel: (012665) 41043

This most attractive, seventeenth-century, historic plantation house has been in the Moore family for nearly 400 years, and is located on the banks of the River Bann. Moore Lodge has been beautifully decorated and furnished. Guests have use of the cosy, lived-in study. The bedrooms are large and all have lovely views. Boats are available to explore the miles of navigable water. No children and no pets.

OWNER Sir William and Lady Moore   OPEN 1 May–1 August
ROOMS 6 double   TERMS B&B from £75.00

BELFAST

Ash-Rowan Town House

12 Windsor Avenue, Belfast, BT9 6EE, Co Antrim
Tel: (01232) 661758, Fax: (01232) 663227

Ash-Rowan Town House is a late-Victorian property in a quiet, tree-lined avenue, situated 10 minutes from the town centre, the King's Hall, Balmoral golf course, Queen's University, the Ulster Museum and the Grand Opera House. The comfortable bedrooms have TVs, tea-makers, bathrobes, linen sheets, telephones, hairdryers, trouser presses and information leaflets. The 2 top-floor rooms are now en-suite, and the others have part bathrooms. This is a most attractive house, with interesting colours and furnishings, and it is cosy and friendly. Breakfasts only are served, but they are substantial, with freshly squeezed orange juice, cereals and home-baked bread, followed by a cooked breakfast. There are flowers and newspapers on the dining room tables. Laundry services are available. Sam and Evelyn have thought of just about everything for their guests, combining all the facilities of a hotel with personal service at a reasonable price. Private parking. No pets. Smoking in some of the bedrooms. Visa, Access and Mastercard accepted.

OWNER Sam and Evelyn Hazlett OPEN All year, except Christmas ROOMS 6 double/twin/single (4 en-suite) TERMS B&B £28.00–£33.00 p.p.; reductions for children; single supplement; evening meal £15.00

The Cottage

377 Comber Road, Dundonald, Belfast, BT16 0XB, Co Antrim

Tel: (01247) 878189

An absolutely charming, low, whitewashed, 250–year-old cottage lying on the Belfast-to-Comber road in open countryside with lovely views. There is a most attractive small rear garden, and one enters the house through a pretty conservatory covered with an enormous passion flower plant which seems to cover half the house as well. The Cottage is owned by the Muldoons, who bought it about 16 years ago as a mostly derelict building and have restored it to a delightful small country retreat. It justifiably became a very popular place to stay, combining proximity to Belfast and rural tranquillity. It has been very prettily decorated and furnished throughout, completely in keeping with its cottage atmosphere. The bedrooms are small, both with antique double beds, pretty wallpaper and fabrics, telephones and hairdryers, and the large breakfast room/lounge with TV and open fireplace is full of character. It is a relaxing, comfortable house with a most delightfully friendly owner. All bedrooms are on the ground floor. Smoking is not permitted.

OWNER Elizabeth Muldoon OPEN All year ROOMS 2 double TERMS B&B £20.00–£35.00

Malone Guest House

79 Malone Road, Belfast, BT9 6SH, Co Antrim
Tel: (01232) 669565

An immaculate, bright and sunny Victorian house in its own gardens, close to the town centre and all amenities. Elsie McClure, a native of Belfast, is a gracious lady, formerly a nurse, who travelled extensively in her profession, staying at B&Bs on her travels. When she opened up her establishment, she wanted to provide all the facilities she had found lacking in other inns, and this has certainly been accomplished. Malone Guest House is a delightful, tastefully furnished house; the lounge has a rich wood fireplace, lots of books to read, and is a pleasant spot to relax in after a busy day. The bedrooms vary in size but are well appointed, all with TVs and tea- and coffee-making facilities. No pets. Not suitable for children. The private parking has been extended to 8 cars.

OWNER Mrs Elsie McClure   OPEN 1 January–1 December
ROOMS 6 twin, 2 single (all en-suite)   TERMS B&B £23.50 p.p.; single supplement

Montpelier

96 Malone Road, Belfast, BT9 6SH, Co Antrim
Tel: (01232) 381831 or 622147

On a main road not far from Queen's University and accessible to central Belfast, Montpelier is a substantial early-Victorian house. The house has belonged to Lord Justice Gibson, Thomas Gilmore (a tea merchant) and the Reverend Hugh Hanna, among others. Mary Carberry, the present owner, bought the house in 1990. The bedrooms are comfortable and individually designed. One large double en-suite is located in the old stables at the rear of the building, and there are 3 en-suite rooms in the main building. Lunch and dinner are available.

OWNER Mary Carberry   OPEN All year   ROOMS 4 double (all en-suite)   TERMS B&B from £35.00 p.p.; evening meal from £20.00

Oakhill Country House

59 Dunmurry Lane, Belfast BT17 9JR, Co Antrim
Tel: (01232) 610658, Fax: (01232) 621566

Only 4 miles (6 km) from Belfast, this country house is approached by a leafy driveway. The first impression is not promising, but walk to the side of the house and you will see that the garden is quite amazing – beautifully designed, with rare and unusual plants, immaculately kept and stretching away into the distance with trees shielding the property from the neighbouring park. The house extends back too, followed by greenhouses and outbuildings. The interior is beautifully decorated and furnished with an enormous formal drawing room and dining room, where May Nobles will put on a dinner party for a group. Upstairs, the 2 front double bedrooms are elegantly furnished and decorated, with bathrooms larger than the average-sized en-suite bedroom. All bedrooms have TVs, telephones, trouser presses and hairdryers. Breakfast is served in a pretty breakfast room, or, during summer, in the conservatory – garden views in every direction. A truly delightful peaceful spot close to Belfast. No pets. No smoking.

OWNER May Noble   OPEN All year, except Christmas   ROOMS 2 double, 1 twin (all en-suite)   TERMS B&B from £35.00; dinner from £15.00

Roseleigh House

19 Rosetta Park, Belfast, BT6 0DL, Co Down
Tel: (01232) 644414

A substantial brick house surrounded by a small garden in a convenient location, close to bus routes leading into the city centre. The McKays bought the house three years ago and completely renovated it. The bedrooms are decorated in pastel colours and are clean, comfortable and all have bathrooms and TVs. The sitting room has leather arm chairs and sofas. Evening meals and lunches, if arranged in advance, are served in the pleasant dining room. There is a car park to the rear of the house.

OWNER Peter and Dorothy McKay   OPEN All year   ROOMS 4 twins, 3 doubles (all en-suite)   TERMS B&B from £19.00; single supplement; dinner from £15.00

Stranmillis Lodge

14 Chlorine Gardens, Belfast, BT9 5DY, Co Antrim
Tel: (01232) 682009, Fax: (01232) 682009

Stranmillis Lodge is a new guest house, opened in 1991 by two sisters-in-law, who both have families and family homes outside Belfast and take it in turns to run the business. They have done an excellent job in doing up the house to a high standard of comfort. Each bedroom has an en-suite bathroom, TV, telephone, trouser press, hairdryer and tea- and coffee-making facilities; a daily newspaper is also provided. There is a pleasant panelled lounge with open fire, and both breakfast and evening meals are served by arrangement in the panelled dining room. The house stands on a bend in the road in the Stranmillis/Malone area close to Queen's University and is handy for shops, restaurants and the city centre. Some car parking is available. Pets are not allowed. Access, Visa and Mastercard accepted.

OWNER J. H. and W. Barton and D. A. Sinnamon   OPEN All year
ROOMS 2 double, 3 twin, 1 single (all en-suite)   TERMS B&B
£28.00 p.p.; single supplement

BROUGHSHANE

Dunaird House

15 Buckna Road, Broughshane, BT42 4NJ, Co Antrim
Tel: (01266) 862117

Built in 1920, this substantial house stands just outside Broughshane. The Grahams bought the house, partly to do B&B and partly because 50 acres went with the house, which extended John's existing farm. They redid the whole house to provide luxuy accommodation. Carpets and wallpapers of all types and varieties adorn every square inch. The Grahams are a friendly young couple, eager to please. Some of the rooms have their original fireplaces and two of the bedrooms are front-facing, with lots of windows and lovely views. All rooms are en-suite with telephones, TV and tea- and coffee-making facilities.

OWNER John and Sylvia Graham   OPEN All year except Christmas
ROOMS 6 double/twin (all en-suite)   TERMS B&B £20.00; single
supplement

BUSHMILLS

Auberge de Seneirl

28 Ballyclough Road, Bushmills, BT57 8UZ, Co Antrim
Tel: (012657) 41536

This famous French restaurant is housed in what was once an old schoolhouse. Auberge de Seneirl has pleasant views and is close to the scenic Antrim coast and the Bushmills distillery. The building has been extended and renovated in a rather dark, French rustic style. The focus is on the restaurant and the food, but to help those who come from far away to enjoy a meal, there are 5 comfortable, attractively decorated rooms, all en-suite and with TVs, and one suite with a sitting room area and a jacuzzi bath in the bathroom. There's also an indoor swimming pool, sauna and sunbed. Mr. Defres comes from Provence, and Mrs Defres lectures in catering. Diners Club and American Express accepted.

OWNER Mr and Mrs B. E. Defres   OPEN All year   ROOMS 5 doubles, 1 suite (all en-suite)   TERMS B&B £21.50–£37.00 p.p.; single supplement; dinner £16.00–£20.00

Montalto Guest House

5 Craigaboney Road, off Priestland Road, Bushmills, BT57 8XD, Co Antrim
Tel: (012657) 31257

This large nineteenth-century farmhouse on 100 acres of mixed farming is in an elevated position, with beautiful views of the surrounding countryside and the sea. A superb combination of a beautiful setting and a most accommodating host, Mrs Taggart, who spends a lot of time ensuring that everything is just right for her guests. Montalto was one of the first B&Bs in the area. The spotless bedrooms are simply furnished, and the house, which is bright and airy, has a lounge and conservatory. There are a couple of shower rooms and 2 bathrooms. Of special interest is the monk seat in the hallway. Montalto is just a few minutes to the old Bushmills Distillery, Dunluce Castle and the Giant's Causeway, with golf, fishing and lovely walks close by. Located off the Bushmills-to-Coleraine road. No pets.

OWNER Mrs Dorothy Taggart   OPEN 1 March–1 November   ROOMS 2 double, 2 single (2 en-suite)   TERMS B&B from £18.00 p.p.; single supplement

White Gables

83 Dunluce Road, Bushmills, Co Antrim
Tel: (012657) 31611

A modern whitewashed house perched on a clifftop with spectacular views, just off the main road. White Gables is very close to Dunluce Castle and is only 4 miles (6 km) from the Giant's Causeway and 2 miles (3 km) from the Bushmills Distillery. The rooms are very comfortable and well furnished and all have lovely views. The pleasant sitting room, where informal suppers are shared with the family, and the dining room, where breakfast and dinner are served, also enjoy the same view. This is a very popular place, so early bookings are recommended. No pets.

OWNER Mrs Ria Johnston   OPEN 1 April–1 October   ROOMS 1 double, 2 twin, 1 single (3 en-suite)   TERMS B&B £21.00 p.p.; reductions for children; evening meal £10.00

CRUMLIN

Caldhame Lodge

102 Moira Road, Nutts Corner, Crumlin, BT29 4HG, Co Antrim
Tel: (01849) 423099

The McKavanaghs built this house for themselves two years ago and then decided to start a B&B business. It is just off the main Moira Road, in its own grounds, and is only five minutes from the Airport. It is comfortable and pleasantly furnished with brand-new furniture. All rooms have bathrooms, TVs, hairdryers and tea- and coffee-making facilities. Mrs McKavanagh is a friendly lady with 3 small children.

OWNER Mrs Anne McKavanagh   OPEN All year   ROOMS 3 double/single, 1 family (all en-suite)   TERMS B&B £16.00; evening meals £10.00; packed lunches available

Keef Halla

20 Tully Road, Nutts Corner, Crumlin, BT29 4AH, Co Antrim
Tel: (01232) 825491

The house got its name, which means "welcome" in Arabic, because Charles Kelly used to work in Saudi Arabia and bought the house with the money he earned there. Keef Halla is an old country house that has been renovated and recently extended. The comfortable sitting room has an open fire, leather sofa and chairs, and leads into the dining room. All bedrooms are en-suite, with TVs and tea- and coffee-making facilities. Evening meals, if arranged in advance. The house stands just off the main road, five minutes from Belfast International Airport.

OWNER Charles and Siobhan Kelly   OPEN All year   ROOMS 6 double/twin (1 en-suite)   TERMS B&B £14.50; single supplement; dinner from £10.00

CUSHENDALL

Glendale

46 Coast Road, Cushendall, BT44 0RX, Co Antrim

Tel: (012667) 71495

An attractive, white, pebble-dashed house on the outskirts of the village, approached by a private drive, in a peaceful location with views of the Antrim plateau and the sea. The house is well maintained and comfortably furnished. Mary O'Neill is an accommodating host and Mr O'Neill, who works on the Larne-Cairnryan ferry, enjoys outlining sight-seeing itineraries for guests. Breakfasts only are served, but there are several venues for eating in the area.

OWNER Mrs Mary O'Neill   OPEN All year   ROOMS 1 double, 5 family (4 en-suite)   TERMS B&B £14.00–£16.00 p.p.; reductions for children under 12

GIANT'S CAUSEWAY

Hillcrest Country House

306 Whitepark Road, Giant's Causeway, BT57 8SN, Co Antrim

Tel: (012657) 31577, Fax: (012657) 31577

Occupying a spectacular position, Hillcrest is an ideal base for touring the Antrim Coast. It lies halfway between Bush-mills and the Giant's Causeway, and is renowned for its cuisine. It also offers four comfortable en-suite bedrooms, two of which have sea views. The lounge is smartly decorated, with a bar at one end. The dining room is immaculately laid out, with enough windows for everyone to enjoy the view. Winners of the Galtee Irish Breakfast Awards 1991, '92, '93 and '94.

OWNER Mr and Mrs Michael McKeever   OPEN February–December   ROOMS 4 double/twin (all en-suite)   TERMS B&B from £22.50; single supplement; dinner from £16.00

LARNE

Cairnview

13 Croft Heights, Ballygally, Larne, BT40 2QS, Co Antrim
Tel: (01574) 583269

A modern house in an area of newer buildings standing above the coast road, with views of the sea and the Glens of Antrim. There is an open-plan sitting/dining room, and the bedrooms have TVs and tea- and coffee-making facilities. Tourism Award Winner. Convenient to Larne, which is only 4 miles (6 km) away, and 500 metres from the beach. Breakfast only is served. No smoking and no pets. Cairndhu Golf Club is one mile away.

OWNER Mrs Jennifer Lough   OPEN All year   ROOMS 2 double, 2 family (2 en-suite)   TERMS B&B from £16.00 p.p.; reductions for children and senior citizens; single supplement available

MUCKAMORE

The Beeches

10 Dunadry Road, Muckamore, BT41 4RR, Co Antrim
Tel: (01849) 433161, Fax: (01849) 433161

Standing in quite a sizeable garden, this Edwardian country house is just off the A6 between Antrim and Templepatrick, 5 miles (7$^{1}/_{2}$ km) from Belfast airport. The Allens, a very friendly couple, offer comfortable accommodation, and good home-cooked food – they have won a Taste of Ulster award for the past 5 years. Two of the bedrooms are in the main part of the house and the remaining 3 in a new pur-pose-built extension. All rooms have tea- and coffee-making facilities, TVs, hairdryers and trouser presses. Evening meals can be arranged if booked in advance. No smoking and no pets. All major credit cards accepted.

OWNER Mrs Marigold Allen   OPEN All year   ROOMS 3 double, 2 single (all en-suite)   TERMS B&B £40.00–£52.00 p.p.; reductions for children

PORTBALLINTRAE

Bayhead Guest House

8 Bayhead Road, Portballintrae, BT57 8RZ, Co Antrim
Tel: (012657) 31441, Fax: (012657) 31725

Built in 1783 as the estate manager's house, Bayhead House is right on the seafront and commands fabulous views over the rest of the town and out to sea. The stables have been turned into flats and the guest house was taken over a year ago by the Cookes, who used to own the next-door Bayview Hotel. They bought the guest house to have a quieter and better lifestyle, and are personable and solicitous hosts. The bedrooms are functional and two of them have sea views. The large, front-facing sitting room doubles as a breakfast room, with several individual tables. There is also a small sitting room on the first floor, overlooking the sea.

OWNER Barbara and Trevor Cooke   OPEN March–October
ROOMS 6 double/twin, 2 family (all en-suite)   TERMS B&B
£17.50–£19.50; single supplement

PORTRUSH

Ardnaree

White Rocks, 105 Dunluce Road, Portrush, BT56 8NB,
Co Antrim
Tel: (01265) 823407

A modern villa-style house on the Causeway road, 1¹/₂ miles (2¹/₂ km) from Portrush. Ardnaree, meaning "top of the hill", certainly describes the location. This must be one of the best views in Northern Ireland; it overlooks the ocean, the Donegal hills and an 18-hole championship golf course. The bedrooms are fairly small, but they are clean and comfortable, all with TVs. There's a guest lounge with TV and a bright dining room where substantial breakfasts are served at separate tables. Elsie Rankin worked in a hotel before opening up her home to visitors, and she certainly knows how to make guests feel at home. Established over 20 years now, this is a popular venue, so early reservations are recommended. There is one ground-floor bedroom. Smoking in the lounge only. Pets outside.

OWNER Mrs Elsie Rankin   OPEN All year except Christmas
ROOMS 3 double, 1 twin, 1 single (2 en-suite)   TERMS B&B £18.00
p.p.; single supplement

Ballymagarry House

46 Leeke Road, Portrush, BT56 8NH, Co Antrim
Tel: (01265) 823737

Ballymagarry House, meaning "house of the enclosed garden",
stands on the site of the home of the Earls of Antrim, who
moved here after the kitchen in Dunluce Castle, the ruins of
which are just below the house, fell into the sea. A converted
sixteenth-century barn is the central feature of the house,
now an enormous drawing room with a large brick fireplace.
The rest of the house has been built around it, slowly
evolving over a period of about 4 years. The ruins of the
walled garden stand in the grounds, purchased when the
Leckeys learned that this historical site was to be torn down
for farmland. Alyson Leckey used to work for Ulster Tele-
vision and is now studying for a philosophy degree. Her
creativity is evidenced by the unusual and interesting decor
and furnishings. There is a great playroom for small children
and a play area outside, which children are invited to share
with Alyson and Paul's 3 children. All the bedrooms have
views over County Donegal. Paul, a keen golfer, would be
happy to advise on golf courses. Alyson is an excellent cook
and prepares an imaginative breakfast selection. On clear
days there are views of the Glens of Antrim and the sea. No
smoking in public rooms and no pets. Off the Ballybogey
Road, or the Coast Road, 2 miles (3 km) from Portrush.

OWNER Alyson Leckey   OPEN 1 April–30 September   ROOMS 2
twin, 2 suites (all en-suite)   TERMS B&B from £17.50–25.00 p.p.;
reductions for children; single supplement

Glenkeen Guest House

59 Coleraine Road, Portrush, BT56 8HR, Co Antrim
Tel: (01265) 822279

This guest house, set back a little from a busy main road
and a short distance from the town centre, has won the title
of Most Attractive Guest House in Northern Ireland. Mrs
Little is a friendly and efficient lady who has been in the bed-
and-breakfast business for ten years. The rooms are comfort-
able and attractively decorated, and all have bathrooms, TV
and tea- and coffee-making facilities. Breakfast and evening
meals are served in the dining room and the pleasant sitting
room has comfortable chairs and sofas. Credit cards accepted.

OWNER Mrs R. Little   OPEN All year   ROOMS 9 twin/double (all en-suite)   TERMS B&B £18.00; single supplement; dinner £5.00

Maddybenny Farm

Loguestown Road, Portrush, BT52 2PJ, Co Antrim
Tel: (01265) 823394, Fax: (01265) 843403

Maddybenny Farm, meaning "sanctified or holy post", dates from the 1600s. It was built as a plantation house on lands belonging to the Earl of Antrim. The first Presbyterian Minister, Rev. Gabriel Cornwall, lived here. Added onto over the years, the house floor plan is unique in that the integral part of the house is in the centre and one can walk completely around the house from the inside. The house is approached up a long track and stands in a wonderful, rural position. It is part of a big complex of buildings: the farm, stables, and 6 self-catering cottages. Newly opened is the riding school, with tuition available for guests by an international rider. Maddybenny Farm is a comfortable, relaxed place – a bright and spacious house – with the dining room and drawing room recently refurbished. The bedrooms are all en-suite and very large, each capable of sleeping 4 people. Rosemary White, the owner, is a marvellous host with a wonderful sense of humour. She also serves the best breakfast in Ireland, a claim backed up by her Irish Breakfast awards: fresh trout, fruit juice, hot and cold cereals, fresh fruit, homemade scones, fresh-baked breads – the menu goes on and on. Maddybenny has a games room and is very near the Royal Portrush Golf Club, the Giant's Causeway, University and beaches. Pets outside only. Access, Visa and Mastercard accepted.

OWNER Mrs Rosemary White   OPEN All year, except Christmas and New Year   ROOMS 3 double/twin/family (3 en-suite)
TERMS B&B £22.50 p.p.; reductions for children; single supplement

County Armagh

County Armagh is the smallest and most varied county in Northern Ireland, ranging from magnificent mountain scenery in the south to rich fruit-growing country in the north, interspersed with small lakes and dairy farms.

Armagh, the ancient capital of Ulster and former great centre of learning, has been the spiritual capital of Ireland for 1,500 years and is the seat of both Protestant and Catholic archbishops. There is little left to see of its early days, the architecture today being predominantly Georgian. The two cathedral churches are prominent features of the city. The Church of Ireland stands on the hill where St Patrick built his stone church, and the twin spires of the Catholic Cathedral of St Patrick, which was finished in 1873, rise from the opposite hill.

In the south of Armagh the mountains of Slieve Gullion contain an unspoilt area of small villages and beautiful scenery. Crossmaglen has the largest market square in Europe and has become the centre of the recently revived lace-making industry. There is an enormous open-air market every Sunday at Jonesborough.

Whilst driving down some country lane you might come across the great Armagh game, road bowls, which is shared with the county of Cork. The object is to hurl a metal bowl weighing 1³/₄ lbs (1kg) as far as possible, covering several miles in the shortest number of shots. Children are dispatched ahead to warn motorists.

The orchard of Ireland, rich fruit-growing country in the northeast, is at its best in May; Apple Blossom Sunday takes place in late May.

ARMAGH

Clonhugh Guest House

College Hill, Armagh, BT61 9DF, Co Armagh

Tel: (01861) 522693

Guests are well taken care of here by Mrs McKenna, a kindly lady who welcomes guests as friends. Clonhugh House is a wisteria-covered 1930s residence set back off the road in a lovely garden. Mrs McKenna is very interested in antiques, as evidenced by the antique furnishings, paintings, china and her collection of over 100 teapots. The bright, airy bedrooms are nicely decorated, and there is one ground-floor en-suite room, suitable for wheelchair access. There are no set times for breakfast, which is served in the attractive dining room with its original fireplace. Tea and biscuits are served in the evening in the cheery lounge, where guests are often joined by Mrs McKenna. Within walking distance of town and all amenities. No smoking in the bedrooms. No pets.

OWNER Mrs P. McKenna OPEN All year ROOMS 2 double, 2

twin, 1 family (1 en-suite)   TERMS B&B £15.00 p.p.; reductions for children; single supplement

Dean's Hill

34 College Hill, Armagh, BT61 9DF, Co Armagh

Tel: (01861) 524923

This substantial Georgian country house was built by a dean from the cathedral in 1760 and it has been in Mr. Armstrong's family since 1870. The house has been restored and offers a large four-poster room, an enormous twin-bedded room and a single room with a newly created large bathroom. Guests have use of a cosy library/study/TV room with comfortable chairs and an open fire. Eighty acres of farmland surround the house, which is ideal for walks. Dean's Hill is located close to the centre of Armagh and is in a superb position for visiting all the local places of interest.

OWNER Jill Armstrong   OPEN All year   ROOMS 1 double, 1 twin, 1 single (all with private bath)   TERMS B&B from £22.00

Padua House

63 Cathedral Road, Armagh, BT61 7QX, Co Armagh

Tel: (01861) 522039 or 523584, Fax: (01861) 527426

Guests are made to feel like part of the family at Padua House. Mr and Mrs O'Hagan are a friendly, welcoming couple who thoroughly enjoy their visitors. The family lounge is shared with guests, who are encouraged to join the owners after a busy day's touring. A hot drink is almost always available, and the O'Hagans are always happy to assist guests with itineraries, recommendations on places to eat, etc. The accommodation is clean and basic; all the bedrooms have a TV. Padua House, built with red brick, is opposite the playing fields and beside St Patrick's Cathedral. Substantial breakfasts are served in the dining room, which has a beautiful antique chaise-longue. Street parking and limited private parking available. No smoking in the bedrooms and no pets.

OWNER Kathleen O'Hagan   OPEN All year except Christmas ROOMS 1 double, 1 twin, 1 family   TERMS B&B £12.00 p.p.; reductions for children; evening meal £4.00

Ballinahinch House

47 Ballygroobany Road, Richhill, BT61 9NA, Co Armagh
Tel: (01762) 870081

On a 120-acre working arable and beef farm, this beautiful early-Victorian house has an old-world atmosphere. The rooms are all spacious, and there are antique and traditional furnishings throughout. The comfortable bedrooms are individually decorated and furnished, one with a coronet (decorative bed canopy). The lounge is large, as is the dining room, which has the original black slate fireplace, and both have recently been refurbished. Exceptionally high standards prevail throughout this lovely home, with its informal and welcoming atmosphere. The owners, John and Elizabeth Kee, are a delightful couple who have been lovingly restoring the house to its original splendour. A peaceful location with lovely walks close by. There is a newly landscaped acre of gardens to the front of the house. No smoking and no pets. To locate Ballinahinch House, turn off the A3 at Junction B131, take second road on the left and continue on over the crossroad; house is approximately 1 mile (1¹/₂ km) on the left.

OWNER Mr and Mrs J. E. Kee   OPEN 1 April–1 September
ROOMS 2 double, 1 twin, 1 single   TERMS B&B £14.00 p.p.; single supplement

County Down

A county rich in monuments of antiquity, County Down has been subject to many invasions throughout its history, the fiercest one of all from the Vikings in the ninth century.

Legend has it that St Patrick landed here in AD 432 at the place where the Slaney River flows into Strangford Lough. In the 30 years between his arrival in Ireland and AD 461, when he died in his abbey at Saul, St Patrick converted the pagan Irish to Christianity.

The Ards Peninsula, bordered by Strangford Lough to the west and the Irish Sea to the east, is a narrow strip of land with a bracing climate, reputedly the sunniest and driest part of the North. It has some charming villages and towns that were first settled by the Scots and English. Bangor was a famous centre of learning from the sixth century, until it was devastated by the Vikings in the ninth century. It was from here that the missionaries St Columbanus, St Gall and many others set off to bring Christianity to the rest of Europe.

The breezy coast road runs from Bangor past Ballycopeland – the only working windmill in Ireland – past the pretty village of Kearney to the attractive town of Portaferry, where the 5-mile-long ferry ride to Strangford affords lovely views up Strangford Lough. The Lough is a famous bird sanctuary and wildlife reserve, and the small rounded hills, called "drumlins", that cover North Down are to be found in Strangford Lough, appearing as small islands. Amongst the historic places to visit are Castle Ward, built by the first Lord Bangor in 1765, and Mount Stewart, the childhood home of Lord Castlereagh, a former British Foreign Secretary. Out of the 4 Cistercian abbeys in medieval County Down, 3 were built around the Lough: Inch Abbey, Grey Abbey and Comber.

Downpatrick, at the southern tip of Strangford Lough, is an attractive Georgian town and contains the burial site of St Patrick, which is in the graveyard of the Church of Ireland Cathedral.

The Mourne Mountains, the best-known mountains in Ireland, cover a small area, 15 miles (22^1/$_2$ km) long and 8 miles (12 km) wide, with 12 rounded peaks. The barren peak of Slieve Donard, climbing steeply to 2,796 feet, dominates this peaceful landscape, which is a paradise for walkers. From the summit you can see the Isle of Man, the Belfast hills and Lough Neagh. There are also two artificial lakes or reservoirs that supply Belfast's water. These are surrounded by a huge dry stone wall over 6 feet (2m) high and 22 miles (33 km) long. The Mourne Wall Walk attracts thousands of walkers from all over the world each June.

The coast south from Newcastle, a lively seaside resort, was notorious for smuggling in the eighteenth century. Newry was once a prosperous mercantile town with large town houses and public buildings, as well as the earliest Protestant church in Ireland, St Patrick's.

BANGOR

Carrig-Gorm

27 Bridge Road, Helen's Bay, Bangor, BT19 1TS, Co Down

Tel: (01247) 853680

A rambling, old white house, standing in its own grounds on the edge of Helen's Bay village. It is thought that the oldest wing of the house dates back around 300 years, and the newest, which includes the elegant, recently refurbished drawing room, from 1870. Some of the older furnishings have a rather worn appearance, but the house exudes a warm, friendly atmosphere. There are sea views from all bedrooms, which have TVs, hairdryers and tea- and coffee-making facilities. Breakfast only is served in the dining room, and guests tend to sit around the open fire in the well lived-in, panelled hall, and in the new conservatory during fine weather. No smoking in the bedrooms or dining room, and no pets.

OWNER Elizabeth Eves   OPEN All year, except Christmas
ROOMS 1 twin, 1 single, 1 family (1 en-suite)   TERMS B&B
£20.00–£25.00 p.p.; single supplement

DOWNPATRICK

Havine Farm Guest House

51 Ballydonnell Road, Downpatrick, BT30 8EP, Co Down
Tel: (01396) 851242

A comfortable, eighteenth-century, pebble-dashed farmhouse with 125 acres of land. The bedrooms are small and cosy, with sloping wooden ceilings and tea- and coffee-making facilities. Mrs Macauley tries to think of everything for her guests' comfort: sewing kits, dressing gowns, slippers, etc. Little wonder that this is a highly acclaimed farmhouse that has received an award for hospitality. Meals are imaginative and nicely presented, with fresh home-cooking, including delicious desserts and homemade gooseberry pickle. Evening snacks are also offered, plus tea and homemade cakes. There are 2 lounges, one with a TV and one for relaxing or reading in. Havine is a place you will look forward to returning to. Pets outside only. No smoking in the bedrooms. Located on the Downpatrick Road 2¼ miles (3½ km) from Clough; turn right at Tyrella – house is 2 miles (3 km) along on left.

OWNER Mrs Myrtle Macauley   OPEN All year, except Christmas
ROOMS 2 double, 1 single, 1 family   TERMS B&B £12.50–£13.00
p.p.; reductions for children; evening meals £10.00

Tyrella House

Downpatrick, BT30 8SU, Co Down
Tel: (01396) 851422, Fax: (01396) 851422

A large, elegant country house, with a porticoed, classical

façade, standing in 300 acres of grounds stretching down to the sea; Tyrella House owns a private beach. David, whose father bought the property in the late 1940s, takes care of the cattle and sheep farm. Sally looks after their two small children and likes to hunt. The grounds include a private event course and also a point-to-point course, which is used a couple of times a year. Horses are available for beach, forest or mountain rides, or guests are welcome to bring their own horses. Croquet and tennis on a grass court are also available. Most of the house dates from around the eighteenth century, with the Georgian front added in the early nineteenth century. The house has a welcoming feeling, with a large hallway and stairs leading up to the three large bedrooms, 2 with en-suite bathrooms and featuring pre-war fittings. Dinner is served by candlelight in the elegant dining room. There is also a TV room. No smoking in bedrooms and no pets. Bookings should be made in advance and it is advisable to get directions.

OWNER David and Sally Corbett   OPEN All year, except Christmas   ROOMS 3 double/twin/family (2 en-suite)   TERMS B&B £35.00–£40.00 p.p.; single supplement; evening meals from £21.00

DROMORE

Sylvan Hill House

76 Kilntown Road, Dromore, BT25 1HS, Co Down
Tel: (01846) 692321

This listed one-and-a-half-storey Georgian house built in 1781 stands in beautiful gardens with mature trees and panoramic views of the Mourne and Dromara mountains. The 3 very large bedrooms, all with tea-makers, overlook the garden, and furnishings are a mixture of antique and traditional, with decor in soft pastel colours. Mr and Mrs Coburn join their guests for dinner. Mrs Coburn is a gourmet cook, and all breads and desserts are homemade. A special treat at breakfast is her elder-flower marmalade. An absolutely wonderful opportunity to experience gracious living in a peaceful and tranquil atmosphere. To find the house, go north from Dromore, turn left off the A1 up Connolystown Road and drive up Kilntown Road; the house is ¹/₂ mile on the right.

OWNER Elise Coburn   OPEN All year   ROOMS 2 double, 1 twin (2 en-suite)   TERMS B&B £20.00 p.p.; single supplement; evening meal £13.00

Ardshane Country House

5 Bangor Road, Holywood, BT18 0NU, Co Down
Tel: (01232) 422044, Fax: (01232) 427506

This large, Edwardian brick family home stands in most
attractive mature gardens. It is approached up a driveway off
the main road at the Bangor end of Holywood, behind the
Presbyterian church. Ardshane means "hill of John" and it is
built on the 800–year-old campsite of King John's army. It is
a restful, spacious and elegant house, beautifully appointed,
with every comfort. The bedrooms are large, with modern
bathrooms, showers, telephones, hairdryers, trouser-presses,
TVs and tea- and coffee-making facilities. There is a TV
lounge and an elegant dining room with a marble fireplace
where table d'hôte dinners are served at separate tables by
waiters and waitresses dressed in Edwardian clothes. The
house is well suited for disabled guests. Ardshane has a wine
licence. Visa, Access, American Express and Eurocard
accepted

OWNER Judith Caughey   OPEN All year   ROOMS 3 double, 3 twin, 2
single, 1 family (8 en-suite)   TERMS B&B £22.50–£65.00 p.p.;
reductions for children; evening meal £16.00

Rayanne House

60 Demesne Road, Holywood, BT18 9EX, Co Down
Tel: (01232) 425859

Standing in its own grounds, Rayanne House enjoys lovely
views across Belfast Lough to Carrickfergus and the Antrim
Hills. It is a substantial brick house dating from the nine-
teenth century that has recently been taken over by the
McClelland family, owners of the successful Schooner
Restaurant in Holywood. Their culinary exploits can also be
enjoyed at Rayanne, as can the six comfortable en-suite
rooms, all of which have TVs, hairdryers, fresh fruit and a
hospitality tray. The restaurant is open to non-residents.
The house was previously a guest house and has been
stylishly revamped by Raymond and Anne. There are two
sitting rooms and a dining room which are comfortable,
informal and filled with all sorts of china and knick-knacks.
There is an excellent breakfast choice and guests are offered
every imaginable extra, such as a laundry service, a video

library, babysitting and mimcom telephone for the deaf. You can be assured of a warm welcome, good food and comfort at Rayanne House. Visa, American Express and Access accepted.

OWNER Raymond and Anne McClelland OPEN All year ROOMS 6 double/twin/family (all en-suite) TERMS B&B from £35.00; reductions for children; single supplement; dinner from £20.00

KILKEEL

Heath Hall

160 Moyadd Road, Kilkeel, BT34 4HJ, Co Down

Tel: (016937) 62612

A turn-of-the-century, stone-built farmhouse set in 16 acres of farmland with sheep and cattle. Heath Hall is ideally situated, with views of the sea and Mourne Mountains. The interior of the house was completely renovated a few years ago. New windows were installed, and the house was attractively decorated. The lounge has the original marble fireplace and a TV. There is also a snooker room. The house was formerly run as a bed and breakfast by Mrs McGlue's mother-in-law and has a good reputation for offering good value meals and accommodation. There is no licence, but guests are welcome to bring their own wine. Some of the rooms have harbour views. Evening meals must be prearranged. Pets outside only. Located on the main Hilltown Road 1½ miles (1½ km) north of Kilkeel.

OWNER Mrs Mary McGlue OPEN All year ROOMS 1 double, 1 twin, 1 single TERMS B&B £12.50 p.p.; reductions for children; evening meal £7.00

Wyncrest Guest House

30 Main Road, Kilkeel, BT34 4NU, Co Down

Tel: (016937) 63012

This small 16-acre farm lies on the main road on the edge of the village of Ballymartin, between Kilkeel and Newcastle. Wyncrest has been in the Adair family for some years, and was recently renovated and extended, giving it a modern appearance. It is close to the sea and is a comfortable house with attractive decor. Mrs Adair is a most friendly lady who in 1991 won both the Taste of Ulster award and the National Galtee Breakfast award. There is a sitting room, and evening meals are served in the large dining room at separate tables. No smoking in the bedrooms and no pets.

OWNER Mrs Irene Adair   OPEN Easter–1 October   ROOMS 1 family, 1 double, 2 twin (all en-suite)   TERMS B&B £19.50 p.p.; reductions for children; single supplement; evening meal £13.00

NEWCASTLE

The Briers

39 Middle Tullymore Road, Newcastle, BT33 0JJ, Co Down

Tel: (013967) 24347 or 24067

A 200–year-old farmhouse, once part of Lord Roden's estate, set in 2 acres. Located half a mile off the main road and 1½ miles (2½ km) from Newcastle, only the twittering birds and visiting squirrels and rabbits break up the silence. The Briers is a low, whitewashed and very pretty house decorated with colourful hanging baskets. The house was almost totally derelict until 8 years ago, when it was lovingly restored. There are thick stone walls, beamed ceilings, and the original fireplace made from local stone. The delightful bedrooms have a mixture of pine and antique furnishings with matching fabrics. A new wing has been added, providing 6 extra bedrooms, 2 on the ground floor suitable for the disabled. The upstairs twin bedroom is very spacious and has a beamed pitched roof. There is a lovely garden, a newly planted arboretum and a sun porch for guests' use. Horse-riding and fishing are available close by. There is no licence,

but guests are welcome to bring their own wine. No pets.
Not suitable for children under 12.

OWNER Mrs Mary Bowater   OPEN All year   ROOM 9 twin/double
(all en-suite)   TERMS B&B £25.00 p.p.; evening meals from
£15.00; high tea £8.00

NEWTOWNARDS

Ballycastle House

20 Mountstewart Road, Newtownards, BT22 2AL,
Co Down

Tel: (01247) 788357

A warm welcome always awaits you at Ballycastle House,
the comfortable home of Mr and Mrs Deering. The house
was built over 150 years ago and is set in 40 acres of lovely
grounds that were once part of the Mount Stewart estate.
The bedrooms have some interesting furniture and the guest
lounge features the original fireplace. Mr Deering collects
and restores old farm machinery and tractors. A conserva-
tory has recently been added. The house is minutes from the
sea, with lovely walks close by, and can be found off the A20,
four miles south of Newtownards.

OWNER Margaret Deering   OPEN All year   ROOMS 2 double, 1
family (all en-suite)   TERMS B&B from £18.00; reductions for
children

Edenvale House

130 Portaferry Road, Newtownards, BT22 2AH, Co Down

Tel: (01247) 814881

Approached up a long driveway, Edenvale House is a small
Georgian country house standing above Strangford Lough. It
stands in its own grounds surrounded by fields and is im-
maculately kept, both inside and out. Diane Whyte is a
welcoming host, and the atmosphere is informal and relaxed.
The house has been beautifully furnished and decorated with
great taste, and there are lovely views from the first-floor rooms.
Guests generally prefer to have breakfast in the large kitchen
at the big kitchen table. Diane's daughter looks after the livery
business, and guests are welcome to bring their horses. The
beautifully kept stables and barn lie to the side of the house.

OWNER Diane Whyte   OPEN All year   ROOMS 3 double/twin (all
en-suite)   TERMS B&B £20.00–£23.00; single supplement

Mrs Marie Adair's

22 The Square, Portaferry, BT22 1LW, Co Down
Tel: (01247) 728412

A spotless house located in the town square within walking distance of the ferry, shops and restaurants. The bedrooms are large and modestly furnished. The family unit has an en-suite room with 2 beds and an adjoining single. There's also a comfortable TV lounge. The house is much larger than it appears from the front, as all of the bedrooms are in an extension to the rear of the house. Street parking available. No smoking in the bedrooms. No pets.

OWNER Tommy and Marie Adair   OPEN All year   ROOMS 2 double/twin/single/family (en-suite)   TERMS B&B £13.00 p.p.; reductions for children

County Fermanagh

County Fermanagh is lake or land – one third of the county is under water – and is traversed by the Erne River, which meanders its way across the forested county into a huge lake dotted with drumlins. A paradise for fishing, boating and other water-related activities, Lough Erne is a magnificent, 50–mile-long (75 km) waterway offering uncongested cruising opportunities with 154 islands and many coves and inlets to explore. It has an interesting mix of pagan and Christian relics and traditions that have withstood the centuries.

The medieval town of Enniskillen is built on a bridge of land between Upper and Lower Lough Erne, and its origins go back to prehistory, when it was on the main highway between Ulster and Connaught. The County museum, housed in the Castle keep, displays the brilliant uniforms, colours and Napoleonic battle trophies of the famous Inniskilling Regiment who fought at Waterloo.

Amongst the many islands to visit, Devenish is particularly interesting, with its perfect twelfth-century round tower, tiny church and remains of a fifteenth-century Augustinian abbey. In the cemetery of the largest island, Boa, are 2 ancient stone Janus idols, thought to date from the first century. Belleek is famous both for its fishing and its china, which comes mostly in the form of *objets d'art*. Two of

Northern Ireland's most attractive Georgian houses are to be found in Fermanagh – Castle Coole, a neo-classical mansion with Paladian features, built in 1795 for the Earl of Belmore, and Florencecourt House, seat of the Earls of Enniskillen, which has wonderful rococo plasterwork.

BALLINAMALLARD

Jamestown

Magheracross, Ballinamallard, BT94 2JP, Co Fermanagh
Tel: (01365) 388209

An attractive country house dating from the 1760s, set in a lovely location in the heart of Fermanagh's lakeland. A wing of the house and the gracious stableyard were added in the early 1820s. The Ballinamallard River runs through the estate, providing excellent fly-fishing, and shooting for pheasant, duck, snipe and woodcock can be arranged. The garden includes a tennis court and croquet lawn, and there are pleasant walks along the river bank. Stabling is available for guests' horses. There are 3 comfortable bedrooms, an elegant, formal dining room, where dinner is served by arrangement, and a relaxing drawing room. No pets in the house.

OWNER Arthur and Helen Stuart   OPEN All year, except Christmas   ROOMS 3 double, 1 twin (all en-suite)   TERMS B&B £25.00 p.p.; evening meal from £15.00

BELCOO

Corralea Forest Lodge

Belcoo, BT93 5DZ, Co Fermanagh
Tel: (01365) 386325

The best thing about this guest house is the location and view. It is in a superb position standing in 34 acres of forested land on the shores of Upper Lough Macnean, with glorious uninterrupted views over the lough to the hills beyond. All rooms share the same views. The bedrooms, which are functional, have TVs and sliding doors opening out onto a terrace. The property has its own private landing stage, and boats are available for hire. Sika deer roam the estate, and in the 1970s, 37,000 trees were planted. When the Catteralls came here 18 years ago and built the house, the property was just a derelict farm. There is a large TV lounge and a dining room where evening meals are available if booked in advance. There is no licence, but guests may bring their own wine. No pets are allowed. The house can be found about 3 miles (4$^{1}/_{2}$ km) outside Belcoo on the road to Garrison.

OWNER Mr and Mrs Peter Catterall   OPEN 15 April–30 September
ROOMS 4 twin (all en-suite)   TERMS B&B £18.00 p.p.; reductions for children; single supplement; evening meal £12.00

DERRYGONNELLY

Drumary Farm Guest House

Drumary North, Glenashaver, Derrygonnelly, BT93 6GA
Co Fermanagh
Tel: (013656) 41420

Drumary Farm is run by the Elliott family and is situated on a 200–acre dairy and sheep farm. The house is 75 years old and is set in glorious scenic countryside. The house has been extended over the years and is in excellent decorative order. The bedrooms are spacious, with pastel wallpapers, TVs and hairdryers. Tasty home-cooked evening meals are served, featuring home baking, fresh produce in season and tasty desserts. There is a craft shop on the premises where guests can purchase Belleek and Donegal pottery. There is also a wide selection of handmade items. Smoking is not encouraged in the house. Pets outside only.

OWNER June Elliott   OPEN All year   ROOMS 3 double/twin/family (all en-suite)   TERMS B&B £16.00 p.p.; reduction for children; single supplement; evening meals from £7.00

Navar Guest House

Derryvary, Derrygonnelly, Co Fermanagh
Tel: (013656) 41384

An immaculately kept, low, whitewashed modern house with black trim and a front garden, standing just above the Enniskillen to Derrygonnelly road. The Loves built this house about 16 years ago, and it has been designed so the guests have one part of the building and the owners the other part. Mrs Love is a most friendly, outgoing lady, who, apart from running the B&B, also teaches. Her husband, whose chief love is fishing (he has represented Ireland twice), helps out in the house and runs their 300–acre farm. Half of this is hill land, where shooting for pheasant, snipe, woodcock and duck is available. There is good game fishing for salmon and trout and, of course, Mr Love is more than happy to offer advice and help to fellow fishermen. The house is most attractive inside; there is a large entrance hall with Italian tiles and a large comfortable lounge with TV and open fire. There is also a separate lounge with a piano and computer, particularly popular with children, who are welcome here. All the bedrooms are on the ground floor. Evening meals are served at 7 pm, if booked in advance, and packed lunches are also available. Pets outside only. The house can be found 8 miles (12 km) west of Enniskillen on the Derrygonnelly road.

OWNER Patrick and Joan Love   OPEN All year   ROOMS 1 double, 2 twin, 2 family (2 en-suite)   TERMS B&B £15.00 p.p.; reductions for children; evening meal from £10.00

ENNISKILLEN

Brindley Guest House

Tully, Killadeas, Enniskillen, BT94 1RE, Co Fermanagh
Tel: (01365) 628065

A purpose-built guest house, about 10 years old, standing in award-winning gardens. This large building is in an elevated position with wonderful views of Lower Lough Erne and the islands. There is an attractive dining room, where evening meals are served at 6 pm, if arranged in advance. A small TV lounge leads to a conservatory where tea- and coffee-making facilities are available. Three of the bedrooms are on the ground floor, and there is a ramp leading up to the front door. No smoking and no pets. The house is signposted off the Enniskillen to Kesh road at Killadeas.

OWNER Mr and Mrs Deane Flood   OPEN All year, except Christmas   ROOMS 3 double, 3 twin, 2 family (6 en-suite)   TERMS B&B from £17.00–£18.00 p.p.; reductions for children; single supplement; evening meals £11.00

Riverside Farm Guest House

Gortadrehid, Culkey, Enniskillen, BT92 2FN, Co Fermanagh
Tel: (01365) 322725

This welcoming, warm, friendly house is an angler's paradise. The house, which is on a 65-acre beef farm, belonged to Ollie Fawcett's grandfather. The oldest part is over 100 years old, though modern stucco and windows give it the appearance of a more modern building. Mollie, who is a trained cook and used to be in charge of a canteen, has been running the bed and breakfast for the last 22 years. The house is simply furnished, with a good ratio of bathrooms to bedrooms, a TV lounge with solid-fuel fire and video and a dining room where evening meals are served if ordered in advance. There is no licence, but guests are welcome to bring their own wine. The Sillies River, at the bottom of the farm, holds the world's record for coarse fishing. The farm has over a mile of private fishing and there is an excellent outbuilding for storage and fridges to keep bait fresh. There is one ground-floor bedroom suitable for disabled guests and a ramp into the house. Pets outside only. The house can be found on the A509, 3 miles (4¹/₂ km) from Enniskillen. Visa accepted.

OWNER Mary Isobel Fawcett   OPEN All year   ROOMS 1 double, 2 twin, 2 single, 1 family (2 en-suite)   TERMS B&B £13.50–£15.00 p.p.; reductions for children; evening meal from £8.00

FLORENCECOURT

Tullyhona Farm Guest House

Marble Arch Caves Road, Florencecourt, BT92 1DE, Co Fermanagh

Tel: (01365) 382452

Fourteen years ago, when the Armstrongs purchased this property, it was just a tiny cottage. It has been extended over the years and is now a good-sized comfortable guest house. Mrs Armstrong is a friendly, chatty, hard-working mother of three who loves to have families and children stay, and the property is ideally suited for them. There is an extensive play area outside, and there are flexible meal times and special menus. Calving tours can be arranged. The house is very close to Florencecourt House and the Marble Arch Caves. There are two lounges, one of which is furnished with antiques and has an open fire, and the other an informal TV lounge. There are two ground-floor rooms suitable for handicapped guests. Excellent breakfasts, featuring home-made jams and marmalades, are served buffet-style. Teas and dinners are served until 7 pm, and there are also barbeque evenings. The focus is on home-cooking, and special diets can be catered for. Smoking only in specific rooms. Pets outside only. Tullyhona Farm is the recipient of several awards, including the Irish Breakfast Award and the Irish Farmers' Journal Award. A popular spot; advance reservations highly recommended.

OWNER Rosemary Armstrong OPEN All year ROOMS 11 double/twin/family/single (10 en-suite) TERMS B&B £18.00 p.p.; reductions for children; single supplement; meals and snacks £2.50–£7.00

IRVINESTOWN

Fletchers Farm

Drumadravey, Irvinestown, BT94 1LQ, Co Fermanagh
Tel: (01365) 621351

A low, whitewashed building about 2 miles (3 km) from Irvinestown on the road to Lisnarick. This 72-acre farm, supporting a suckling herd, has belonged to the Knoxes for the last 22 years. They always wanted to build a new house on the site, which they finally did about 3 years ago, and then Mrs Knox, who retired from her career as a nurse, started doing B&B, which she loves. The property is immaculately kept, with the farmyard behind the house and pleasant farmland views. The house has been comfortably furnished, and all bedrooms are on the ground floor. Evening meals are served by prior arrangement, and there are good hotels nearby. The bedrooms have tea-making facilities, hairdryers, trouser presses and electric blankets. The lounge has a TV and open fire. An equestrian facility is now available. There is a barbecue area, children's play area and bicycles for guests. Smoking in the lounge only. Pets are not allowed in the bedrooms.

OWNER Myrtle Knox OPEN All year ROOMS 2 double, 1 twin, 1 family (3 en-suite) TERMS B&B £13.00 p.p.; reductions for children; evening meal £8.00

KESH

Ardess House

Kesh, BT93 1NX, Co Fermanagh
Tel: (01365) 31267

The house is located in the tiny hamlet of Ardess, a couple of miles out of Kesh, and is approached up a winding driveway with the house at the top of a hill. It is an old, square, grey stucco building, built in 1780 as the rectory for the church opposite, and has lovely views. The Pendrys bought it in 1984 and have done a great deal of work on restoring the house. Dorothy Pendry was a teacher in a girls' school in Belfast, and did weaving and spinning as a hobby. Now she has turned the basement of the house into small workshops, where courses on different crafts are taught, by herself and other tutors. There is also a small shop. The students who attend the courses get full board in the house, though even those not attending courses can partake of evening meals if they wish. Guests are also welcome to join in the activities in the craft centre. The kitchen is the preferred place for breakfast, but there is a dining room as well, and a drawing room. The bedrooms have been freshly decorated and good-sized bathrooms have been added. The former are large, airy rooms, with high ceilings and wonderful views and furnished with antiques. The house has been awarded a British Airways Tourism Endeavour Award. Smoking is not encouraged. Pets by arrangement. Follow the signs to Kesh; turn off onto the B72 before you reach the village.

OWNER Dorothy Pendry OPEN 1 January–1 November ROOMS 3 double, 1 twin (all en-suite) TERMS £21.00 p.p.; reductions for children; single supplement; evening meal £12.00; lunch £4.00

Rosscah Lodge

11 Crevenish Road, Kesh, BT93 1RG, Co Fermanagh
Tel: (01365) 631001

A most attractive, modern house situated on a quiet side road. The well-appointed bedrooms are tastefully decorated, and although only one has en-suite facilities, there are two additional bathrooms for guests' use. There is a very large lounge available to guests. Breakfast is served in the conservatory overlooking the garden. There are several establishments serving evening meals within walking distance. Astrid is always happy to assist guests in every way to ensure their stay is as comfortable as possible. Electric blankets are provided. Smoking is not permitted and pets are not allowed. Rosscah Lodge is located opposite Lough Erne hotel.

OWNER Astrid Geddes OPEN Easter–October ROOMS 3 double/ twin (1 en-suite) TERMS B&B £15.00–£27.00 p.p.; single supplement

Willowdale

Drumbarna, Kesh, BT93 1RR, Co Fermanagh
Tel: (01365) 631596

This warm and welcoming house is situated on the scenic
Kesh/Enniskillen Road in glorious surroundings. There are
spectacular views from the bedrooms. Breakfast is served in
the dining room which overlooks the famous Lough Erne.
Tea and coffee are served in the TV lounge upon arrival and
there is a vast breakfast menu, including a substantial
traditional Irish breakfast. The owners are local people and
are always happy to assist with sightseeing and fishing
information. Water sports and horse-riding are available
locally. There is a TV lounge.

OWNER Mrs Shirley McCubbin   OPEN Easter–October   ROOMS 2
double   TERMS B&B £14.00 p.p.; reductions for children

LETTER

Manville Guest House

Aughnablaney, Letter, BT93 2BB, Co Fermanagh
Tel: (01365) 631668

Manville House is set in an idyllic location with a superb
view of Lower Lough Erne and Boa Island. Standing in its
own grounds, it is hard to pin down the exact date of its
origins, as it has been added to and modernised over the
years. The house is clean, comfortable and furnished simply,
and is an ideal location for tourists and anglers, with seasons
for brown trout and salmon, and fishing all year for pike,
perch, rudd and bream, which are plentiful. There are boats
and engines for hire. There is a lounge with a TV and a
separate dining room. Evening meals are not served, but
there is no shortage of good eating establishments in the
area. Manville House is one of the first B&Bs in Letter, and
Mrs Graham is a congenial host, always happy to give advice
and recommend restaurants. Pets by arrangement.

OWNER Mr and Mrs R. H. Graham   OPEN All year except
Christmas   ROOMS 5 double/twin/family   TERMS B&B £15.00
p.p.; reductions for children

Aghnacarra House

Carrybridge, Lisbellaw, BT94 5NFCo Fermanagh
Tel: (01365) 387077

The Ensors came here from Coventry and, after scouring
the countryside, finally settled on this site where they
purpose-built a guest house designed with the angler in
mind. Dave Ensor is a great fisherman and he spends most
of his time making sure his guests get just the fishing they
want. The house has tackle storage space, and bait can be
ordered in advance ready for a guest's arrival. Previously,
Dave was in the plumbing and building trade, and the
couple built the house themselves; the name "Aghnacarra"
means "hill of the fort", although the house is not actually
on a hill. Set in 2½ acres of lawns and gardens with a lake,
there is a nice view from the terrace, which runs the length
of the house, overlooking farmland and the lake. The house
stands beside a country road in the small village of
Carrybridge, halfway between the 2 major Erne loughs. The
house is clean, freshly decorated and comfortably furnished,
with a TV lounge and a dining room. Evening meals, if
ordered in advance, are served at 7 pm; special diets are
catered for, and packed lunches are also available. There is
no licence, but guests are welcome to bring their own wine.
There is a new games room with pool table, TV and video.
There are 4 ground-floor bedrooms. Pets are not allowed.

OWNER Dave and Norma Ensor   OPEN All year except Christmas
ROOMS 3 triple, 1 family (2 en-suite)   TERMS B&B £14.00–
£16.00 p.p.; reductions for children; evening meal £8.00

County Londonderry

Londonderry is probably best known for the tune "London-
derry Air", better known as "Danny Boy". The city of
Londonderry, situated on a hill on the banks of the Foyle
estuary, acquired its name when the City of London sent
money and builders to rebuild it in the seventeenth century.
The seventeenth-century walls, about a mile (1½ km) round
and 18 feet (5½ m) thick, have withstood several sieges and
are still complete, giving magnificent views of the surround-
ing countryside. The city still preserves its medieval layout,
and amongst the historic buildings is the 1633 Gothic
Cathedral of St Columb. From the quay behind the Guild-

hall, hundreds of thousands of Irish emigrants left Derry for America during the eighteenth and nineteenth centuries, amongst them the families from which Davy Crockett and U.S. President James Polk were descended.

The Mussenden Temple, built by the eccentric Earl Bishop of Derry as testimony of his affection for Lady Mussenden, stands on a windswept headland on the coast at Downhill; adjacent, the castle itself, now in ruins but exuding an aura of romance and grandeur, is certainly worth visiting. One of Ulster's finest fortified farmhouses can be seen at Bellaghy, and whiskey is produced at Bushmills, near Coleraine, the town allegedly founded by St Patrick.

CASTLEROCK

Carneety House

120 Mussenden Road, Castlerock, Coleraine, BT51 4TX, Co Londonderry

Tel: (01265) 848640

An attractive farmhouse on the A2, on the edge of Castlerock, standing in a beautifully kept, compact garden. The house is 300 years old and has been in Mr Henry's family for some time. It is immaculately kept and attractively decorated and furnished. Mrs Henry is a young mother of 2 who also runs an outside catering business. Her husband takes care of the dairy and beef farm. The dining room, with one table at which breakfast only is served, is a cosy room with a nice fireplace and family silver, and the drawing room has a piano, TV and open gas fire. There are TVs in all the bedrooms. Stabling is available, and pony trekking, golf, and forest and beach walks are close by.

OWNER Mrs Carol Henry   OPEN All year   ROOMS 2 double, 1 twin (1 en-suite)   TERMS B&B £15.00 p.p.; reductions for children

COLERAINE

Blackheath House

112 Killeague Road, Blackhill, Coleraine, BT51 4HH, Co Londonderry

Tel: (01265) 868433, Fax: (01265) 868433

This fine old house is set in 2 acres of gardens and was built in 1791 as a rectory. It was, at one time, home of Archbishop William Alexander, whose wife, Cecil, wrote "There is a

Green Hill Far Away" and "All Things Bright and Beautiful". The present owners were originally teachers in London and took over the house when it was derelict. Now it is difficult to imagine the state it once was in, as they have done a wonderful job in creating a warm, comfortable house, beautifully furnished and decorated. All bedrooms have TVs and hairdryers. There is a breakfast room, and the drawing room is a gracious room with a grand piano, a warm, open fire and shelves to each side reaching to the ceiling, full of collectable items; the room has a pleasant, lived-in feeling. Joey and Margaret are a friendly, relaxed couple with 2 teenage children. Margaret is in charge of cooking, with an assistant chef. Macduff's Restaurant was the first part of the house to be open to the public. It is located in the basement and has its own entrance. The restaurant has the atmosphere of a cellar, with its low ceilings and arches, and is most attractively furnished with pink tablecloths, flowers on every table, green chairs and, with only a few tables, a cosy, intimate atmosphere. It offers country-house cooking using freshly grown produce, local game, salmon and seafood. There is a full licence and a heated indoor swimming pool. Not suitable for children. No pets. Blackheath House can be found $4^1/_2$ miles ($6^1/_2$ km) north of Garvagh. Visa and Access cards accepted.

OWNER Joey and Margaret Erwin   OPEN All year except Christmas   ROOMS 4 double, 1 twin (4 en-suite)   TERMS B&B £30.00 p.p.; evening meal à la carte

Camus House

27 Curragh Road, Coleraine, BT51 3RY, Co Londonderry
Tel: (01265) 42982

Camus House may have been built on the site of an old monastery. It is the oldest house in the area, a listed building dating from 1685. The house is in a charming setting close to the River Bann and Mrs King owns a mile of river frontage. The lovely, old ivy-covered house is approached by a driveway through parklike grounds and has a pretty front garden. Mrs King's parents bought the house in 1914. The land is now let out and, when her 2 children moved away from home, she started doing bed and breakfast. Mrs King is a most friendly, characterful lady who does all the work herself. Her passion is fishing, and this is a great fishing family; her daughter has represented Ireland. The house has a lot of character and is comfortably furnished as a family home. In winter, guests use Mrs King's own sitting room, a cosy room with an open fire. However, there is another sitting room and a nice old dining room where breakfast only is served. The bedrooms are large, fresh and bright, and simply furnished. Mrs King was the recipient of the Galtee Breakfast award in 1991. There is partial central heating. Not suitable for children under 14. No pets. No smoking in the dining room.

OWNER Mrs Josephine King   OPEN All year   ROOMS 1 double/family/twin   TERMS B&B £16.50 p.p.

Greenhill House

24 Greenhill Road, Aghadowey, Coleraine, BT51 4EU,
Co Londonderry
Tel: (01265) 868241

A nice old Georgian country house, standing in its own grounds of trees, lawns and shrubs, with lovely views over farmland to distant hills. The Hegartys bought the house about 12 years ago, mostly because they wanted the land, now a 150–acre beef and arable farm. Mrs Hegarty was a teacher but now devotes her time to running the bed and breakfast; she is a most friendly and cheerful lady. The bedrooms are large, well equipped and furnished with TVs, hairdryers, tea- and coffee-making facilities and minute shower rooms, cleverly disguised. There is a large lounge and dining room with 4 tables. Evening meals can be served, by arrangement. No pets. The house lies off the B66 to Ballymoney, 3 miles (4¹/₂ km) north of Garvagh and 7 miles (10¹/₂ km) south of Coleraine. Visa, Access and Eurocard accepted.

OWNER Mrs James Hegarty   OPEN 1 March–1 October   ROOMS 2 double/twin/family (all en-suite)   TERMS B&B £22.00 p.p.; reductions for children; single supplement; evening meal £15.00

Inchadoghill House

1 Agivey Road, Aghadowey, Coleraine, BT51 4AD,
Co Londonderry
Tel: (01265) 868232 or 868250

An old brick farmhouse, standing back from the A54, 9 miles

(13¹/₂ km) south of Coleraine, in a pleasant lawned front garden, part of a mixed farm. The house has been in the same family for 5 generations and was built by them. Mrs McIlroy is helped in the business by her daughter-in-law, who lives next door. They offer comfortable, simple farm-house accommodation. The dining room has a piano and family memorabilia in the dresser. There is also a TV lounge. No pets.

OWNER Mamie and Ann McIlroy   OPEN All year   ROOMS 2 double, 1 family   TERMS B&B £14.00 p.p.; reductions for children; single supplement available

Killeague House

Blackhill, Coleraine, BT51 4HJ, Co Londonderry
Tel: (01265) 868229

From the outside, Killeague House looks quite modern, with newly applied stucco, an addition of arches and a garage. This square house, standing in its own garden, is, however, about 300 years old. The farm buildings adjacent serve the 120-acre dairy farm. It is a comfortable house with a friendly atmosphere and a lot of steps to negotiate. The bathroom is downstairs and the pleasant dining room, with 2 tables, family silver on the sideboard and cabinets filled with china and glass, is in the basement. The TV lounge has both an organ and piano. Evening meals are served, by arrangement. No smoking. Pets by arrangement. The house can be found on the A29, 5 miles (7¹/₂ km) south of Coleraine.

OWNER Mrs Margaret Moore   OPEN All year   ROOMS 1 double, 1 single, 2 family (2 en-suite)   TERMS B&B from £16.00 p.p.; reductions for children; single supplement; evening meal £10.00

EGLINTON

Longfield Farm

132 Clooney Road, Eglinton, BT47 3DX, Co Londonderry
Tel: (01504) 810210

A spacious old house in a pleasant garden with lawn and shrubs, set off the main Londonderry to Limavady road. The farmyard, which serves the 200–acre farm of potatoes, beef and cereals, is to the back of the house. It is a comfortable family home with a lived-in feeling. A cosy smaller lounge with open fire is used in winter; in summer, the large lounge is preferred, and the dining room has a TV. The bedrooms are a good size and there are 2 bathrooms. Longfield Farm is well placed for visiting Donegal and Londonderry. No smoking in the bedrooms.

OWNER Mrs E. M. Hunter   OPEN 1 March–1 October   ROOMS 1 double, 1 single, 1 family   TERMS B&B £15.00 p.p.; reductions for children; single supplement

LIMAVADY

Ballyhenry House

172 Seacoast Road, Limavady, BT49 9EF, Co Londonderry
Tel: (01504) 722657

An attractive house, close to the sea, on the B69 between Limavady and Castlerock. The house was built around the turn of the century by Mr Kane's grandfather, who subsequently sold it. Mr and Mrs Kane bought it back when they got married. The acreage at that time was 53 acres, but thanks to prudent acquisitions it now exceeds 350 acres. The land is very flat and fertile, and the fields are enormous, some in excess of 100 acres. Mr Kane died about 8 years ago, and the farm is now managed by his 2 sons and their uncle. It is an extremely successful operation, and they have won all kinds of awards. Mrs Kane is a most friendly lady who prepares excellent evening meals, if arranged in advance. The rooms are nicely proportioned and pleasantly decorated and furnished, with some good pieces of furniture. There is a dining room, TV lounge, snooker room, and a pub within 100 yards, which serves food some evenings. The bedrooms have hairdryers and trouser presses. Smoking downstairs only and pets outside.

OWNER Rosemary Kane   OPEN All year   ROOMS 1 double, 1 twin, 1 family (1 with private shower)   TERMS B&B £15.00 p.p.; reductions for children; evening meal £9.50

LONDONDERRY

Number Ten

10 Crawford Square, Londonderry, BT48 7HR,
Co Londonderry
Tel: (01504) 265000

Number Ten is a family-run, modernised Victorian house in an unspoilt Victorian square, five minutes' walk from the city centre. Grace Broderick is a very personable and helpful lady who keeps a spotlessly clean house. There are TVs, radios and tea- and coffee-making facilities in all rooms. There are no en-suite rooms, but they all have washing facilities and there are two bathrooms for guests' use. A home-cooked and very tasty breakfast is served in the attractive dining room. A popular venue with tourists and business people.

OWNER Gerry and Grace McGoldrick OPEN All year
ROOMS 5 double/single/family TERMS B&B from £15.00 p.p.;
reductions for children; single supplement

Robin Hill

103 Chapel Road, Londonderry, BT47 2BG,
Co Londonderry
Tel: (01504) 42776

A country setting right in the heart of the city, Robin Hill was built as a Presbyterian manse 117 years ago. It is a large, square house standing in an acre of gardens and parklike grounds right on top of a hill, with wonderful views of the city and hills. The Muirs have been here for about 10 years. Mrs Muir is a teacher and Mr Muir looks after the two small children and runs the bed and breakfast. This is a warm, comfortable family home with large rooms, freshly decorated and with new carpets and double-glazed windows. There is a TV lounge, dining room and small sitting room. All bedrooms have TVs. Evening meals can be served if booked in advance. Non-smoking rooms are available. No pets.

OWNER Malcolm and Gemma Muir OPEN All year ROOMS 9
double/twin/single/family (6 en-suite) TERMS B&B £14.50–
£16.50 p.p.; reductions for children; evening meal £9.50

PORTSTEWART

Lis-Na-Rhin

6 Victoria Terrace, Portstewart, BT55 7BA, Co Londonderry
Tel: (01265) 833522

Lis-na-Rhin is a bright and fresh house, located in a pleasant spot a few feet away from the sea, overlooking the golf course. The town centre and the promenade are just a few minutes' walk away. The owner, Mrs Montgomery, takes pride in her house, and high standards pervade throughout.

The beds are comfortable and some bedrooms have sea-views. There is information on the area available and the Montgomerys are happy to give advice on local activities and local places for evening meals. Guests enjoy congregating in the spacious, well-furnished lounge, which has a TV. There is also an enclosed car park.

OWNER Mr and Mrs Montgomery   OPEN March–October
ROOMS 9 double/twin/single/family (4 en-suite)   TERMS B&B
£16.00–£17.00 p.p.; reductions for children

Oregon Guest House

168 Station Road, Portstewart, BT55 7PU, Co Londonderry
Tel: (01265) 832826

About half a mile from the sea, and within walking distance of the city centre, this guest house lies on the outskirts of Portstewart, just off a fairly busy main road. The house is immaculately kept, with a high standard of furnishings and fresh, bright rooms prettily decorated with floral curtains and bedcovers. The small, cosy, panelled dining room, with pretty floral china and flowers on tables, overlooks the sunny patio with pond and small fountain. There is a comfortable TV lounge and off it a supplementary dining room, very bright, with windows all around. One of the double rooms has a corner bath, separate shower, bidet and sauna. All bedrooms have TVs and hairdryers. Evening meals are served if ordered in advance, and some rooms are on the ground floor. No smoking in the bedrooms. No pets. The house is located ¹/₂ mile south of Portstewart, on the B185.

OWNER Mrs Vi Anderson   OPEN 1 February–30 November
ROOMS 3 double, 2 twin, 3 family (all en-suite)   TERMS B&B
£18.00–£20.00 p.p.; reductions for children; single supplement;
evening meal £12.00

Strandeen

63 Strand Road, Portstewart, BT55 7LU, Co Londonderry
Tel: (01265) 833159

Situated overlooking the ocean, this attractive house offers three en-suite rooms, all with TVs and tea-makers. One bedroom is on the ground floor. Strandeen is impeccably maintained by owner, Elizabeth Caskey, who worked in London for 12 years prior to returning home to Ireland.

Breakfast and evening meals, if prearranged, are served in the spacious dining-room-cum-lounge, which affords a panoramic ocean view, and is furnished with original paintings. Guests can also enjoy the cliff walks nearby, which are maintained by the National Trust. No smoking. No pets. Guests may bring their own wine to dinner.

OWNER Elizabeth Caskey   OPEN All year including Christmas
ROOMS 1 double, 1 twin, 1 single (all en-suite)   TERMS B&B from £20.00 p.p.; reductions for children; single supplement; evening meals from £12.50

County Tyrone

The least populated of the 6 counties of Northern Ireland and the heart of Ulster, Tyrone is bordered to the north by the Sperrin Mountains, bare hills with fertile green valleys. The main towns are Omagh, the county town, Cookstown and Dungannon, which has a textile industry and crystal factory.

The meaning of the Beaghmore stone circles, consisting of seven Bronze Age stone circles and cairns, is still unknown. The Ulster-American Folk Park at Camphill, Omagh, which recreates the America of pioneering days and the Ireland those pioneers left from, grew up round the cottage where Thomas Mellon was born in 1813.

Also in County Tyrone is the ancestral home of Woodrow Wilson. The farm is still occupied by Wilsons, who will show callers round the house.

BALLYGAWLEY

The Grange Guest House

15 Grange Road, Ballygawley, BT70 2LP, Co Tyrone
Tel: (016625) 68053

Situated on the edge of Ballygawley, this old house, dating from 1720, had a thatched roof until recently. It stands in a lovely, large walled garden of lawns surrounded by flower beds, and has now the appearance of a more modern house, with white stucco and new windows. Mrs Lyttle is a very friendly, older lady and the house has a pleasant, lived-in feeling. The attractive lounge has a piano and TV, and the dining room, from which stairs lead to the next floor, has lots of character, is full of knick-knacks and has sideboards decorated with silver and china. There is one ground-floor bedroom with a bathroom next to it. Pets outside only.

OWNER E. Lyttle OPEN All year ROOMS 2 double, 1 twin (2 en-suite) TERMS B&B £14.00–£15.00 p.p.; single supplement; evening meal £9.00

DUNGANNON

Grange Lodge

7 Grange Road, Dungannon, BT71 7EJ, Co Tyrone
Tel: (018687) 23891

An attractive Georgian country house just off the Dungannon to Moy road, set in over 3 acres of pleasant gardens. The Browns, who also own a retail concern in Dungannon, bought the house about 6 years ago and have done a great deal to bring it up to a very high standard of comfort. It is a spacious house with well-proportioned reception rooms, and the bedrooms all have telephones, TVs and tea- and coffee-making facilities. There is a large drawing room and a cosier, smaller study with TV, which is normally the preferred sitting area for guests, especially in winter. Other facilities include a panelled snooker room with piano. Grange Lodge offers its guests comfort and a friendly atmosphere in peaceful surroundings. A stay here would not be complete without sampling Norah Brown's cooking. She is quite superb and an utter perfectionist, both in terms of the extremely high standard of the food itself and the way in which it is presented. Dinner is served in the elegant dining room, with separate tables covered in white tablecloths and decorated with pretty flowers and candles. The dining room is open to non-residents, but prior bookings are absolutely essential. There is no licence, but guests are welcome to bring their own wine. Not suitable for children under 12. Pets outside only.

OWNER Ralph and Norah Brown OPEN All year, except Christmas ROOMS 3 double, 1 twin, 1 single (all en-suite) TERMS B&B £29.50 p.p.; single supplement; dinner £18.50

Muleany House

86 Gorsetown Road, Moy, Dungannon, BT71 7EX, Co Tyrone
Tel: (018687) 84183

A substantial, porticoed whitewashed building, purpose-built 9 years ago, close to the town of Moy. Mrs Mullen is a most friendly, chatty lady, who does her own baking and enjoys meeting her guests. The bedrooms are good-sized, all with tiny shower rooms, and there are 2 extra public bathrooms with bathtubs. An excellent place for children, Muleany House offers a babysitting service, laundry facility and a large games room with pool table, small organ and open fire. There is also a smaller lounge with a TV, and a dining room where evening meals are served, if ordered in advance. There is no licence, but guests are welcome to bring their own wine. Two bedrooms are on the ground floor. There are also 2 self-catering apartments available in the grounds. The house can be found about 1 mile (1½ km) from Moy; from the B106 to Benburb, take the right fork towards Ballygawley.

OWNER Mary Mullen   OPEN All year   ROOMS 5 twin, 2 single, 2 family (all en-suite)   TERMS B&B £14.00 p.p.; reductions for children; single supplement; evening meal £8.00

FIVEMILETOWN

Al-Di-Gwyn

103A Clabby Road, Fivemiletown, BT75 0QY, Co Tyrone
Tel: (013655) 21298

This large, colour-washed building, in a good centre for touring, stands just off the road between Fivemiletown and Clabby. Originally it was a 3-roomed bungalow, but it has been added to over the years. The rooms are functional and there is one small sitting room and a larger TV lounge. There is a ground-floor room with en-suite shower room, and a ramp and wide doors leading into the house. No smoking in the bedrooms. Pets outside only.

OWNER Mrs Vera Gilmore   OPEN 1 January–30 November   ROOMS 4 double, 4 twin (all en-suite)   TERMS B&B £15.00–£17.00 p.p.; reductions for children; single supplement

MOY

Charlemont House

4 The Square, Moy, Dungannon, BT71 7SG, Co Tyrone
Tel: (018687) 84755 or 84895

A lovely Georgian townhouse occupying a corner site on the central square of the small town of Moy, which lies halfway between Armagh and Dungannon. Until recently it was owned by a doctor, and has been taken over by the McNeice family, who have been associated with innkeeping in Moy for many generations. A sign to one side of the house reads "Enquire at Tomney's Bar and Lounge or Moy Reproductions" which are located just a few doors down the square. The bar is quite an amazing place, completely authentic, with small, dark rooms and a great atmosphere. The house is also amazing, full of Victorian furnishings and furniture. The lounge has old floral wallpaper, pinkish chintzes, black-and-pink patterned carpeting, black furniture, including a piano, romantic pictures and all kinds of glass and china. The house has elegant proportions, with the breakfast room in the basement, a less flamboyant room with an Aga cooker and pottery adorning the high shelf around the room. The property stretches right down to the River Blackwater at the back, reached through a courtyard. Guests can sit here on fine days, surrounded by old coach houses (destined to be converted into bedrooms), then through an archway to a pretty, partly walled, compact garden with more tables and chairs. The bedrooms have TVs and tea- and coffee-making facilities, and there are 2 sitting rooms. All major credit cards accepted.

OWNER Margaret McNeice   OPEN All year   ROOMS 1 twin, 2 double   TERMS B&B £15.00 p.p.; reductions for children.

OMAGH

Bankhead

9 Lissan Road, Omagh, BT78 1TX, Co Tyrone
Tel: (01662) 245592

A small house, built by the Clementses in 1970, with farm buildings to the rear. The beef and sheep farm consists of 27 acres and is located about 1½ miles (2½ km) outside Omagh on the Ballygawley Road. The bedrooms are furnished simply, but fresh and bright; there is a small, neatly kept TV lounge with an open fire, and the dining room has a TV and sitting area. Outside, the terrace is pleasant for sitting out on fine days, and guests have use of a garden. Smoking is not allowed in bedrooms, and pets are not permitted. All the bedrooms are on the ground floor. Bankhead is a quarter of a mile from the golf course.

OWNER Mrs S. C. Clements   OPEN All year   ROOMS 2 double, 1 single   TERMS B&B £12.00; reductions for children

Greenmount Lodge

58 Greenmount Road, Gortaclare, Omagh, BT79 0YE,
Co Tyrone
Tel: (01662) 841325, Fax: (01662) 840019

The house stands in a very quiet position on a country
estate, with an eighteenth-century courtyard to the rear of
the modern house. Open to non-residents for evening meals
on Fridays and Saturdays. The bedrooms are all en-suite
and reasonably sized with TVs and tea- and coffee-making
facilities. Disabled accommodation, purpose-built with a
NITB category 1 classification, is also available. Evening
meals are available if prearranged. The lodge can be found 7
miles (10½ km) from Ballygawley off the Omagh road,
turning left at the Travellers' Rest and travelling a further
mile.

OWNER Frances Reid OPEN All year ROOMS 2 double, 2 twin, 3
family, 1 single (all en-suite) TERMS B&B £16.00 p.p.; reductions
for children; single supplement

STRABANE

Mrs Jean Ballantine's

38 Leckpatrick Road, Artigarvan, Strabane, BT82 0HB, Co
Tyrone
Tel: (01504) 882714

A family home just off the B49 Strabane-to-Dunnemana
road, with lovely distant views of farmland and hills. This
modern house has a friendly atmosphere and 3 small bed-
rooms as well as 2 bathrooms. There is a fairly large TV
lounge with an open fire, a new conservatory and the family
dining room, with one table, where evening meals can be
served, by arrangement. No smoking. Pets outside only.

OWNER Mrs Jean Ballantine OPEN All year, except Christmas
ROOMS 1 double, 1 twin, 1 single TERMS B&B £13.00; reductions
for children; evening meal £6.00

Area Maps

Malin Head

▲ C

INISHOWEN

Downings

Dunfanaghy

▲ Falcarragh

▲ Buncrana

▲ Derrybeg

N56

▲ Ramelton

N13

L
(D

D O N E G A L

N1

A5

Letterkenny ▲

▲ Portnoo

N56

▲ Lifford

▲ Castlefinn

▲ Strabane

N15

▲ Dungloe

T

A5

▲ Ardara

N15

▲ Glencolumbkille

Carrick ▲ ▲ Killybegs

Inver ▲ ▲ Donegal

▲ Omagh

Dunkineely

▲ Laghy

▲ Ballyshannon

A35

Kesh

A32

▲ Bundoran

A46

A38

▲ Irvinestown

▲ Ballinamallard

Fivemiletown

▲ Derrygonnelly

▲ Cliffoney

F E R M A N A G H

▲ Enniskillen

▲ Drumcliff

▲ Belcoo

A4

L E I T R I M

▲ Lisbellaw

A34

▲ SLIGO

Florencecourt

A509

crone

▲ Collooney

S L I G O

▲ Riverstown

▲ Ballymote

▲ Ballinamore

▲ Tobercurry

▲ Carrick-on-Shannon

N55

N83

N61

N60 N60

R O S C O M M O N

L O N G F O R D

Longford ▲

N60

Scale

0 — 5 — 10 — 15 — 20 — 25 Miles
0 — 10 — 20 — 30 — 40 Kilometres

▲ Tipperary = Guide entry

Area 2

▲ Tipperary = Guide entry

Area 3

Ballycastle ▲

Killala ▲   ▲ Enishcrone

Crossmolina ▲   ▲ Ballina

M A Y O

ACHILL
ISLAND

▲ Newport   ▲ Castlebar

N84

N60

▲ Westport   ▲ Knock

▲ Louisburgh   N59

N84

▲ Leeane   Clonbur ▲

CONNEMARA   N59

▲ Clifden   Annaghdo ▲

N84

N17

▲ Cashel   Oughterard ▲

N59

Moycullen ▲

GALWAY   N6

Spiddal ▲

Salt Hill ▲

N67

▲ Bell Harb

THE
BURREN

▲ Lisdoonvarna

▲ Doolin

▲ Ennistymon

▲ Lahinch

N67

▲ Milltown Malbay   Ennis ▲

N68

N67

N68

0	5	10	15	20	25 Miles
0	10	20	30	40 Kilometres	

▲ Tipperary = Guide entry

Area 4

Bell Ha
THE
BURRE

▲ Lisdoonvarna
▲ Doolin

N67

▲ Ennistymon
▲ Lahinch

N67

▲ Milltown Malbay   Ennis ▲

N68

N67

N68

▲ Ballybunion

L

Newcastle West ▲

N21

N21

▲ Tralee

N21

N21

DINGLE
PENINSULA

N23

▲ Castleisland

K E R R Y

N72

▲ Dingle   ▲ Anascaul

▲ Caragh Lake   ▲ Killarney

N70

▲ Cahirsiveen

IVERAGH
PENINSULA

N70

▲ Kenmare

N22

Waterville

▲ Sneem

Caherdaniel
▲

▲ Glengarriff

N71

BEARA
PENINSULA

N71

▲ Bantry

N71

Skibbereen ▲

N66

N62

N8
Stradbally

N65 N52
Ballinderry

N52

L A O I S

N52

N78
N7

N62

N7
Nenagh ▲

N62

N8

N77

market on Fergus

Thurles
▲

N75

Kilkenny ▲

▲ Bunratty

N10

▲ **LIMERICK**

T I P P E R A R Y

K I L K

N62

N24

Cashel ▲

I C K

▲ Tipperary

N8

N76

dare

▲ Bansha

N76

N74

Cahir ▲

N74 N76

N74

N8

Clonmel
▲ Nire Valley

Pilto
▲

N73

WATERF

N73

N8

▲ Ballymacarbry

N25

Ba

N20

W A T E R F O R D   Tramo

N72

Cappoquin ●   ▲ Millstreet

N25

▲ Kanturk

N72

N72

Dungarvan ▲

N8

N25

▲ Castlelyons

N72

▲ Conna

O R K

N20

Youghal ▲

Blarney ▲

▲ Killeagh

room

N25

▲ Ardmore

▲ **CORK**

▲ Midleton

N22
Douglas ▲

▲ Shanagarry

▲andon ▲

Kinsale

▲ Court-
macsherry

▲

Butlerstown

▲ Tipperary = Guide entry

0   5   10   15   20   25 Miles

0   10   20   30   40 Kilometres

Index of towns and cities